CASES AND COMMENT ON
IRISH COMMERCIAL LAW
AND LEGAL TECHNIQUE

RAYMOND BYRNE

BCL, LLM (NUI)
of the King's Inns, Dublin
Barrister-at-Law
Assistant Lecturer in Law,
National Institute for Higher Education, Dublin

THE ROUND HALL PRESS
DUBLIN

The typesetting for this book was keyboarded by Noelette Crosse for The Round Hall Press Ltd, Kill Lane, Blackrock, Co. Dublin.

Printed in Ireland

© *Raymond Byrne 1985*

ISBN 0-947686-07-X hb
ISBN 0-947686-08-8 pb

ACKNOWLEDGMENTS

The author and publishers gratefully acknowledge permission to reproduce extracts from the cases in this collection from the following bodies:

The Department of Justice, in respect of extracts from unreported judgments.

The European Law Centre, in respect of the extract from the Fleet Street Reports.

The Incorporated Council of Law Reporting for Ireland, in respect of extracts from cases in *the Irish Reports*.

The Round Hall Press, in respect of extracts from cases in *the Irish Law Times Reports* and *Irish Law Reports Monthly*.

To Séamus and Nora

Contents

Chapter 11   Restrictions on Unfair Competition

Chapter 12   Remedies

Preface

This collection of cases is aimed primarily at students in Irish third level colleges taking commercial law as part of a business studies course. In selecting material I have attempted to provide instances of the application of relatively well accepted rules and principles. I have, therefore, omitted some cases which would require quite elaborate, and not necessarily conclusive, comment to place them in context. As an example there is the difficult case of *British Leyland Exports Ltd.* v. *Brittain Manufacturing Ltd.* [1981] I.R. 335 on the validity of exemption clauses. This case is complicated by the fact that the High Court judge was required to apply English law in an Irish court and thus to place to one side any relevant Irish authority. The further problem might arise then whether the authorities relied on were correctly applied, and that is a 64 dollar question.

In terms of structure, I have tried in the introductory comments to the extracts in each chapter to give some overall perspective on the subject-matter covered. In some instances this has meant filling in some gaps which are not dealt with in the extracts themselves. In no sense, however, should these introductory comments be regarded as substitutes for full texts. I am conscious of the value of existing works in the area, including Clark, *Contract* (Irish Law Texts, 1982), Linehan, *Irish Business and Commercial Law* (1981) and O'Malley, *Business Law* (Irish Law Texts, 1982).

With this in mind the cases have been chosen with an eye to introducing students to a sense of the process involved in legal reasoning. It is probably more helpful, and less off-putting, to talk about this simply as reasoning and argument in the context of legal rules, rather than to refer to legal reasoning as an extra-terrestrial form of knowledge.

Each extract is preceded by a summary of what I consider the salient facts of the case, together with a couple of pointers to the reader as to the legal issues dealt with by the judge. This is in the hope that the reader will know what to look for when it comes to examining the extract itself. Without exception, the extracts have to a greater or lesser degree been edited, but I hope the flavour of the original has not been lost. In a few instances, particularly with unreported judgments, I have attempted some hygienic checking of references and quotations for accuracy. Otherwise, the text given is as handed down by the original author.

While the first three chapters deal with the legal technique aspect of the text there is an inevitable degree of overlap with the remaining nine. For instance Extract 1.1, *Wall* v. *Hegarty and Callnan* is an important case on the liability of professional persons in negligence as well as illustrating techniques of dealing with, and creating, precedent. Similarly, Extract 8.6, *O'Callaghan* v. *Hamilton Leasing Ltd.* illustrates some basic principles of statutory interpretation.

Where appropriate, I have given cross-references to relevant extracts in the introductory remarks to each chapter.

I hope I can be forgiven for not providing either tables of cases and statutes or an index. It seemed to me that in a text of this small size the chapter headings and extracts speak for themselves and that it would be an undue burden on readers to add an extra element to the price for a relatively small return.

There are a number of people who made publication of this text possible, and it is a great pleasure to thank those behind-the-scenes people here. Thanks to Bart Daly and Michael Adams for agreeing to take on the project in the first place. In N.I.H.E. Dublin, I am very grateful to the Registrar Mr. D. Clarke and Head of Accounting and Finance Dr. J. A. Walsh for smoothing the administrative waters to make available the Institute's considerable facilities for producing the final printed version of this text. I must, however, reserve my best thanks to Noelette Crosse for transforming increasingly spidery script and poor quality photocopies into superb condition, and all with a smile. Without her, this text would simply not have reached the printers. Finally, thanks for encouragement from my colleagues in the School of Accounting and Finance, and in particular Patricia Barker and Marie Baker for arranging valuable "market research" when this text was no more than a gleam in my eye.

Raymond Byrne,
N.I.H.E. Dublin,
1st September 1985.

CHAPTER 1

Precedent and Legal Reasoning

When a judge sits down to decide civil cases, he performs a dual role. Firstly, he must listen to what the witnesses on both sides have to say and if there is a conflict between them, to decide which account he believes; in other words, it is the judge who decides what the facts of a case are for the purposes of the law. His second function is to hear legal arguments on both sides where this is necessary, and then to determine the rules and principles of law which are applicable in the case. In a legal system, such as Ireland's, based on the common law where the judges develop the law through the decisions they arrive at in individual cases, the lawyers on both sides will attempt to convince the judge of their legal arguments by referring him to previous decisions of judges in similar cases. The judge is expected to arrive at a conclusion which fits into some consistent pattern for the development of the law, and he will usually rely on some previous decision in arriving at whatever conclusion he reaches. In doing so, the judge employs the doctrine of precedent, a central part of the legal system in Ireland.

The doctrine of precedent has a number of facets to it, and in the Irish context this would include matters such as that any decision of a higher court in the hierarchy of courts binds a lower court. This means that a decision of the Supreme Court binds all other courts and indeed, except in exceptional cases, binds the Supreme Court itself. This important facet of the doctrine of precedent means that once a precedent has been established, for example, in the Supreme Court, all other courts are bound to follow that lead by saying, in effect, "let the decision stand", as the relevant phrase *stare decisis* indicates. This allows lawyers to advise clients about how a legal issue will, or at least ought to, be decided. In turn this certainty allows businessmen to rely on settled legal rules and principles in going about their ordinary business affairs. This facet of the doctrine relates to the consequences of its operation but this chapter is more concerned with the techniques used by judges, and by extension legal writers and lawyers, in developing the law through reliance on precedent.

Textbooks on the law use statements by judges in many cases to build up a picture of the law, and these are often helpful to student and practitioner alike. Actual cases do not, however, consist of a narrative of legal issues alone; they also involve interaction between persons which must then be fitted into some legal framework. Thus, when a judge arrives at a particular legal conclusion, he has done so within the context of a particular live conflict which has been re-enacted before him in a courtroom. Judges frequently make the point that they are not in the business of deciding questions of purely academic legal interest and that their main function is to resolve actual disputes. The doctrine of precedent in turn has a firm footing in actual conflict resolution because only conclusions of law secured to the facts of a case which a judge is resolving are said to create legally binding precedents in subsequent cases. Such conclusions are said to form, or perhaps be simply a part of, the *ratio decidendi* of the case, indicating that this fairly narrowly defined "reason for a decision" must be adhered to. Where legal conclusions cannot be said to be rooted in the facts of the case resolved by a judge, they are described as *obiter dicta*. The translation of this phrase, "statements by the way" hides the reality that statements of legal rules by judges which might technically be described as *obiter* are nonetheless treated with a great deal of reverence by other judges and textbook writers. In other words, the distinction which has been drawn between *ratio decidendi* and *obiter dictum* proposes some kind of guiding rule of thumb, not a mathematical formula, within which judges can deal with precedent.

Common sense dictates that a High Court judge is not likely to turn his back on any statement in a Supreme Court judgment which commands the respect of all the then Supreme Court judges simply because the lawyer for one of the parties in the case before him can describe the statement in question as *obiter* and not necessary for the resolution of the earlier case. In some instances, of course, a statement in an earlier case may be unavoidably relevant to the present case before the judge and so he may be reluctantly forced by the strictures of *stare decisis* to apply that case to the issues before him. But this type of situation is more the exception than the rule. In the majority of cases the judge can exercise a choice about whether he accepts what was stated in a previous case. Where he agrees with what was said in the earlier case, he can say he is prepared to follow what was said. If, however, he does not agree then he may be able to say the statement was *obiter* or that there are crucial differences of fact between the case and the one with which he himself has to deal. And it is important to note that he, not the earlier judge, decides this. Broadly speaking, this is referred to as the art of distinguishing cases; it is an indispensible tool to the judge and to any person who becomes involved in the law either as a student or as a lawyer. It involves the use of argument by analogy, and as a result the focus of attention here is on the fusing of the facts of a case to the legal conclusions reached. In this process the link in time btweeen a case being relied on as a precedent and a case calling for resolution by a judge can be seen. If there is a close analogy between the facts of the case being relied on and those of the case today, the lawyer relying on that case will find it relatively easy to convince the judge that he should follow the legal conclusion reached in the earlier decision, and at least he will force the judge today to use a convincing argument to reject the case, a rejection which must be rooted in a legal conclusion gleaned from some other precedent; otherwise the judge risks being reversed on appeal to a higher court. If, on the other hand, the lawyer is relying on a precedent bearing little resemblance to the present case, his opponent will quickly point this out to the judge and attempt to convince him that it should not be used by the judge in arriving at his conclusion.

Argument by analogy is, therefore, central to legal reasoning and this is illustrated in the judgment of Barrington J. on solicitors' liability for negligence in *Wall* v. *Hegarty and Callnan* (1980) (Extract 1.1). The law relating to negligence has developed in Ireland and England since the important decision of the House of Lords in England in *Donoghue* v. *Stevenson* [1932] A.C. 562. That development has been based on the general comments made by Lord Atkin in that case in which he formulated what became known as the neighbour principle. The case itself established the liability of the careless manufacturer of ginger beer to the ultimate consumers of his product who suffer physical injury. Lord Atkin's principle, which is referred to in Barrington J.'s judgment, is, however, stated in extremely broad terms. Strictly speaking, it was not necessary for Lord Atkin to put forward the principle in order to decide the particular case, so that it could be described as an *obiter dictum* and not part of the *ratio decidendi* (even had Lord Atkin been the only judge in the case). After some initial hesitation, the neighbour principle has, however, been applied to a variety of situations far removed from the original context of *Donoghue* v. *Stevenson*. Those applications have been based on the use of *Donoghue* v. *Stevenson* as an analogy, with the neighbour principle being regarded as a general proposition which should be applied to all other similar cases unless some justification, such as public policy, makes it application inappropriate: see *Anns* v. *Merton London Borough Council* [1978] A.C. 728. The use of argument by analogy is even stronger in *Wall* v. *Hegarty and Callnan* since the English cases relied on by Barrington J. can at best be described only as persuasive precedents, and whatever the *ratio decidendi* of any of those cases might be, they could never be binding on Irish judges of any rank. But leaving that point aside, Barrington J. was being asked to decide whether the neighbour principle should be applied where because of a solicitor's carelessness in not witnessing a will properly a person due a legacy under the will loses out on that legacy. Should the solicitor be made responsible for that person's loss in the same way as the manufacturer of beer in *Donoghue* v. *Stevenson*? The answer lies, ultimately, in the balance of analogy between the circumstances arising in the two instances. There is the similar type of relationship in which the "consumer" is, in theory at any rate, relying on the skill and expertise of the manufacturer or professional person. There are sharp differences in terms of the activity involved and also in terms of the type of injury sustained, but clearly these differences in detail are outweighed in Barrington J.'s mind by the broader similarities of the situations. This is an important factor in his conclusion that the solicitor must be held responsible to the person who lost out on his legacy.

Having seen how the use of analogy is important in legal reasoning, it is as well to balance this with an instance of how the more technical process of analysing a case in terms of its core, its *ratio decidendi*, can also play a part in the development of precedent. The process of distinguishing has been mentioned already and in many cases an old decision may be got around by using this technique or by describing a statement in the old case as *obiter*. But there may be situations where the central part of a court's decision 30 years ago has been overtaken by more recent decisions and the day comes when that 30 year old case must be faced squarely and overruled. Most of these factors are at work in the extract from the judgment of Henchy J. in *The State (Lynch)* v. *Cooney* (1982) (Extract 1.2). At least three steps can be seen in his process of concluding that the courts must be able to review the exercise of discretionary powers granted by legislation in permissive and wide terms. First, Henchy J. makes a painstaking analysis of a statement in the Supreme Court decision *In re the Offences Against the State (Amendment) Bill, 1940* [1940] I.R. 470 that the courts have no function to review such powers. The conclusion reached, based on this analysis, is that the statement was an *obiter dictum*. The second stage of his analysis is to conclude that the adoption of this statement by the Supreme Court in 1957 in *In re Ó Laighléis* [1960] I.R. 93 was a central part of that decision. The third step involved Henchy J. asking whether the *Ó Laighléis* decision, its *ratio decidendi*, should be overruled, and answering this in the affirmative. The answer is based on the simple premise that the view being put forward in 1940 as an aside, or *obiter*, and as part of the central reasoning of the Supreme Court in 1957 had been overtaken by more recent events in judgments of the Supreme Court itself which made it necessary to sweep those older decisions aside in order to establish a consistent picture of the law, which, as was stated at the beginning of this chapter, is an important element in the idea of precedent.

1.1   Wall v. Hegarty and Callnan
[1980] I.L.R.M. 134   High Court

[The defendants were a firm of solicitors who were instructed by a client to draw up his will.   They did this without attesting it as required by s.78 of the Succession Act, 1965.   Relatives of the testator succeeded in having the will declared invalid after his death.   The plaintiff was to receive £15,000 as a legacy under the will.   He issued these proceedings against the solicitors, claiming £15,000 as damages suffered as a result of the negligence of the solicitors in failing to ensure that the will they drew up for their client was properly attested.   The case thus raised the net point of law whether in the circumstances the solicitors owed a duty of care in law to persons other than their client.

In deciding that the plaintiff was entitled to succeed, Barrington J. brought together a number of strands.   First, he dealt with the old decision of *Robertson* v. *Fleming* (1861) 4 Macq. 167, which was an authority against the plaintiff.   It is of note that Barrington J. was prepared to deal with the decision on its own terms and was not content to dismiss it merely because the statements made by the judges in the case might be described as *obiter dicta*.   As it happened, this was not so difficult as in the second part of his discussion of the precedents in this area, stemming from *Donoghue* v. *Stevenson* [1932] A.C. 562, Barrington J. was able to conclude that the statements from the 1861 decision had been overtaken by later developments.   This he supports by referring to the only Irish case in his judgment, *Finlay* v. *Murtagh* [1979] I.R. 249.   At issue in that case was whether the plaintiff was entitled to a hearing in the High Court with a jury in his action against his solicitors.   Only if he could show that his solicitors owed him a duty other than in contract could he succeed.   The Supreme Court held in his favour on this issue.   The passages from the judgments in the case which Barrington J. relies on go further than was absolutely necessary to decide *Finlay* v. *Murtagh* and so might be described as *obiter dicta* but again he does not deal with the statements on this basis but is content to take them at face value.   Finally, by using the decision in *Ross* v. *Caunters* [1980] Ch. 297 as a further useful analogy in support of the plaintiff's claim, Barrington J. reaches a conclusion that fits easily within a consistent pattern in the development of the law on negligence and at the same time shows clearly why *Robertson* v. *Fleming* should no longer be regarded as a correct statement of the law.]

Barrington J.:

The plaintiff, in his statement of claim, pleads that a solicitor retained by a testator to prepare a will owes a duty to an executor and beneficiary named in the will to ensure that the testator's benevolent intentions in respect of the executor and beneficiary are not frustrated through lack of reasonable care on the part of the solicitor... Traditionally, English law did not regard a solicitor as owing any such duty to a legatee named in a testator's will and, so far as I am aware, the law of Ireland was no different in this respect. A passage which appears on p. 184 of the 1961 edition of *Cordery's Law Relating to Solicitors*, puts the matter as follows:

> "Since the solicitor's duty to his client is based on the contract of retainer, he owes no duty of care to anyone other than his client, save where he is liable as an officer of the court".

The chief authority relied on, in support of that proposition was *Robertson* v. *Fleming* (1861) 4 Macq. 167. That was a decision of the House of Lords in a Scottish case. It is arguable that the central question in that case was whether an issue which had been settled in the Second Division of the Court of Session properly raised the question of fact in dispute between the parties. But it is also arguable that this question of fact would have been irrelevant if a solicitor owed a duty, not only to his client, but also to the person for whose benefit his services had been retained. In any event, as Sir Robert Megarry has stated in the recent case of *Ross* v. *Caunters* [1980] Ch. 297, at p.304 the *dicta*, whether they were of the *ratio* or not, are clearly of high authority.

In that case, Lord Campbell L.C. rejected in the strongest possible terms the suggestion that a solicitor retained by a testator might owe any duty to a legatee who was a stranger to him... While Lord Campbell was in a minority in other aspects of the case, it would appear that a majority of his colleagues agreed with him on this point.

However, since *Robertson* v. *Fleming* was decided, there have been two major advances in the law, material to the consideration of the present question. First was the development of negligence as an independent tort and the line of authority running from *Donoghue* v. *Stevenson* [1932] A.C. 562 to *Hedley Byrne & Co. Ltd.* v. *Heller & Partners Ltd.* [1964] A.C. 465. In particular was the famous passage in Lord Atkin's speech in *Donoghue* v. *Stevenson*, where he stressed the duty to take reasonable care to avoid injuring one's neighbour, and went on to inquire:

> "Who, then, in law is my neighbour? The answer seems to be - persons who are so closely and directly affected by my act that I ought reasonably to have them in contemplation as being so affected when I am directing my mind to the acts or omissions which are called in question."

Lord Atkin went on to stress that the concept of 'neighbour' did not include merely persons in close physical proximity to the alleged tortfeasor; but also, all such persons as stood in such direct relationship with him, as to cause him to know that they would be directly affected by his careless act: see [1932] A.C. 562, at p.580.

The second important legal development which has taken place since *Robertson* v. *Fleming*, is that it is now finally established, so far, at any rate, as the law of Ireland is concerned, that a solicitor owes two kinds of duties to his client. First is his duty in contract to carry out the terms of his retainer. Second is a duty in tort to show reasonable professional skill in attending to his client's affairs. It is clear that this duty in tort arises simply because he is purporting to act as a solicitor for his client and is independent of whether he is providing his professional services voluntarily or for reward: see the judgment of the Supreme Court in *Finlay* v. *Murtagh* [1979] I.R. 249 and also the judgment of Oliver J. in *Midland Bank Trust Co. Ltd.* v. *Hett, Stubbs & Kemp* [1979] Ch. 384.

The Supreme Court in *Finlay* v. *Murtagh* was merely dealing with a net point of law as to whether a solicitor owed a duty to a client in tort as well as in contract, but it is quite clear that the Court, in holding that he did, derived the duty from the proximity principle outlined by Lord Atkin in *Donoghue* v. *Stevenson*. For instance, the following passage appears in the judgment of Kenny J. (at p. 264):

> "The professional person, however, owes the client a general duty, which does not arise from contract but from the "proximity" principle (*Donoghue* v. *Stevenson* [1932] A.C. 562 and *Hedley Byrne & Co. Ltd.* v. *Heller & Partners Ltd.* [1964] A.C. 465) to exercise reasonable care and skill in the performance of the work entrusted to him. This duty arises from the obligation which springs from the situation that he knew or ought to have known that his failure to exercise care and skill would probably cause loss and damage. This failure to have or to exercise reasonable skill and care is tortious or delictual in origin."

Indeed, Henchy J. in a passage in his judgment appears to anticipate the situation which has arisen in the present case. He says (at p. 257):

> "The solicitor's liability in tort under the general duty of care extends not only to a client for reward, but to any person for whom the solicitor undertakes to act professionally without reward, and also to those (such as beneficiaries under a will, persons entitled under an intestacy, or those entitled to benefits in circumstances such as a claim in respect of a fatal injury) with whom he has made no arrangement to act but who, as he knows or ought to know, will be relying on his professional care and skill. For the same default there should be the same cause of action. If others are entitled to sue in tort for the solicitor's want of care, so also should the client."

Since the decision of the Supreme Court in *Finlay* v. *Murtagh*, the specific question which arises in the present case arose for consideration in the English High Court in the case of *Ross* v. *Caunters* [1980] Ch. 297.

In that case, the testator instructed solicitors to draw up his will to include gifts of chattels and a share of his residuary estate to the plaintiff, who was his sister-in-law. The solicitors drew up the will naming the plaintiff as legatee. The testator requested the solicitors to send the draft will to him at the plaintiff's home where he was staying, to be signed and attested. The solicitors sent the will to the testator with a covering letter giving instructions on executing it, but failed to warn him that under section 15 of the Wills Act, 1837, attestation of the will by the beneficiary's spouse would invalidate the gift to the beneficiary. The plaintiff's husband attested the will which was then returned to the solicitors who failed to notice that he had attested it. In fact, prior to the execution of the will, the testator had, in correspondence, raised with his solicitors, the question "Am I right in thinking that beneficiaries may not be witnesses?" The solicitors unfortunately did not answer this question which clearly provided them with an opportunity to warn the testator that the spouse of a beneficiary should not be a witness either.

The testator died two years after the execution of the will. Some time later, the solicitors wrote to the plaintiff informing her that the gifts to her under the will were void because her husband had attested it. The plaintiff brought an action against the solicitors claiming damages for negligence for the loss of the gifts under the will. Sir Robert Megarry V.-C., after an exhaustive analysis of the authorities, held that she was entitled to succeed.

In the present case, [counsel for] the plaintiff has relied strongly on *Ross* v. *Caunters*. [Counsel for] the defendants has drawn the distinction that in *Ross* v. *Caunters* there was a valid will - only the bequest was invalid - whereas in the present case there was no valid will. He has also stated that I should not, by following *Ross* v. *Caunters* extend the traditional boundaries of the law of negligence in this country. However, it appears to me that the decision of the English High Court in *Ross* v. *Caunters* was already anticipated by the decision of our own Supreme Court in *Finlay* v. *Murtagh* and, for my own part, I find the reasoning of Sir Robert Megarry in *Ross* v. *Caunters* unanswerable.

I do not think that the fact that there was a valid will in *Ross* v. *Caunters* and that there is not a valid will in the present case is a material distinction. The question is whether the testator's solicitor owes any duty at all to the named legatee. If he owes such a duty and if the legacy fails because of his failure to observe it, it is immaterial whether the gift fails because of a defect in the words granting the legacy or because of a defect in the will itself.

I fully accept the reasoning of Sir Robert Megarry that in a case such as the present, there is a close degree of proximity between the plaintiff and the defendant. If a solicitor is retained by a testator to draft a will, and one of the purposes of the will is to confer a benefit on a named legatee, the solicitor must know that if he fails in his professional duty properly to draft the will, there is considerable risk the legatee will suffer damage. To use Sir Robert's words, his contemplation of the plaintiff is "actual, nominate and direct."

Likewise, I accept Sir Robert's reasoning that there can be no conflict of public policy in holding that a solicitor has a duty to take care in drafting a will, not only to the testator but also to a named legatee in the will. There is no possible inconsistency between the duty to the testator and the duty to the legatee. Recognising a duty to a legatee tends to strengthen the chances that the testator's wishes will in fact be properly expressed in the will. The two duties march together.

The authorities are, as I said, analysed by Sir Robert Megarry with consummate ability in his judgment in *Ross* v. *Caunters*, and it would be otiose for me to repeat here the exercise which he has carried out in his judgment. Suffice it to say that I am satisfied on the basis of the decision in *Finlay* v. *Murtagh* that a solicitor does owe a duty to a legatee named in a draft will, to draft the will with such reasonable care and skill as to ensure that the wishes of the testator are not frustrated and the expectancy of the legatee defeated through lack of reasonable care and skill on the part of the solicitor.

20

1.2 The State(Lynch) v. Cooney
[1982] I.R. 337 Supreme Court

[Mr. Lynch was a candidate for Sinn Féin in the February 1982 general election.   Radio Telefís Éireann decided to allow airtime to his party to make party political broadcasts during the election campaign.   Mr. Cooney, the then Minister for Posts and Telegraphs, made an order under s.31 of the Broadcasting Authroity Act, 1960, as amended in 1976, directing R.T.E. not to allow any spokesman for Sinn Féin to make a party political broadcast.   S.31 allows such directives to be issued where the Minister "is of the opinion" that a broadcast would be likely to promote to, or incite to, crime or would tend to undermine the authority of the State.   Sinn Féin challenged the validity of the Minister's directive.   In the High Court, O'Hanlon J. held that the courts had no power to review the evidence on which the Minister based his opinion, and he therefore held s.31 was unconstitutional because it conflicted with the constitutional right of freedom of expression.   The Supreme Court, on appeal, reversed that decision. The extract from the judgment of Henchy J. discusses the cases on which O'Hanlon J. had based his decision.

O'Hanlon J. had referred to the statement of the Supreme Court in *In re the Offences Against the State (Amendment) Bill, 1940* [1940] I.R. 470 that "opinion" based powers could not be reviewed by the courts.   By carefully placing that statement in the context of the overall reasoning of the entire judgment of the Supreme Court, and the decision in *The State (Burke) v. Lennon* [1940] I.R. 136, Henchy J. is able to conclude that the statement was *obiter*.   He then contrasts this with the position in *In re Ó Laighléis* [1960] I.R. 93 when the Supreme Court rejected the possibility of reviewing the same opinion power, this time as part of the central reasoning in the case.   Finally, having established there did exist a Supreme Court judgment *ratio* stating these powers could not be reviewed, Henchy J. felt that the decision must be overruled because it has been overtaken by more recent decisions in the Irish courts which had stated that analogous powers were capable of being reviewed.   Had Henchy J. wanted to he could have referred to such Supreme Court decisions as *East Donegal Co-Op. Ltd.* v. *The Attorney General* [1970] I.R. 317 and *Loftus* v. *The Attorney General* [1979] I.R. 221.]

Henchy J.:

It appears from the judgment under appeal that the reason why the judge held that ... the Minister's opinion was excluded from judicial review was because the judge felt bound to follow a statement to that effect in the judgment of the then Supreme Court in *In re the Offences Against the State (Amendment) Bill, 1940* [1940] I.R. 470.   If that statement could be said to be part of the *ratio decidendi* of that judgment, I would agree that the doctrine of *stare decisis* would have obliged the judge to follow it - even though the Supreme Court which gave that judgment was the Supreme Court which was empowered to function as such under the transitory provisions of the Constitution of Ireland, 1937, and was not the Supreme Court which was required by Article 34, s.1, of the Constitution to be established by law and which was eventually so established by the Courts (Establishment and Constitution) Act, 1961. The maintenance of judicial order and continuity would support such a conclusion.

However, I do not consider that the statement relied on could be said to be part of the *ratio decidendi* of that decision of the former Supreme Court. The reference by the President of Ireland to the Supreme Court of the Bill in question was deemed necessary because of the decision of Gavan Duffy J. in 1939 in *The State (Burke)* v. *Lennon* [1940] I.R. 136. In that case Gavan Duffy J. ordered the release by habeas corpus of an internee who was being detained under Part VI of the Offences Against the State Act, 1939; the judge made the order primarily because, in his opinion, Part VI of the Act of 1939 was repugnant to the Constitution. Part VI had contained a provision (s. 54) whereby the Government was empowered in certain emergency circumstances to bring that Part of the Act into operation by making and publishing a proclamation to that effect. The Government had made and published such a proclamation. Part VI had also provided (s. 55, sub-s.1) as follows:

> "Whenever a Minister of State is satisfied that any particular person is engaged in activities calculated to prejudice the preservation of the peace, order, or security of the State, such Minister may by warrant under his hand order the arrest and detention of such person..."

...As the report shows, when the respondents brought an appeal to the Supreme Court from [the High Court] decision, the Supreme Court held that an appeal did not lie. In what was apparently an effort to circumvent this impasse, the Government introduced the Offences Against the State (Amendment) Bill, 1940, and it was passed by both Houses of the Oireachtas. When the Bill was presented to the President of Ireland for signature he, in exercise of the power vested in him by Article 26 of the Constitution, referred the Bill to the Supreme Court for a ruling as to its constitutionality... Possibly to justify the enactment of the Bill as an amendment, the text of the Bill differed in a few minor respects from that of Part VI of the Act of 1939. The main difference was that under the Bill a warrant of internment could issue "whenever a Minister of State is of opinion" that the proposed internee is engaged in the specified activities, whereas under the condemned Part VI the warrant could issue whenever a Minister "is satisfied" that the proposed internee is engaged in those activities.

A study of the judgment of Gavan Duffy J. shows that, even if s. 55, sub-s. 1, of the Act of 1939 had used the words "is of opinion" instead of "is satisfied", he would still have found Part VI to be unconstitutional. I say that because it is clear from that judgment that it was the effect of the ministerial warrant (which was held to be "an authority, not merely to act judicially, but to administer justice and an authority to administer criminal justice") and not the mental element leading to the making of the warrant that was the foundation for the opinion of Gavan Duffy J. that Part VI of the Act of 1939 was unconstitutional. Indeed, it might well be contended that if s. 55, sub-s. 1, of the Act of 1939 had used the words "is of opinion" - thus connoting a laxer and more arbitary level of ministerial assessment - Gavan Duffy J. might very well have treated those words as an *a fortiori* reason for his finding of unconstitutionality.

Upon the hearing of the reference by the President, the Supreme Court rejected the argument that the Bill was unconstitutional. In doing so, the Court set aside the conclusion of Gavan Duffy J. that, in making and issuing a warrant for detention, the Minister of State was administering justice within the meaning of Article 34; it rejected the argument that the impugned provisions created a criminal offence; and it dismissed the contention that those provisions fell short of the guarantees as to personal rights contained in Article 40. In short, the Supreme Court overthrew the conclusion of Gavan Duffy J., as well as the rationale for that conclusion, as to the effect, in the constitutional perspective, of the making and issuing of a warrant of detention. In neither decision was the adjudicative process, whereby the Minister of State decided in that case to make and issue a warrant, a crucial element. Each decision would have reached the conclusion actually reached, whether the impugned provisions used the expression "is of opinion" or the expression "is satisfied."

It is true, however, that in *In re the Offences Against the State (Amendment) Bill, 1940* [1940] I.R. 470 the Supreme Court expressed itself (p. 479) as follows in the course of its decision:

> "The only essential preliminary to the exercise by the Minister of the powers contained in s. 4 [*i.e., as to the making and issue of a warrant of detention*] is that he should have formed opinions on the matters specifically mentioned in the section. The validity of such opinions is not a matter that could be questioned in any Court."

On a perusal of the judgment as a whole, I am satisfied that the opinion expressed in that quotation was purely *obiter*. It is a parenthesis which has no necessary connection with either the conclusions or the reasoning of the judgment. It is no more than a passing remark, superfluous to the disposition of any of the reported submissions of counsel in the case. On the application of any of the tests for distinguishing *obiter dicta* from that which is part of the *ratio decidendi* of a case, I would deem that by-the-way observation to be *obiter*. Therefore, it has not the authority of a binding precedent.

I regret, therefore, that I cannot agree with the conclusion reached in the decision under appeal in this case, i.e., that the judgment given by the then Supreme Court is a conclusive authority for the proposition that the expression "is of opinion" does not permit of a judicial review of the opinion actually formed, so as to determine whether it was legally valid or not. Considering the commendable speed with which this case was dealt with in the High Court, one might excuse counsel for not having directed the judge's attention to a binding decision on the point, i.e., the decision of the then Supreme Court in *In re Ó Laighléis* [1960] I.R. 93. It is less understandable why, despite the fact that counsel on each side had an opportunity to file written submissions for the purpose of the appeal, this Court's attention has not been directed by counsel to that case, either in the written submissions or in the course of the argument.

Notwithstanding that lapse, however, once the case has come to our notice it has to be considered for the purpose of overruling or approving its decision on this point.

The *Ó Laighléis* case came before the Supreme Court on appeal from a decision of the High Court to the effect that Ó Laighléis, who was being held in internment pursuant to a warrant made by the Minister for Justice under s. 4 of the Offences Against the State (Amendment) Act, 1940, was not entitled to be released by *habeas corpus.* The appeal by the internee was dismissed. While not questioning the bona fides of the Minister for Justice in making and issuing the warrant, counsel for Ó Laighléis submitted that, as the internee had averred in his affidavit that he was not engaged in illegal activities at the time of his arrest, he was entitled to question the validity of that Minister's opinion. The Court ruled otherwise. In doing so it quoted (at p. 130) and applied the dictum, supra, appearing at p. 479 of the report of the judgment of the Court in *In re the Offences Against the State (Amendment) Bill, 1940,* which dictum states that the validity of such opinions cannot be questioned in any court. What was merely *obiter* in the 1940 case thus became part of the *ratio decidendi* in the *Ó Laighléis* case. The question, then, is whether that ruling should be still adhered to. In my opinion, it should not. It should be overruled in exercise of the power of this Court to do so as stated in *The Attorney General* v. *Ryan's Car Hire Ltd.* [1965] I.R. 642, and in *Mogul of Ireland Ltd.* v. *Tipperary (N.R.) County Council* [1976] I.R. 260.

While it might be argued that the opinion of the then Supreme Court expressed in those decisions of 1940 and 1957 was part of what was then current judicial thinking, that could not be said if the same opinion were expressed today. Decisions given in recent years in this and other jurisdictions show that the power of the courts to subject the exercise of administrative powers to judicial review is nowadays seen as having a wider reach than that delimited by those decisions of 1940 and 1957. The more recent decisions in this and other jurisdictions - I do not cite them, because counsel have not referred to them - show that there is good foundation for the conclusion stated in *de Smith's Judicial Review of Administrative Action* (4th ed. p. 326) as follows: "As we have already observed, nowadays the courts will not readily be deterred by subjectively worded statutory formulae from determining whether acts done avowedly in pursuance of statutory powers bore an adequate relationship to the purposes prescribed by statute."

I conceive the present state of evolution of administrative law in the courts on this topic to be that when a statute confers on a non-judicial person or body a decision-making power affecting personal rights, conditional on that person or body reaching a prescribed opinion or conclusion based on a subjective assessment, a person who shows that a personal right of his has been breached or is liable to be breached by a decision purporting to be made in exercise of that power has standing to seek, and the High Court has jurisdiction to give, a ruling as to whether the pre-condition for the valid exercise of the power has been complied with in a way that brings the decision within the express, or necessarily implied, range of the power conferred by the statute. It is to be presumed that, when it conferred the power, Parliament intended the power to be exercised only in a manner that would be in conformity with the

Constitution and within the limitations of the power as they are to be gathered from the statutory scheme or design. This means, amongst other things, not only that the power must be exercised in good faith but that the opinion or other subjective conclusion set as a precondition for the valid exercise of the power must be reached by a route that does not make the exercise unlawful - such as by misinterpreting the law, or by misapplying it through taking into consideration irrelevant matters of fact, or through ignoring relevant matters. Otherwise, the exercise of the power will be held to be invalid for being *ultra vires*.

CHAPTER 2

The Interpretation of Statutes

The drafter of legislation has the difficult task of attempting to state a general legal rule in a vacuum; he does not have the assistance of the particular facts of an actual case before him to help put that rule in context. Instead, it is the role of a statute to attempt, in a series of general words, to anticipate future events. Some statutes try to get around this inherent problem by setting out detailed clauses and subclauses, but invariably no matter how detailed the law, an actual case arises which may not have been foreseen and then the words used must be analysed by a judge to decide if they are sufficiently clear to indicate that had this case been adverted to then the intention was to cover it. To a large extent the judges have been left to decide for themselves the rules for interpreting statutes.

There are no set of hard and fast rules which must be followed by a judge when he is asked the meaning of a particular provision in a statute. He does, however, have a wide range of guidelines from which he may choose in order to find what lawyers describe as the intention of the legislature which passed the law, but which is in reality the intention which the judges assume that body to have had. This is because is most instances the problem being addressed by the judge is one which was probably not debated by the legislature at all. Before looking at the rules of interpretation, it is as well to mention a controversial point with judges: should they look at the debates which took place between members of the legislature when passing a piece of legislation to assist in finding the meaning of that law? The answer in England is an emphatic no, but the Irish situation is that at least one judge of the High Court is prepared to use Dail Debates to assist in the process of interpretation: *Wavin Pipes Ltd.* v. *Hepworth Iron Co. Ltd.* [1982] F.S.R. 32. The pros and cons of this argument are dealt with by Professor Casey, who favours the decision in the *Wavin Pipes* case, in his article "Statutory Interpretation - A New Departure" (1981) 3 D.U.L.J.(n.s.)110.

Legal writers sometimes talk about three main rules of statutory interpretation, the literal, golden and mischief rules, and these do give some idea of the process through which judges go in finding the meaning of legislative provisions. Briefly, the literal rule requires the judges to keep strictly to the words used in the statute and not go outside them to achieve a different meaning. The golden rule modifies this to a limited extent by stating that if the application of the literal approach would achieve an absurd or unreasonable result, then it must be assumed that this could not have been intended by the legislature. The mischief rule allows the judges to investigate the purpose behind the legislation to see what defect or "mischief" in the previous law it attempted to remedy. Even this short description of the general rules should show that they are not easily compatible, since two of them allow the judges to roam around at least to some extent in finding the meaning of legislation.

In fact the judges do tend to take a fairly broad approach in this area and words such as contextual, schematic or even teleological are used to explain the role of the judge, as the extracts below show. One point judges make over and over is, however, that their function is not to mend a piece of legislation to make it fit a particular situation: this is a function of a legislature. In the majority of cases the judges try to reach a sensible conclusion and one which ordinary people would recognise as correct. There may be exceptions where special rules apply. One common instance is where a statute imposes some penalty, for example a tax liability. In this instance the approach is particularly strict and the literal rule is predominant, as *Inspector of Taxes* v. *Kiernan* (1981) (Extract 2.3) illustrates. A more particular instance as far as Irish law is concerned is that in some cases the judges are prepared to give the benefit of the doubt to legislation passed since 1937 (when the Constitution came into force) which might appear to have ignored some constitutional requirements. This occurred when the Supreme Court was prepared to assume that the mart licensing system contained in the Livestock Marts Act, 1967 would be operated in a procedurally fair manner: *East Donegal Co-Op Ltd.* v. *The Attorney General* [1970] I.R. 317. In effect, the Court added on a scheme for the procedural implementation of the Act which allowed it to withstand constitutional challenge.

The three extracts provide some idea of the variety of approaches required to tackle problems of statutory interpretation. *Nestor* v. *Murphy* (1979) (Extract 2.1) shows the Supreme Court looking at the background to legislation, a modern day "mischief" approach, as well as adopting the golden rule of construction to the actual words used.
In *Dillon* v. *Minister for Posts and Telegraphs* (1981) (Extract 2.2) Henchy J. used the literal and contextual approaches to arrive at the same conclusion, but the lesson is that in difficult cases such as this the contextual approach provides a safer and less subjective basis for the conclusion actually reached. Finally, *Inspector of Taxes* v. *Kiernan* (1981) (Extract 2.3) provides a useful collection of specialised rules to deal with particular problems of interpretation, including that of legislation creating a liability to tax.

2.1. Nestor v. Murphy [1979] I.R. 326
Supreme Court

[The defendants were a married couple who agreed to sell the leasehold interest in their family home to the plaintiff. They refused to complete the sale to him on the ground that the agreement, which both the husband and wife had signed, was in breach of the provisions of s.3(1) of the Family Home Protection Act, 1976. That subsection of the Act states: "Where a spouse, without the prior consent in writing of the other spouse, purports to convey any interest in the family home to any person except the other spouse, then ...the purported conveyance shall be void." The Supreme Court rejected the objection by the defendants and ordered them to complete the sale to the plaintiff.

Two points may be noted about Henchy J.'s judgment. Firstly, he explains the basic intention behind the 1976 Act as a whole, referring to the "spirit and purpose" of its provisions. This, together with the "evil" which he feels s.3(1) is aimed at, might be described as a modern version of the mischief rule. The second point is that when he addresses the actual words used, Henchy J. admits that a literal interpretation would not give effect to the general intent of the Act; so a more limited meaning must be given to the subsection. The quotation from Lord Reid in *Luke* v. *Inland Revenue Commissioners* [1964] A.C. 557 illustrates the application of the golden rule to solve this problem.]

Henchy J.:

The basic purpose of the sub-section is to protect the family home by giving a right of avoidance to the spouse who was not a party to the transaction. It ensures that protection by requiring, for the validity of the contract to dispose and of the actual disposition, that the non-disposing spouse should have given a prior consent in writing. The point and purpose of imposing the sanction of voidness is to enforce the right of the non-disposing spouse to veto the disposition by the other spouse of an interest in the family home.

The sub-section cannot have been intended by Parliament to apply when both spouses join in the "conveyance". In such event no protection is needed for one spouse against an unfair and unnotified alienation by the other of an interest in the family home. The provisions of s. 3, sub-s. 1, are directed against unilateral alienation by one spouse. When both spouses join in the "conveyance," the evil at which the sub-section is directed does not exist.

To construe the sub-section in the way proposed on behalf of the defendants would lead to a pointless absurdity. As is conceded by counsel for the defendants, if their construction of s.3, sub-s. 1, is correct then either the husband or the wife could have the contract declared void because the other did not give a prior consent in writing. Such an avoidance of an otherwise enforceable obligation would not be required for the protection of the family home when both spouses have entered into a contract to sell it. Therefore, it would be outside the spirit and purpose of the Act.

In such circumstances we must adopt what has been called a schematic or teleological approach. This means that s. 3, sub-s. 1, must be given a construction which does not overstep the limits of the operative range that must be ascribed to it, having regard to the legislative scheme as expressed in the Act of 1976 as a whole. Therefore, the words of s. 3, sub-s. 1, must be given no wider meaning than is necessary to effectuate the right of avoidance given when the non-participating spouse has not consented in advance in writing to the alienation of any interest in the family home. Such a departure from the literal in favour of a restricted meaning was given this justification by Lord Reid in *Luke* v. *Inland Revenue Commissioners* [1964] A.C. 557 when he said, at p. 577 of the report:

> "To apply the words literally is to defeat the obvious intention of the legislation and to produce a wholly unreasonable result. To achieve the obvious intention and produce a reasonable result we must do some violence to the words. This is not a new problem, though our standard of drafting is such that it rarely emerges.
> The general principle is well settled. It is only where the words are absolutely incapable of a construction which will accord with the apparent intention of the provision and will avoid a wholly unreasonable result, that the words of the enactment must prevail."

2.2 Dillon v. Minister for Posts and Telegraphs (1981) Supreme Court

[Mr. Dillon was a candidate in the 1981 general election. To qualify for distribution of his election literature free of charge, he submitted a sample to the Department of Posts and Telegraphs. The Department rejected the literature for free postage. The main ground on which the Department objected was that it was in breach of the statutory regulations governing postal packets, which are referred to in the extract from the judgment of Henchy J., but the objection was rejected by the Supreme Court.

In the extract, it is notable that Henchy J. rejects the Minister's objection to the leaflet, and the particular passage to which he objected, on the application both of a literal view of the regulations and also on the application of the maxim *noscitur a sociis,* a rule which requires the courts to look not only at the text of legislation but also the context.]

Henchy J.:

The Minister rests his case on certain restrictions imposed by the Post Office Act, 1908, and regulations made thereunder. Assuming (without necessarily so holding) that the Act and those regulations have application to this case, one notes that Reg. 6 of the relevant regulations (The Inland Post Warrant, 1939) prohibits the posting, conveyance, or delivery by post of "any postal packet...[h]aving thereon, or on the cover thereof, any words, marks, or designs of an indecent, obscene or grossly offensive character". Again assuming (without necessarily so deciding) that this brochure falls within the definition of "postal packet" given in the 1908 Act, or within the more restricted definition of "postal packet" given in the 1939 regulations, I would find it impossible to hold that the brochure is debarred from the benefit of free post because of the passage in it to which the Minister takes exception. That passage, and it is the only passage relied on for the purpose of this point, runs as follows:

> "Today's politicians are dishonest because they are being political
> and must please the largest number of people".

I am far from saying that even if the prohibition were simply against words of a grossly offensive character, I would have held that sentence would offend against such a prohibition. And I venture to think that those who practise what is often dubbed the art of the possible would not feel grossly offended by such an expression of opinion which, denigratory and cynical though it might be thought by some, is no more than the small coinage of the currency of political controversy. Some of the most revered and successful politicians who have lived have failed, at least in the eyes of reputable historians, to align great political acumen and success with moral or intellectual honesty. A charge of dishonesty is one that rarely penetrates the epidermis of any seasoned politician.

But the embargo is not simply against words of a grossly offensive character. So I do not have to reject the Minister's objection on that ground. The embargo is against "any words, marks, or designs of an indecent, obscene or grossly offensive character". That assemblage of words gives a limited and special meaning to the expression "grossly offensive character". As Stamp J. said in *Bourne* v. *Norwich Crematorium Ltd.* [1967] 1 W.L.R. 691, at p. 696:

> "English words derive colour from those which surround them.
> Sentences are not mere collections of words to be taken out of the
> sentence, defined separately by reference to the dictionary or
> decided cases, and then put back again into the sentence with the
> meaning which one has assigned to them as separate words..."

Applying the maxim *noscitur a sociis,* which means that a word or expression is known from its companions, the expression "grossly offensive character" must be held to be infected in this context with something akin to the taint of indecency or obscenity. Much of what might be comprehended by the expression if it stood alone is excluded by its juxtaposition with the words "indecent" and "obscene". This means that the Minister may not reject a passage as disqualified for free circulation through the post because it is apt to be thought displeasing or distasteful. To merit rejection it must be grossly offensive in the sense of being obnoxious or abhorrent in a way that brings it close to the realm of indecency or obscenity. The sentence objected to by the Minister, while many people would consider it to be denigratory of today's politicians, is far from being of a "grossly offensive character" in the special sense in which that expression is used in the regulations.

30

2.3   Inspector of Taxes v. Kiernan
[1981] I.R. 117   Supreme Court

[Mr. Kiernan was a farmer who specialised in buying, fattening and selling pigs.   He was assessed for income tax under the provisions of s. 78 of the Income Tax Act, 1967, which applied to a taxpayer who is "a dealer in cattle".   He appealed against that assessment and the Supreme Court, affirming the High Court, upheld that appeal.

While it might seem strange that the courts should have spent so much time deciding that "cattle" did not refer to pigs, the problem was not quite so simple.   In the extract, Henchy J. points out that in some legislation the word cattle had been given a special definition which actually encompassed pigs, amongst other animals.   He then points out that such special definitions were not relevant in deciding the issue of the meaning of s.78 of the 1967 Act.   When he turns to that issue he applies two general and one special rule of interpretation.   The special rule is the one applied to legislation imposing any form of penalty such as a law imposing a tax liability: the courts will be strict in interpreting such a provision.   The other two rules to which he refers amount to giving words in a statute the meaning which ordinary people would give them.   The important key to this approach to the meaning of s.78 of the 1967 Act is that Henchy J. is able to conclude that the word cattle is directed to the public at large rather than to a selected section of the public who might use the word in a specialised sense.]

Henchy J.:

There is no doubt that, at certain stages of English usage and in certain statutory contexts, the word "cattle" is wide enough in its express or implied significance to include pigs.   That fact, however, does not lead us to a solution of the essential question before us.   When the legislature used the word "cattle" in the Act of 1918 and again in the Act of 1967, without in either case giving it a definition, was it intended that the word should comprehend pigs?

That the word has, or has been held to have, that breadth of meaning in other statutes is not to the point.   A word or expression in a given statute must be given meaning and scope according to its immediate context, in line with the scheme and purpose of the particular statutory pattern as a whole, and to an extent that will truly effectuate the particular legislation or a particular definition therein.   For example, s. 1 of the Towns Improvement (Ireland) Act, 1854, defines the word "cattle" as including "horse, mare, gelding, foal, colt, filly, bull, cow, heifer, ox, calf, ass, mule, ram, ewe, wether, lamb, goat, kid or swine."   Unlike such an instance, the question posed here is whether the word "cattle" includes pigs in a taxing Act when the word is left undefined.

Leaving aside any judicial decision on the point, I would approach the matter by the application of three basic rules of statutory interpretation.   First, if the statutory provision is one directed to the public at large, rather than to a particular class who may be expected to use the word or expression in question in either a narrowed or an extended connotation, or as a term of art, then, in the absence of internal evidence suggesting the contrary, the word or expression should be given its ordinary or colloquial meaning. As Lord Esher M.R. put it in *Unwin* v. *Hanson* [1891] 2 Q.B. 115 at p. 119 of the report:

> "If the Act is directed to dealing with matters affecting everybody generally, the words used have the meaning attached to them in the common and ordinary use of language. If the Act is one passed with reference to a particular trade, business, or transaction, and words are used which everybody conversant with that trade, business, or transaction, knows and understands to have a partcular meaning in it, then the words are to be construed as having that particular meaning, though it may differ from the common or ordinary meaning of the words."

The statutory provisions we are concerned with here are plainly addressed to the public generally, rather than to a selected section thereof who might be expected to use words in a specialised sense. Accordingly, the word "cattle" should be given the meaning which an ordinary member of the public would intend it to have when using it ordinarily.

Secondly, if a word or expression is used in a statute creating a penal or taxation liability, and there is looseness or ambiguity attaching to it, the word should be construed strictly so as to prevent a fresh imposition of liability from being created unfairly by the use of oblique or slack language: see Lord Esher M.R. in *Tuck & Sons* v. *Priester* (1887) 19 Q.B.D. 629 (at p. 638); Lord Reid in *Director of Public Prosecutions* v. *Ottewell* [1970] A.C. 642 (at p. 649) and Lord Denning M.R. in *Farrell* v. *Alexander* [1976] Q.B. 345 (at pp. 358-9). As used in the statutory provisions in question here, the word "cattle" calls for such a strict construction.

Thirdly, when the word which requires to be given its natural and ordinary meaning is a simple word which has a widespread and unambiguous currency, the judge construing it should draw primarily on his own experience of its use. Dictionaries or other literary sources should be looked at only when alternative meanings, regional usages or other obliquities are shown to cast doubt on the singularity of its ordinary meaning, or when there are grounds for suggesting that the meaning of the word has changed since the statute in question was passed. In regard to "cattle", which is an ordinary and widely used word, one's experience is that in its modern usage the word, as it would fall from the lips of the man in the street, would be intended to mean and would be taken to mean no more than bovine animals. To the ordinary person, cattle, sheep and pigs are distinct forms of livestock.

It was submitted on behalf of the appellant that it should be borne in mind that the Act of 1967 is a consolidating Act and that the Act of 1918 is also a consolidating Act which incorporated, inter alia, the Income Tax Act, 1842, which contained an almost identical provision for persons who were dealers in "cattle". Accordingly, it was contended, the prevalent meaning of the word in 1842 is the meaning that should be applied for the purposes of the Acts of 1918 and 1967, and it was submitted that there were grounds for believing that at that time the word had a wider usage and meaning which would comprehend pigs. However, as has been pointed out by Mr. Justice McWilliam in his

32

judgment in the High Court, a consideration of the definition of the word "cattle" contained in the edition of the Oxford Dictionary published at the end of the 19th century clearly confirms the meaning as restricted to bovine animals. Therefore, I would so construe it in the context in question here.

CHAPTER 3

The Constitution and Constitutional Rights

The basic law of a State is contained in its Constitution, a fact recognised by the Irish name given to the Constitution of 1937, Bunreacht na hÉireann. The majority of the Constitution's provisions, which are called Articles, are devoted to a description of the basic organisation of the political and legal structures of the State, in particular the executive (cabinet government), legislative (Houses of the Oireachtas) and judical branches of government. Most legal systems of Western democracies are organised on this three way separation of powers with, at least in theory, separate areas of function for each branch. What this chapter focuses on, however, is the relatively powerful function conferred by the Constitution on the judical branch which has had a profound impact on the other two branches. This is the power which the High Court and, on appeal, the Supreme Court have to declare that a piece of legislation, passed by the Oireachtas or its predecessors, has no legal effect because it is in conflict with one of the many rights which the constituional text sets out. The list of explicitly stated rights is long. The rights include political rights, such as to vote at Dail elections by means of a secret ballot (Article 16.1.4⁰), freedom of expression, assemble peaceably and join associations and unions (Article 40.6.1⁰), social rights regarding the protection of private property (Article 43) and the protection of the family and the education of children (Articles 41 and 42) as well as religious freedom (Article 44) and traditional legal rights, such as protection against the arbitrary taking away of personal liberty (Article 40.4) and the right to jury trial in most serious criminal matters (Article 38.5). At some time or another since 1937 the courts have been asked to adjudicate on claims that legislation has conflicted with these constitutional rights and in consequence the courts have declared such legislation to have had no legal effect where the conflict has been established. In addition to the wide-ranging list of these explicit constitutional rights, the courts have found a further source of rights. Using the text of Article 40.3 of the Constitution, the High Court and Supreme Court have established that there exists an unspecified list of rights, sometimes called unenumerated rights, which arise from what might be termed the spirit of the Constituion and are sometimes to be implied from the more explicit rights contained in the Constitution.

It is not possible to discuss in any depth here whether the courts should have the power to declare legislation to be unconstitutional or whether the idea of unenumerated constitutional rights is too vague to be left to the courts to expound and expand in the future. What can be done is to accept that the courts do at present have such powers and to describe their impact in the social and economic spheres. Two cases have been chosen for this purpose.

In *Madigan & Ors.* v. *The Attorney General* (1983 and 1984) (Extract 3.1), the High Court and Supreme Court were asked to decide whether the residential property tax contained in Part VI of the Finance Act, 1983 conflicted with the property rights of the plaintiffs guaranteed in Article 40.3 and Article 43 of the Constitution. In the course of his judgment in the High Court, O'Hanlon J. discusses most of the recent cases which have involved constitutional challenges to taxation laws of one form or another and in so doing attempts to place the role of the judges in this sensitive area in perspective. The judges have consistently pointed out that it is not their function to decide the wisdom or otherwise of legislative provisions, whether tax laws or laws involving social or moral questions, but that it is merely to decide whether such legislation meets constitutional tests. The problem is that in most areas where the courts are asked to adjudicate on constitutional matters, the dividing line between harsh laws which are constitutional and laws which seem desirable but are unconstitutional is difficult to draw, and this leaves the courts open to a certain degree of criticism normally confined to the political arena. The *Madigan* case, like its predecessor on the taxation of married couples *Murphy* v. *The Attorney General* [1982] I.R. 241, is an example of the spillover of a political argument into the legal sphere and there is an understandable, though misplaced, tendancy to confuse the different arguments used in the these respective spheres. This leads in turn to the frequent disclaimers by the courts regarding their role in constitutional adjudication.

The Madigan case also raises more subtle problems of legal technique, since in explaining the scope of property rights the courts must have regared to two differing constitutional provisions. Article 40.3.2⁰ recites that in relation to, amongst others, the property rights of every citizen the State "shall... by its laws protect as best it may from unjust attack and, in the case of injustice done, vindicate", those rights. Article 43, on the other hand, acknowledges the natural right of man, as a rational being, to the private ownership of external goods; protects against any attempt by the State to abolish that right; and recognises that the right may be regulated by principles of social justice and that the State may delimit its exercise in light of the exigencies of the common good. Since the Supreme Court judgment in the *Blake* case, mentioned by O'Hanlon J. in *Madigan,* the courts have attempted to describe the appropriate weight to be given to each of these constitutional protections of property rights. This is a matter which has yet to be finally determined. The main emphasis in *Madigan* was on Article 40.3, although in the Supreme Court judgment Article 43 was referred to, so it is clear that it has some relevance to discussing the extent of the property rights of the individual, rather than simply being a limit on the State's rights in this area.

As mentioned above, Article 40.3 has also been interpreted as a source of constitutional rights which the courts graft on to the list of explicity stated rights. In part, Article 40.3 fuses into other constitutional provisions such as Article 43 and this may account for the difficulty which judges have found in tackling the problem of constitutional rights which they say can only be found by reading something into the Constitution. The extracts from the judgments of Walsh and Henchy JJ. in *McGee* v. *The Attorney General* (1973) (Extract 3.2) illustrate the problem here. Both judges agree that the State was not entitled to intrude into the private area of decision-making in which Mrs. McGee and her husband resolved not to have more children. But Walsh J. appeared to rest his judgment on the protection given to the family unit in Article 41; Henchy J. felt that Mrs. McGee's right to privacy arose not merely from Article 41 but also from a right as an individual which he found to be implicit in Article 40.3. While both judges were in a sense finding rights implicit in the constitutional text (there being no explicit reference to a right to privacy in either Article 41 or Article 40.3) the fact that Henchy J. linked privacy to Article 40.3 opened up a broader area of potential application outside the family unit circumstances of *McGee* itself.

Here, in the context of the basis on which rights are said to be implicit in the Constitution just as with the property rights cases, the courts have yet to clarify completely the relationship between Article 40.3 and, in this area, the rest of the constitutional text.

3.1   Madigan and Ors. v. The Attorney General (1983) High Court

[The plaintiffs challenged the constitutionality of Part VI of the Finance Act, 1983, which introduced a residential property tax, the tax being levied at the rate of 1.5% of the amount by which the market value of residential properties exceeded £65,000. Exemption from the tax could be obtained if the person assessed could show that his income, together with that of any other person normally residing in the property, did not exceed £20,000. Marginal relief for income up to £25,000, as well as reductions of one-tenth for each dependent child resident with the person assessed, were also provided for by the Act. The market value of the property was to be self-assessed, subject to a right of the Revenue Commissionsers to have this valuation reviewed. The plaintiffs owned and occupied property for which they would have been liable to tax under the Act. Their main challenge to the Act was that it failed to respect their constitutional rights regarding property contained in Articles 40.3 and 43. The claim was rejected by O'Hanlon J. in the High Court and, on appeal by the Supreme Court.

The extract from the judgment of O'Hanlon J. begins by pointing to the problem of achieving a balance between, on the one hand, the leeway to be given to the Oireachtas when drafting taxation laws and, on other, to the ultimate superiority of constitutional rights. When O'Hanlon J. goes on to deal with case law in the area he focuses on two decisions. The *Cityview Press* case involved a flat rate levy on a particular class of persons, similar to the tax in the 1983 Act, but as O'Hanlon J. admits the main argument in the case did not deal with the taxation issue as such. In the *Brennan* case, the poor law valuation system as applied to agricultural land was found unconstitutional. O'Hanlon J. points out that the anomalies present there were not present in the system as applied to residential properties and the analogy with that system appears later on in his judgment. Turning to the 1983 Act, his view is that although it singles out a particular class of property owners for tax purposes, this is not inherently unconstitutional and in particular the exemptions and income thresholds ameliorated the effects of the tax.

The Supreme Court, in affirming O'Hanlon J.'s decision, agreed with his description of the tax as a tax on the occupation of property and his conclusion that its imposition based on the market value of property over the stated limit did not conflict with the property rights contained in Articles 40.3 or 43. The Court also noted that the provisions of the Act which aggregated together the incomes of all occupants of assessed property reflected reality and were unobjectionable.]

O'Hanlon J.:

In challenging the validity of a taxation statute enacted by the Oireachtas, it appears to me that a plaintiff faces a very uphill battle. In the first place, there is the presumption of constitutionality which exists in favour of an Act of the Oireachtas. This principle has been reiterated in many cases, commencing with *In re the Offences against the State (Amendment) Bill, 1940* [1940] I.R. 470. It must be accepted as an important principle of construction and one which cannot be disregarded.

Secondly, it has been recognised, both in our own jurisdiction and in the

United States, where the constitutional guarantees are closely analogous to those provided by the Irish Constitution, that tax laws are in a category of their own, and that very considerable latitude must be allowed to the legislature in the enormously complex task of organising and directing the financial affairs of the State. Equality of treatment may be a desirable goal, but absolute equality can never be achieved. Each year's budgetary provisions bring with them a chorus of protest from sections of the community who feel they have been called upon to bear a disproportionate share of the tax burden. Very often these complaints are perfectly legitimate and well founded, but it is necessary to go much further to sustain a constitutional challenge to the validity of such financial provisions - otherwise the affairs of State would grind to a halt each year while the courts were called upon to review the contents of successive Finance Acts.

In a proper case, however, even tax laws must yield to the overriding requirements of the Constitution. The test to be applied has been expressed in a number of different ways. Mr. Justice Pitney, delivering the opinion of the U.S. Supreme Court in *Royster Guano Co.* v. *Virginia,* 253 U.S. 412 (1920) said, at p.415:

> "It is unnecessary to say that the "equal protection of the laws" required by the 14th Amendment does not prevent the states from resorting to classification for the purposes of legislation. Numerous and familiar decisions of this court establish that they have a wide range of discretion in that regard. But the classification must be reasonable, not arbitrary, and must rest upon some ground of difference having a fair and substantial relation to the object of the legislation, so that all persons similarly circumstanced shall be treated alike. The latitude of discretion is notably wide in the classification of property for purposes of taxation and the granting of partial or total exemptions upon grounds of policy...Nevertheless, a discriminatory tax law cannot be sustained against the complaint of a party aggrieved if the classification appear to be altogether illusory."

...While these were statements of legal principles based on the guarantees of "due process" and "the equal protection of the laws" as found in the American Constitution, with particular reference to he 5th and 14th Amendments, it appears to me that they are apposite when endeavouring to determine whether any part of our own taxation code is repugnant to the Constitution of Ireland, and I propose to apply them accordingly, in determining whether Part VI of the Finance Act, 1983 fails to respect the personal rights (in particular, rights of property) of the citizen, but rather represents an unjust attack on such rights....

In the Rent Act cases [*Blake and Ors.* v. *The Attorney General* [1982] I.R. 117]... the courts had to consider a situation where one section of the community, the landlords, were made to provide residential accommodation for another section of the community, the tenants, at artificially depressed rents, without regard to the means of either landlord or tenant. There were and are, rich landlords and poor landlords; rich tenants and poor tenants; but the income of the landlords from controlled tenanted property was frozen, in most cases by reference to already depressed rents payable in 1966, and remained frozen throughout a period of high inflation when incomes generally multiplied several times over. As well as controlling rents in this manner, the Acts also virtually dispossessed the landlord by curtailing severely his right ever to recover vacant possession of his property. These provisions were... found by the High Court and the Supreme Court to be indefensible. They represented an unjust attack on the property rights of landlords of controlled properties.

Conversely, in *Cityview Press Ltd.* v. *An Chomhairle Oiliúna and Ors.* [1980] I.R. 381 the High Court and, on appeal, the Supreme Court rejected a challenge to the constitutionality of something akin to a form of taxation imposed under the provisions of the Industrial Training Act, 1967. A levy was imposed on employers in the printing industry, based on 1% of the wage bill of the firm in excess of £20,000 per annum, to finance a training scheme for apprentices. The plaintiffs gave up employing apprentices and derived no benefit from the scheme. They objected to paying the levy which was imposed on them without regard to their turnover, their profitability, or their ability to pay, but almost the entire argument in the case was concerned with the constitutionality of giving to An Chomhairle Oiliuna (AnCO) the power to make the regulations under which the levy was imposed, and the further complaint that the Act permitted AnCO to impose different kinds of levy on different industries and sets of employers. It appears to have been accepted that it was permissible under the Constitution: (a) to impose a levy on employers in one section of industry, while not imposing it on employers generally; (b) to impose a levy based on a percentage of all emoluments paid to persons employed in firms in that section of industry, without regard to whether any particular firm had a small or large turnover, or was trading profitably or was in a loss-making situation with no means of paying the levy when imposed; and (c) to exempt from all liability to pay the levy, firms whose annual wage bill fell below a certain figure.

To revert to the circumstances of the present cases, I have to consider whether the provisions of Part VI of the Act of 1983 represent "an unjust attack" on the plaintiffs' rights of property; whether they can be regarded as "unreasonable", "arbitrary" or "hostile discrimination against particular persons or classes", to use the phrases which have found currency in previous decisions in this field of constitutional law.

The new system of taxation appears to me to have much in common with the former scheme involving the payment of rates on domestic premises. In each case a payment is levied in respect of the occupation of premises for residential purposes, and in each case such payment is exacted without regard to the income of the occupier or his ability to pay the amount demanded. In each case the payment must be made at the same rate whether the occupier is the freehold owner without incumbrances, or a lessee or owner of a lesser interest in the premises, or a person whose property is heavily mortgaged. The constitutionality of the rating system was never challenged until the case of *Brennan and Ors.* v. *The Attorney General and Anor.* [1983] I.L.R.M 449 highlighted the extreme anomalies which had been allowed to persist for over a century in the system of rating agricultural land, resulting in a finding by Mr. Justice Barrington in the High Court that the relevant provisions of the Valuation Acts, 1852 to 1864 were inconsistent with the Constitution and were no longer valid. These anomalies did not exist in relation to the rating system which was formerly applicable to domestic premises.

The residential property tax created by Part VI of the Finance Act, 1983, was described by counsel for the defendants as "a tax on the occupation of property", which I think is correct, and which I would regard as a fair description also of the rates which were payable on domestic premises until a few years ago.

I do not find it offensive to principles of justice or fair play that a tax should be imposed on occupiers of residential premises, or that it should be measured by reference to the market value of such premises rather than by reference to Poor Law Valuation, or that exemption from the tax should be given to occupiers of premises whose market value falls below a certain figure. The tax is imposed without reference to the means of the occupier or his ability to pay, but so were domestic rates as long as they continued to be payable and no one appears to have regarded them as unconstitutional. Before liability arises under the Act the assessable person must have available for occupation by him for residential purposes, property of very substantial value, considerably in excess of the value of the general run of house property in this country. I think it is quite legitimate under the Constitution to impose a tax by reference to the occupation of such property, and without regard to the fact that the occupation of such property, and without regard to the fact that the occupier may not be the freehold owner, or that the property may be heavily mortgaged, or that the occupier may only enjoy a small income in his own right.

"You are the occupier of this valuable property - you must pay for the privilege", is the message spelt out by the Act. One can criticise the thinking behind the imposition of this new form of taxation and say that it is discriminatory, but it is much more difficult to say that it is unconstitutional...

If it is accepted that there is nothing untoward in imposing a tax on the occupation of residential property and measuring the amount of tax to be paid by reference to the market value of the unencumbered freehold interest in the property, then I see nothing unreasonable in allowing the assessable person to make his own valuation of the property in the first place, reserving to the Revenue Commissioners a right to review this valuation if they feel that it is incorrect.

...Turning to the provisions which refer to the income exemption limit these appear to me to be intended to ameliorate the rigour of the Act, and to succeed in this purpose. S.96 of the Act imposes the new tax as an annual tax upon the net market value of all relevant residential property, at the rate of 1.5% of that net market value, so one commences with a starting point of a tax imposed on the excess of the aggregate amount of the market value of all residential properties of an assessable person over the market value exemption limit, which stands for the time being at £65,000. If the Act contained no further exemptions from liability, it would, in my opinion, stand the test of constitutionality, just as the conventional method of exacting payment of rates in respect of the occupation of residential premises had no obvious constitutional infirmity.

The Act then proceeds to grant exemption from tax if it can be established to the satisfaction of the Revenue Commissioners that the aggregation of the incomes of all relevant persons living in the residential property does not exceed the income exemption limit (at present fixed at £20,000 per annum, with marginal relief granted up to a figure of £25,000 per annum). This seems to me to put the assessable person in a considerably better position than he would have if the simple expedient had been adopted of reimposing liability for domestic rates, as such rates would have been payable regardless of the ability of the occupier, with or without the help of other members of the household, to discharge the liability.

...Viewing the Act as objectively as I can, I am unable to find in Part VI any features which would justify one in describing it as "arbitrary", "unreasonable", "an unjust attack on rights of property" or "hostile or invidious discrimination" against the plaintiffs or other persons captured within the residential property tax net. The classification of persons rendered liable to pay the tax appears to me to "rest upon some ground of difference having a fair and substantial relation to the object of the legislation, so that all persons similarly circumstanced shall be treated alike", to hark back to the words of Mr. Justice Pitney in the *Royster Guano Co.* case.

3.2 McGee v. The Attorney General
[1974] I.R. 284 Supreme Court

[Mrs. McGee had decided with her husband that they should not have any more children. That decision was taken on medical advice. Her doctor advised a particular form of contraception which required the importation of certain spermicidal jelly. Pursuant to s.17 of the Criminal Law Amendment Act, 1935, which prohibited the importation of any contraceptive, custom officials seized and impounded the material which Mrs. McGee had attempted to import. She began proceedings claiming that s.17 was unconstitutional. In the Supreme Court, a majority of the judges agreed with her claim.

The majority agreed that the legislation intruded into an area of private decision making by a husband and wife which the Constitution protected. What they differed on was the constitutional provision which was the source of this protection. In the extracts from the judgments of Walsh and Henchy JJ. this differnt emphasis in arriving at the same conclusion is evident. Walsh J. takes the view that the most important aspect of the case is the fact that the Constitution, in Article 41, gives special protection to the family as the fundamental unit group of society. Confining most of his comments to this part of the Constitution, Walsh J. concludes that the private decisions taken by members of that family unit were implicity given protection by Article 41. Henchy J. also talks about rights implicit in the Constitution, but he is prepared to link Article 41 with the more general provisions of Article 40.3 which guarantees protection for the implicit rights of all citizens.   This seems to indicate that the notion of privacy envisaged by Henchy J. is potentially wider than the one referred to by Walsh J. The extracts illustrate that the judges themselves find some difficulty in defining precisely the scope of application of rights which they are agreed are protected by the Constitution.]

Walsh J:

Articles 40, 41, 42 and 44 of the Constitution all fall within that section of the Constitution which is titled "Fundamental Rights".   Articles 41, 42 and 43 emphatically reject the theory that there are no rights without laws, no rights contrary to the law and no rights anterior to the law.   They indicate that justice is placed above the law and acknowledge that natural rights, or human rights, are not created by law but that the Constitution confirms their existence and gives them protection.   The individual has natural and human rights over which the State has no authority; and the family, as the natural primary and fundamental unit group of society, has rights as such which the State cannot control.   However, at the same time it is true, as the Constitution acknowledges and claims, that the State is the guardian of the common good and that the individual, as a member of society, and the family, as a unit of society, have duties and obligations to consider and respect the common good of that society.

...The private morality of its citizens does not justify intervention by the State into the activities of those citizens unless and until the common good requires it.   Counsel for the Attorney General did not seek to argue that the State would have any right to seek to prevent the use of contraceptives within marriage.   He did argue, however, that it did not follow from this that the State was under any obligation to make contraceptives available to married couples.   Counsel for the [Revenue Commissioners] put the matter somewhat further by stating that, if she had a right to use contraceptives within the privacy of her marriage, it was a matter for the plaintiff to prove from whence the right sprang.   In effect he was saying that, if she was appealing to a right anterior to positive law, the burden was on her to show the source of that right.   At first sight this may appear to be a reasonable and logical proposition.   However, it does appear to ignore a fundamental point, namely, that the rights of a married couple to decide how many children, if any, they will have are matters outside the reach of positive law where the means employed to implement such decisions do not impinge upon the common good or destroy or endanger human life.   It is undoubtedly true that among those persons who are subject to a particular moral code no one has a right to be in breach of that moral code.   But when this is a code governing private morality and where the breach of it is not one which injures the common good then it is not the State's business to intervene.   It is outside the authority of the State to endeavour to intrude into the privacy of the husband and wife relationship for the sake of imposing a code of private morality upon that husband and wife which they do not desire.

In my view, Article 41 of the Constituton guarantees the husband and wife against any such invasion of their privacy by the State. It follows that the use of contraceptives by them within that marital privacy is equally guaranteed against such invasion and, as such, assumes the status of a right so guaranteed by the Constitution. If this right cannot be directly invaded by the State it follows that it cannot be frustrated by the State taking measures to ensure that the exercise of that right is rendered impossible.

Henchy J.:

As has been held in a number of cases, the unspecified personal rights guaranteed by sub-s. 1 of s.3 of Article 40 are not confined to those specified in sub-s. 2 of that section. It is for the Courts to decide in a particular case whether the right relied on comes within the constitutional guarantee. To do so, it must be shown that it is a right that inheres in the citizen in question by virtue of his human personality. The lack of precision in this test is reduced when sub-s. 1 of s. 3 of Article 40 is read (as it must be) in the light of the Constitution as a whole and, in particular, in the light of what the Constitution, expressly or by necessary implication, deems to be fundamental to the personal standing of the individual in question in the context of the social order envisaged by the Constitution. The infinite variety in the relationships between the citizen and his fellows and between the citizen and the State makes an exhaustive enumeration of the guaranteed rights difficult, if not impossible.

The dominant feature of the plaintiff's dilemma is that she is a young married woman who is living, with a slender income, in the cramped quarters of a mobile home with her husband and four infant children, and that she is faced with a considerable risk of death or crippling paralysis if she becomes pregnant. The net question is whether it is constitutionally permissible in the circumstances for the law to deny her access to the contraceptive method chosen for her by her doctor and which she and her husband wish to adopt. In other words, is the prohibition effected by s.17 of the Act of 1935 an interference with the rights which the State guarantees in its laws to respect, as stated in sub-s. 1 of s.3 of Article 40?

The answer lies primarily in the fact that the plaintiff is a wife and a mother. It is the informed and conscientious wish of the plaintiff and her husband to maintain full marital relations without incurring the risk of a pregnancy that may very well result in her death or in a crippling paralysis. Section 17 of the Act of 1935 frustrates that wish. It goes further; it brings the implementation of the wish within the range of the criminal law. Its effect, therefore, is to condemn the plaintiff and her husband to a way of life which, at best, will be fraught with worry, tension and uncertainty that cannot but adversely affect their lives and, at worst, will result in an unwanted pregnancy causing death or serious illness with the obvious tragic consequences to the lives of her husband and young children. And this in the context of a Constitution which in its preamble proclaims as one of its aims the dignity and freedom of the individual; which in sub-s. 2 of s. 3 of Article 40 casts on the State a duty to protect as best it may from unjust attack and, in the case of injustice done, to vindicate the life and person of every citizen; which in Article 41, after recognising the family as the natural primary and fundamental unit group of society, and as a moral institution possessing inalienable and imprescriptible rights antecedent and superior to all positive law, guarantees to protect it in its constitution and authority as the necessary basis of social order and indispensable to the welfare of the nation and the State; and which, also in Article 41, pledges the State to guard with special care the institution of marriage, on which the family is founded, and to protect it against attack.

...In my opinion, s.17 of the Act of 1935 violates the guarantee in sub-s. 1 of s. 3 of Article 40 by the State to protect the plaintiff's personal rights by its laws; it does so not only by violating her personal right to privacy in regard to her marital relations but, in a wider way, by frustrating and making criminal any efforts by her to effectuate the decision of her husband and herself, made responsibly, conscientiously and on medical advice, to avail themselves of a particular contraceptive method so as to ensure her life and health as well as the integrity, security and well-being of her marriage and her family.

CHAPTER 4

Formation of a Contract

To the law, contracts concern agreements made directly between persons involving some element of negotiation. For agreement to be reached, one party must make a definite statement of intention that he is willing to enter into a contractual arrangement on terms (the offer) and this must be unequivocally agreed to by the other party (the acceptance). This, however, is not enough; a further basic requirement is that in return for a promise made by one party, the other must provide some benefit of minimal economic value, called the consideration. Without consideration of some kind, the promise made is worthless in law, because the courts will not force a person to fulfil a voluntary promise where he is not receiving something in return. The thorny problem of the courts developing at the same time an increasing tendancy to prevent a person from going back on his word where that word or promise has been relied on by another, the idea of estoppel, is examined later in this chapter.

Sometimes it is difficult to fit particular contractual arrangements into the rigid offer and acceptance framework created by the law, though even in modern conditions where standard form contracts abound the courts have yet to change their basic approach. A glimpse of what the courts may do in the future is provided by the judgment of Henchy J. in *McCord* v. *Electricity Supply Board* (1980) (Extract 4.1), in which he points out the essential unreality of transferring 19th century ideas of freedom of contract to the latter part of the 20th century. This may be especially true for Irish law, because the *laissez-faire* philosophy, with its emphasis on the rights of property only may not fit easily into a legal system whose Constitution guarantees protection not just to property but also a host of other express and implicit rights. The courts have already suggested that constitutional influences of fair procedures may be imposed in the context of private contractual arrangements: see *Glover* v. *B.L.N. Ltd.* [1973] I.R. 388. Therefore, the comments of Henchy J. in *McCord*, in linking his criticism of potential arbitrariness to constitutional law, should provide some food for thought.

Aside from these reservations, contractual arrangements can still be found which fall into the more traditional framework set out in *Boyers & Co.* v. *Duke* (1904) (Extract 4.2) where Madden J. discusses the common problem of whether an offer can be said to have been made, both in its legal and policy setting. While it is clear that the courts find little problem of thinking in terms of intention to enter into a binding agreement in such cases, where they are faced with two standard form agreements with conflicting terms passed between companies on an impersonal basis, only an unreal view of the parties intentions can be attempted. Such a "battle of forms", which is different in kind from the inequality dealt with in *McCord*, is discussed in the English cases *Butler Machine Tool Co. Ltd.* v. *Ex-Cell-O Corp.* [1979] 1 W.L.R. 401 (decided in 1977) and *Gibson* v. *Manchester City Council* [1979] 1 W.L.R. 294 where the judges indicate they will struggle on with the offer and acceptance formula.

Two elements mentioned at the beginning of this chapter as essential to enforceability of promises were directness and certainty, the latter in the context of offer and acceptance. Put another way, the law requires personal participation and the achievement of a clear consensus for enforceability. Both these elements were at issue in *Cadbury (Irl.) Ltd.* v. *Kerry Co-Op. Ltd.* (1981) (Extract 4.3) and ultimately the lack of both proved to be insurmountable problems.

The case does illustrate, however, an important feature of the courts' general outlook in commercial law issues, namely a presumption that agreements entered into between businessmen are intended to be legally binding. But this is only a presumption and the case shows that parties themselves can indicate through their actions that the presumption must be overthrown. A similar presumption, this time not overthrown, is at work in the judgment of McWilliam J. in *Folens & Co. Ltd.* v. *Minister for Education* (1982) (Extract 4.4). Here the judge was prepared to allow a remedy to Folens, where, although it was clear that no final contract had been entered into between the parties, it was implicit that both sides realised that the considerable professional expertise deployed by Folens was not being provided on a voluntary and gratis basis. This area of law, where someone is given restitution under the umbrella of *quantum meruit* (as much as he deserves), is not strictly speaking part of the law of contract but it frequently arises in settings where a contract was contemplated by parties but did not actually come to fruition.

The other prerequisite to enforcing a promise made is that consideration must be provided by the person to whom the promise was made. While this remains the basic approach of judges to contract formation, there is a rule of the courts of equity which prevents, or estops, a person from going back on his word where another person relies on that word and acts to their detriment in relying on it. This rule of equitable estoppel could potentially undermine the consideration requirement if taken to its ultimate. As yet this has not occurred in the Irish courts. But in *Revenue Commissioners* v. *Moroney* (1971) (Extract 4.5), the High Court judge, Kenny J., was prepared to decide the case on the basis of equitable estoppel principles, even though at the time the promise or representation concerned was made there was no existing legal relationship between the parties. That remains the only definite Irish decision, and recent developments in English cases tend to support this extension of estoppel. Decisions such as those in *Amalgamated Investment & Property Co. Ltd.* v. *Texas Commerce International Bank Ltd.* [1982] Q.B. 84, if considered, would force the courts here to re-examine the importance of the concept of consideration in contract law. It would be difficult to avoid that problem question. Some of the English developments were accepted by Finlay P. in *Smith* v. *Ireland* [1983] I.L.R.M. 300.

4.1   McCord v. Electricity Supply Board
[1980] I.L.R.M. 163 Supreme Court

[The E.S.B. has a statutory monopoly to supply electricity under the Electricity (Supply) Act, 1927. The plaintiff's house was supplied with electricity by the Board, and this supply was subject to the Board's General Conditions Relating to Supply. Clause 13 of the Conditions provided that the Board "may disconnect supply without prior notice to the consumer" where the consumer was in breach of any of the other Conditions. The Board discovered that its meter in the plaintiff's house had been tampered with and was not registering electricity used. When the plaintiff refused to sign a document setting out his involvement, if any, in this and undertaking to repay by instalments the sums, to be agreed, due for electricity consumed, the Board disconnected supply. One point that was agreed between the parties when the case went to the Supreme Court was that the Board was entitled to discounnect supply under s.99 of the 1927 Act without the need for a court order where a debt was due for electricity consumed, contrary to what had been said by the High Court judge.

The extract from the judgment of Henchy J. clears up that point regarding the Board's powers. But, along with the other judges, he decided that in the circumstances the Board was not entitled to disconnect because the plaintiff's refusal to sign the Board's document was not in breach of any of the General Conditions Relating to Supply. What is of more general interest is the judge's attitude to the interpretation of the General Conditions. First, his comment that the courts might adopt a special approach to them in view of the difficulty of fitting such contracts of adhesion into the traditional *laissez-faire* idea on which many contract law rules depend. Second, the view that constitutional requirements may also be a factor in that approach in determining the validity of general conditions. In *McCord* itself, of course, these comments arose against a statutory background, but the Introduction to this Chapter discusses how the constitutional perspective may apply in a non-statutory context also.]

Henchy J.:

Specific power to cut off the supply of electricity, where a debt for electricity consumed is due, is given to the Board by s.99 of [the Electricity (Supply)] Act. This statutory power (which is repeated in more drastic terms in condition 13(a) of the General Conditions) must be deemed to be exercisable only in a reasonable manner, that is, after due notice and after giving the debtor a fair and reasonable opportunity, having regard to all the circumstances, of discharging the debt. Admittedly, any comment on this aspect of the case must be *obiter*, but because of the widespread publicity given to the [High Court] judge's statement that the Board is not entitled to disconnect electricity to premises because of an unpaid account, until it gets a court order, it is important to clear the air by recording that it is common case that such a conclusion is unwarranted and in fact is in the teeth of the statutory powers vested in the Board.

The real question in this case is whether the Board has power to disconnect the supply of electricity to premises when the meter has been wrongfully interfered with (in this case without the proven knowledge of the occupier) and the occupier has refused to give a statement in writing setting out what he knows of the wrongdoing and giving an undertaking to pay by instalments for the electricity consumed but unrecorded.

Before proceeding to answer this question, it is important to point out that the contract made between the plaintiff and the Board (incorporating the General Conditions Relating to Supply) is what is nowadays called a contract of adhesion: it is a standardised mass contract which must be entered into, on a take it or leave it basis, by the occupier of every premises in which electricity is to be used. The would-be consumer has no standing to ask that a single iota of the draft contract presented to him be changed before he signs it. He must lump it or leave it. But, because for reasons that are too obvious to enumerate, he cannot do without electricity, he is invariably forced by necessity into signing the contract, regardless of the fact that he may consider some of its terms arbitrary, or oppressive, or demonstrably unfair. He is compelled, from a position of weakness and necessity vis-a-vis a monopolist supplier of a vital commodity, to enter into what falls into the classification of a contract and which, as such, according to the theory of the common law which was evolved in the *laissez-faire* atmosphere of the 19th century, is to be treated by the courts as if it had emerged by choice from the forces of the market place, at the behest of parties who were at arm's length and had freedom of choice.

The real facts show that such an approach is largely based on legal fictions.

When a monopoly supplier of a vital public utility - which is what the Board is - forces on all its consumers a common form of contract, reserving to itself sweeping powers, including the power to vary the document unilaterally as it may think fit, such an instrument has less affinity with a freely negotiated interpersonal contract than with a set of bye-laws or with any other form of autonomic legislation. As such, its terms may have to be construed not simply as contractual elements but as components of a piece of delegated legislation, the validity of which will depend on whether it has kept within the express or implied confines of the statutory delegation and, even if it has, whether the delegation granted or assumed is now consistent with the provisons of the Constitution of 1937.

However, since the present proceedings raise no issue as to the question of the validity, on constitutional or other grounds, of the contract between the plaintiff and the Board, the terms of reference of this case rule out a consideration of such a question; while, for similar reasons, judicial self-control requires that I withhold adverse comment on certain terms of the contract, such as that which purports to give contractual force to the idea that notices of intended disconnection may be taken as having been delivered on the weekday following the day they were posted; or on even the final term of the contract by which "the Board reserves to itself the right to add to, alter or amend any of the foregoing terms and conditions, AS IT MAY THINK FIT". However, having regard to my conclusion that the contractual powers of the Board are in the nature of delegated legislation, and because a statute replacing the powers conferred on the Board by the 1927 Act may result from this case, it might not be out of place to refer to what was laid down by this Court in the following passage in its judgment in *Cityview Press Ltd.* v. *An Chomhairle Oiliúna* [1980] I.R. 381, at p. 398:

"The giving of powers to a designated Minister or subordinate body to make regulations or orders under a particular statute has been a feature of legislation for many years. The practice has obvious attractions in view of the complex, intricate and ever-changing situations which confront both the Legislature and the Executive in a modern State. Sometimes, as in this instance, the legislature, conscious of the danger of giving too much power in the regulation or order-making process, provides that any regulation or order which is made should be subject to annulment by either House of Parliament. This retains a measure of control, if not in Parliament as such, at least in the two Houses. Therefore, it is a safeguard. Nevertheless, the ultimate responsibility rests with the Courts to ensure that constitutional safeguards remain, and that the exclusive authority of the National Parliament in the field of law-making is not eroded by a delegation of power which is neither contemplated nor permitted by the Constitution. In discharging that responsibility, the Courts will have regard to where and by what authority the law in question purports to have been made. In the view of this Court, the test is whether that which is challenged as an unauthorised delegation of parliamentary power is more than a mere giving effect to principles and policies which are contained in the statute itself. If it be, then it is not authorised, for such would constitute a purported exercise of legislative power by an authority which is not permitted to do so under the Constitution. On the other hand, if it be within the permitted limits - if the law is laid down in the statute and details only are filled in or completed by the designated Minister or subordinate body - there is no unauthorised delegation of leglislative power."

4.2 Boyers & Co. v. D. & R. Duke
[1905] 2 I.R. 617 King's Bench Division

[The plaintiffs wrote to the defendants: "Please give us your lowest quotation for 3,000 yards of canvas... to the enclosed sample, or near, and your shortest time for delivery." The defendants replied stating: "We enclose sample...nearest we have to match yours, also enclosed. Lowest price... is 4 5/8 d. per yard.... Delivery of 3,000 yards in 5/6 weeks." The plaintiffs responded, again by letter: "Please get made for us 3,000 yards of canvas... as per your quotation... at 4 5/8 d. per yard; deliver same as quickly as possible." The issue for the court was whether the letter from the defendants amounted to an offer and the plaintiff's reply an acceptance of that offer. If not there would be no binding agreement between the parties.

The judgment of Madden J. focuses on two points. First, the legal issue as to whether a price quotation can "import an offer to sell", in other words whether there is a clear intention to enter into a contract on terms. *Harvey* v. *Facey* [1893] A.C. 552 provided authority for concluding quotations were not offers. Second, having looked at the purely legal angle the judge points out that it would make commerce impossible to describe quotations as offers. This policy view is interesting since, ultimately, many contract law rules can be traced to business practice requirements. This approach continues to the present, as can be seen in a case on the related topic of communicating acceptance: see *Brinkibon Ltd.* v. *Stahag Stahl G.m.b.H.* [1983] 2 A.C. 34.]

Madden J.:

The defendants in this case were asked for a "quotation". Now the word "quotation" is capable of different meanings according to the connection in which it is used, but there is a common idea underlying them all, that of notation or enumeration. The things quoted may be passages in an author, the prices of specific articles, or the terms upon which work is to be done. In the case before us both parties agree that the documents before us must be read and construed, giving the words the ordinary meaning which they bear in the English language, having regard to the subject-matter to which they relate; for neither party has contended that evidence should have been taken as to the use of the word "quotation" in mercantile transactions.

A quotation might be so expressed as to amount to an offer to provide a definite article, or to do a certain work, at a defined price. But the ideas of a quotation, and of an offer to sell, are radically different. The difference is well illustrated by the case of *Harvey* v. *Facey* [1893] A.C. 552. There, to a telegram in these terms, "Will you sell us Bumper Hall Pen? Telegraph lowest cash price", the answer was returned, "Lowest price for Bumper Hall Pen £900". The inquirer telegraphed, "We agree to buy Bumper Hall Pen for £900 asked by you". An exceptionally strong judical committee of the Privy Council, in a judgment delivered by Lord Morris, held that this statement, or quotation, of the lowest price at which a definite thing will be sold, does not import an offer to sell.

The principle on which this case was decided applies with a greater force to mercantile transactions than to an application for a statement of the price of a single parcel of land. It is a matter of common knowledge that quotations of prices are scattered broadcast among possible customers. Business could not be carried on if each recipient of a priced catalogue offering a desirable article - say a rare book - at an attractive price, were in a position to create a contract of sale by writing that he would buy at the price mentioned. The catalogue has probably reached many collectors. The order of one only can be honoured. Has each of the others who write for the book a right of action? Wholesale dealers have not in stock an unlimited supply of the articles the prices of which they quote to the public at large. This stock usually bears some proportion to the orders which they may reasonably expect to receive. Transactions of the kind under consideration are intelligible and business-like, if we bear in mind the distinction between a quotation, submitted as the basis of a possible order, and an offer to sell which, if accepted, creates a contract, for the breach of which damages may be recovered.

These observations seem to apply with special force to a quotation furnished by a manufacturer, in the position of the defendants, stating the terms on which he is prepared to work, as to price and time for completion. He may receive and comply with many applications for quotations on the same day. If his reply in each case can be turned into a contract by acceptance, his looms might be burdened with an amount of work which would render it impossible for him to meet his engagements. In my opinion, a merchant, dealer, or manufacturer, by furnishing a quotation invites an offer which will be honoured or not according to the exigencies of his business. A quotation based on current prices usually holds good for a limited time. But it remains a quotation, on the basis of which an offer will not be entertained after a certain date. I have arrived at this conclusion irrespective of the terms of the [third] letter... as to which I will only say that it suggests to my mind that the writer knew well that he was giving an order, not accepting an offer for sale.

4.3 Cadbury (Irl.) Ltd. v. Kerry Co-Op. Ltd. and Dairy Disposal Co. Ltd. [1982] I.L.R.M. 77 High Court

[The plaintiff owned a factory which manufactured chocolate. They were supplied milk by a local creamery. The creamery was acquired by Dairy Disposal, a company which was set up by the Department of Agriculture to purchase small creameries and resell them to larger concerns to rationalise the dairy industry. When Cadbury discovered that Dairy Disposal had purchased the local creamery, it made strong respresentations, through a lengthy series of correspondence and meetings, to the Department to ensure continued supply of milk to its factory when Dairy Disposal resold the creamery. The Department, through Dairy Disposal, made known these views to Kerry Co-Op which eventually purchased the creamery, and a commitment from Kerry Co-Op regarding continued supply was ultimately incorporated into the contract of sale between Dairy Disposal and Kerry Co-Op as clause 19 of that agreement. When, a number of years after this agreement of 1974 Kerry Co-0p declined to continue the supply of milk to the Cadbury factory, Cadbury brought this action to enforce the terms of clause 19, whose main provisions are quoted in the extract.

As the extract from the judgment of Barrington J. shows, two contract law problems stood in Cadbury's way. First, Cadbury had not been party to the agreememt which it was now attempting to enforce, and so had to establish that it could claim the benefit of one of the limited exceptions to the privity rule. While the judge was not prepared to state immediately that the Cadbury case fell at this hurdle, his approach was to note the reluctance of the courts to allow this type of claim. He did, however, fuse this issue with the second one raised which was that the wording of clause 19 of the 1974 agreement was difficult to interpret. Reviewing the law in this area, Barrington J. pointed out that courts are prepared to give the benefit of the doubt to businessmen and attempt as far as possible to make vague or uncertain clauses workable, by applying a business efficacy test. The judge's reference to English cases is important here. Despite this, the court concludes that clause 19 of the agreement, whatever about the rest of the contract, was not a statement intended to have legal consequences for Kerry Co-Op, but was merely a commitment of the good faith of the Department and Kerry Co-Op. At the end of the extract, Barrington J. points out that he would not have been prepared to overlook the privity problem either in such a complex and unusual case.]

Barrington J.:

In my view clause 19 was inserted in the agreement by [Dairy Disposal] for the benefit of the plaintiffs. The plaintiffs accordingly maintain that, though not a party to the contract, they are entitled to sue upon clause 19 of it because the Dairy Disposal Co. Ltd. is, in the circumstances of this case, a trustee of the benefit of that clause for the plaintiff company. They rely upon the principle laid down in *Lloyd's* v. *Harper* (1880) 16 Ch.D. 290 and in particular on the law as stated by Fry J. at 309:

"It appears to me from the cases which were cited in the course of the argument, especially *Tomlinson* v. *Gill* (1756) Amb.330 and *Lamb* v. *Vice* (1840) 6 M. & W. 467, that where a contract is made for the benefit and on behalf of a third person, there is an equity in that third person to sue on the contract, and the person who has entered into the contract may be treated as a trustee for the person for whose benefit it has been entered into".

The principle that the parties to a contract can create a trust of contractual rights for the benefit of a third party and that the third party can himself enforce those rights, if his trustee does not enforce them for him, by suing the person placed under a duty to him by the contract and by joining his trustee as a co-defendant, is well established... *Cheshire and Fifoot's Law of Contract* (1975)... (at p. 442) quote Lord Wright as referring to the doctrine of a trust of contractual rights as "a cumbrous fiction" and suggest that the courts are reluctant to extend it....[I]n the 24th edition of *Chitty on Contracts* Vol. 1, p.528, paragraph 1122, it is stated that the trust device has so far only been applied to promises to pay money or to transfer property. The passage continues:

"It is sometimes suggested that it might be applied to other kinds of promises, e.g. that an employer might hold the benefit of an exemption clause on trust for his employee. In view of the present judicial tendency to confine the trust device within narrow limits, it seems unlikely that such extension will be made; though other techniques may be used for making the benefit of exemption clauses available to third parties".

As previously stated, it seems clear to me that in the present case the Minister and the Dairy Disposal Co. Ltd. intended to benefit Cadburys, not indeed because they wished to confer any favours on Cadburys, but because they wished, through the Cadbury factory at Rathmore, to advance their view of what the public interest required. One fact which makes the courts more ready to infer that the promisee in a contract is a trustee for the third party, is that the promisee should have some contractual or fiduciary duty to the third party. In the present case there was certainly no fiduciary relationship between the Dairy Disposal Co. Ltd. and the plaintiffs. It seems improbable that there was any contractual relationship between them.

What there was was an undertaking given by the Dairy Disposal Co. Ltd. to the plaintiffs with the knowledge and approval of the Minister. The value of such an undertaking to the plaintiffs lay not so much in any legal sanction as in the fact that it committed the good faith of the public authority. This undoubtedly provided the motive for the Dairy Disposal Co. Ltd. to attempt to protect the interest of the plaintiffs when they were selling creameries the produce of which was covered by the undertaking, but it does not necessarily follow that the Dairy Disposal Co. Ltd. intended to, or did in fact, constitute itself a trustee of its rights under clause 19 for the benefit of the plaintiffs. The answer to this question depends, at least in part, on whether clause 19 in fact created legal rights which either the Dairy Disposal Co. Ltd or the plaintiffs can now enforce.

Leaving aside for the moment, the fact that the person seeking to enforce clause 19 is not a party to the agreement, clause 19 presents a number of unusual features:

1. The obigation imposed on the purchasing society, under the clause, is to "take all the necessary steps to ensure that there will after the possession date be no diminution in the milk supply (as in 1973)'' to the Rathmore factory. There is no mention of the term during which this obligation is to last and the term appears to be of indefinite duration or to extend as long as the factory referred to is at Rathmore. The plaintiffs have argued that this point is not relevant to these proceedings as the first named defendants have not purported to terminate the agreement but, they submit, that the agreement is one which could be terminated by the first, named defendants on reasonable notice.

2. The obligation imposed on the first named defendant appears to be one to supply milk "to the factory premises at Rathmore''. If therefore the clause is legally enforceable by the plaintiffs it would appear to be enforceable also by the owners for the time being of the factory premises at Rathmore. The obligation of the first named defendant to supply milk would therefore appear to continue as long as the factory exists at Rathmore unless that obligation can be terminated by reasonable notice.

3. The obligation of the first named defendants to supply milk is however subject to the price available being "comparable to that receivable from potential other purchasers''... The plaintiffs say that to understand the reference to "potential other purchasers'' it is necessary to know something about other creameries and co-operative societies in Kerry, Limerick and Cork...

4. The first named defendants are obliged to sell their milk to Rathmore only if the price available is "comparable'' to that receivable from potential other purchasers. I find it hard to understand this word in this context. It cannot mean "equal''. If the parties to the agreement had intended to say "equal'' to the best price available from other potential customers or "equal to the average price availabe'' from other potential purchasers they could easily have said so. [Counsel for the defendants] suggests that in the context "comparable'' means "approximately equal''. Counsel for the plaintiffs have submitted that, despite the difficulties in clause 19, it is the duty of the court to interpret the clause in such a way as to give it business efficacy. If, they say, the clause was not intended to be legally binding the parties would not have taken so much trouble in drafting it. They point to the fact that the first named defendants themselves amended the clause by adding the proviso. This, the plaintiffs suggest, was a pointless exercise unless the first named defendants knew that the clause would be legally binding on them.

Mr. Blayney (for the plaintiffs) submitted that the courts are extremely reluctant to hold a clause in an agreement void for uncertainty once it is established that the agreement was intended to have business efficacy. He relied on the case of *Brown* v. *Gould* [1972] Ch. 53. In that case a lease between a landlord and a tenant contained a clause giving the tenant an option to renew the lease for a further term of 21 years "at a rent to be fixed having regard to the market value of the premises at the time of exercising this option taking into account to the advantage of the tenant any increased value of such premises attributable to structural improvements made by the tenant during the currency of this present lease such new lease also containing the like covenants and provisions as are herein contained with the exception of the present covenant for renewal"...

Megarry J. held that this clause was not void for uncertainty. He applied the principle that the courts are extremely reluctant to hold void for uncertainty any provision that was intended to have legal effect. It may be of some significance however, that it was apparently conceded in argument that the option was intended to have business efficacy.

Since the main argument in the present case, the English Court of Appeal has carried the principle of business efficacy even further in its decision in *Beer* v. *Bowden* [1981] 1 W.L.R. 522 [decided in 1976]. I gave the parties an opportunity to discuss this case... The case was also a landlord and tenant case.

Under the terms of a lease demising premises for a term of years the rent payable by the tenant was to be £1,250 per annum for a number of years and was to be reviewed at intervals thereafter, the new rent to be "such rent as shall... be agreed between the landlords and the tenant but no account shall be taken of any improvements carried out by the tenant in computing the amount of increase, if any, and in any case [the rent shall be] not less than the yearly rental" of £1,250 payable under the lease.

The Court of Appeal held that on the true construction of this rent review clause the "rent to be agreed" by the parties was a "fair" rent (excluding the tenant's improvements) of not less than £1,250 per annum. So the court first implied a term stipulating a "fair" rent and then set about giving that term business efficacy.

In these circumstancs Mr. Blayney, on behalf of the plaintiffs, claims that *Beer* v. *Bowden* is helpful to his clients. In the present case, he claims that there is no necessity to imply any term; it is merely a question of giving business efficacy to clause 19. Moreover, he submits that the fact that the Court of Appeal in *Beer* v. *Bowden* followed *Foley* v. *Classique Coaches Ltd.* [1934] 2 K.B. 1 (a case concerning the supply of petrol) shows that the principle of *Beer* v. *Bowden* is applicable to all commercial contracts including contracts for the supply of milk. Moreover he claims that the fact that the parties operated clause 19 successfully for so long shows that they could continue to do so with the minimum of assistance from the court.

Mr. Liston on the other hand says that the principle in *Beer* v. *Bowden* has no relevance for this case. Reserving his major point that, before attempting to give business efficacy to clause 19, one would have to be satisfied that clause 19 created a legal relationship between the plaintiffs and the first-named defendants and was intended to have business efficacy, he says that it would be quite impracticable for the court to attempt to operate clause 19. There might be a dispute and an application to the court every time an increase was proposed in the price of milk and special problems would arise from the fact that milk is a perishable commodity.

PRACTICE OF THE PARTIES

The plaintiffs rely not only on their statement of the law concerning business efficacy but, they state, that the parties themselves were, over a number of years, able to give business efficacy to the clause. It is suggested that they did this by having regard to a number of objective factors which determined the price of milk from time to time in accordance with the provisions of clause 19.

There is no doubt that, over a number of years, the parties were able to resolve their problems as businessmen by striking a bargain on the price of milk from time to time. When an increase came through from Brussels the parties were able to decide how much of the increase should go to the processors to cover increased costs of production and how much should be passed on to the farmer. In striking their bargains the parties had regard to what was being done by other co-operative societies and other processors... But it appears to me that what took place was a series of bargains arrived at by parties engaged in an ongoing business relationship rather than a series of determinations of milk prices in accordance with a preordained formula.

It will be noted that [in correspondence agreeing a particular price increase] both parties refer to it as a "compromise". This appears to me to be more consistent with a bargaining process than with a search for a factor which would determine the price already agreed by contract.

While therefore the parties undoubtedly carried on business to their mutual advantage for a number of years I am not satisfied that this proves that the formula set out in clause 19 had business efficacy or that what transpired between the parties during those years was governed by clause 19.

CONCLUSION

I have referred already to four peculiar features of clause 19. If for instance one takes the statement that the price available must be "comparable" to that receivable from potential other purchasers and one takes "comparable" as meaning "approximately equal" one gets a strange result. If X is the price "receivable from potential other purchasers" and Y represents the tolerance above or below X contained in the word "approximately" then "comparable" price could range from X + Y to X-Y. If therefore clause 19 is a clause having business efficacy and the plaintiffs were to tender to the first named defendants a price equal to X-Y the first named defendants would be committeed to supply to the plaintiffs a milk supply equal to the 1973 supply. This would be so despite the fact that the first-named defendants could, more profitably, sell the milk elsewhere or process it through their own subsidiary. But the plaintiffs would be under no corresponding duty to tender for or to accept any milk at all.

It appears to me that the imprecision of the language in clause 19 is explained by the fact that the clause was concerned with policy considerations and that the draughtsman assumed that clause 19 would be supplemented by a bilateral agreement between the plaintiffs and the first named defendants in which the precise rights and duties of both parties would be set out. Put another way one could say that clause 19 contemplated a further agreement between the plaintiffs and the first-named defendants to give it business efficacy.

....I do not think that the court is competent to interpret or apply clause 19 in such a way as to give it business efficacy as between the plaintiffs and the first named defendants even assuming that *Beer* v. *Bowden* should be followed in Ireland. The task which would confront the court in attempting to apply clause 19 to the facts of the present case would be infinitely more complex and difficult than that with which the Court of Appeal was confronted in *Beer* v. *Bowden.* Moreover I do not believe that the concept of a trust of contractual rights for the benefit of a third party can be extended to cover a case as complex and unusual as the present one.

4.4 Folens & Co. Ltd. v. Minister for Education
[1984] I.L.R.M.   265 (1982) High Court

[Folens approached the Department of Education with the idea of producing a children's encyclopedia in Irish. The Department was in favour of the idea and between 1970 and 1975 a substantial amount of preliminary work had been completed on the project. Officials from the Department made it clear from the beginning that the Department of Finance would have to be consulted to provide funds for publication and that the estimates furnished by Folens would require approval by a contracts committee. In January, 1975, the Department wrote to the plaintiffs saying no further commitments should be made relating to the production of the encylopedia as there were no funds availale for the project. Folens claimed damages for the works they had put into preparation of the encyclopedia.

McWilliam J. decides, on the basis of the English cases he refers to, that even though no contract to publish ever existed between the parties Folens were being told implicity that the preparatory work would be paid for by the Department. His paraphrase of Romer L.J. in the *Brewer Street* case is of particular importance here.]

McWilliam J.:

I am satisfied that there was no concluded contract for the production of the encyclopedia although it was alleged and was vigorously urged by Mr. Folens in evidence, that he had, in effect, received assurances that, if he produced the encylopedia, he would be adequately remunerated for it.

I am also satisfied that the Department was anxious to have the encyclopedia published, that the plaintiff was anxious to produce it and that both parties proceeded on the basis that a contract would be made between them for its publication. This being the situation, the plaintiff went ahead with the preliminary work with the full approval of the supervisory committee and of the Department and all steps taken by the plaintiff were either approved or, as in the case of the paper to be purchased, actually directed by the supervisory committee. Although the plaintiff hoped and expected to make a profit out of the production of the encyclopedia, the work was being done for the benefit of the Department.

On this basis I am of opinion that the case should be considered by reference to the principles adopted in the case of *William Lacey Ltd.* v. *Davis* [1957] 1.W.L.R. 932 and *Brewer Street Investments Ltd.* v. *Barclay's Woollen Co. Ltd.* [1954] 1 Q.B. 428, although I am in full agreement with Somervell L.J. when he said, at p. 434 of the *Brewer Street* case, that the area of this class of case is somewhat difficult and that each case must be judged on its own circumstances, and with Lord Denning who said, at p.435 of the same case, that it is not easy to state the legal basis of the plaintiff's claim.

Barry J. in the *William Lacey* case rejected the proposition that a common expectation that a contract would ultimately come into being, and that the plaintiff's services would ultimately have been rewarded by the profits of that contract if it had come into being, negatives the suggestion that these services could be paid for on any other ground. He was of opinion that an action could be founded on "quasi-contract" so that the court may look at the true facts and ascertain from them whether or not a promise to pay should be implied, irrespective of the actual views or intentions of the parties at the time when the work was done or the services rendered.

Adapting the words of Romer L.J. at p.438 of the *Brewer Street* case, I have no doubt that had the Department said "We want you to put this work in hand but we are only going to pay for it provided we eventually agree upon the terms of contract between us", the plaintiff would not have done the work at its own risk as to cost. On this basis, I am of opinion that the plaintiff is entitled to be paid for all the work which had been done with the approval or at the direction of the Department.

4.5 Revenue Commissioners v. Moroney
[1972] I.R. 372 High Court and Supreme Court

[Two sons, the defendants, agreed to a transfer to them and their father of their father's property. The agreement was carried out by an assignment of the premises to the father and the sons "in consideration of the sum of £16,000 paid by the purchasers", the sons thus becoming liable to two-thirds of the purchase price under this agreement. The father and sons agreed before signing the deed of assignment that no money would ever be paid over in respect of the transfer, and none was ever in fact paid. When the father died and the Revenue Commissioners discoverd that no money had been paid, they began proceedings claiming that the two-thirds due from the sons was an asset of the father and that estate duty was payable on that amount. The case turned, therefore, on the question whether if the father was still alive he would have been successful in a claim against the sons for the amount concerned. In Extract 5.1 a different aspect of this case is examined, but at this stage the extracts given relate to whether the father would have been prevented from going back on his statement to his sons that he would not look for the amount they committed themselves to pay in the deed of assignment.

The High Court judgment in the case dwells on the potential application of the idea of equitable estoppel. In the High Court, Kenny J. took the view that the father could be estopped from going back on his representation to his sons even though at the time he made it there was no existing contractual relationship between him and his sons. In doing this the judge rejected some of the limitations placed on the view of estoppel which emerged after the *High Trees* case in England. The Supreme Court did not see any circumstances in which estopped could apply because, on its view of the case there was never any debt owed by the sons to the father so the representation had no effect in law. Extract 5.1 indicates why the Supreme Court came to this conclusion. The result as far as estoppel is concerned is that the judgment of Kenny J. remains the only discussion of how far Irish courts are prepared to apply estoppel in situations where consideration would otherwise be the basic requirement of enforceability.]

Kenny J. (High Court):

In the course of the hearing I asked whether the sons could succeed on a plea that the parent was estopped from claiming any part of the "purchase" money. Counsel for the defendants did not show any enthusiasm for this point and so I did not have the advantage of hearing counsel for the plaintiffs on it. Despite this, I think that in an action by the parent against the sons they would succeed on what is now called promissory estoppel.

This doctrine first appeared in *Hughes* v. *Metropolitan Railway Co.* (1877) 2 App. Cas.439... In the course of his speech the Lord Chancellor, Lord Cairns, said at p. 448 of the report:

> "... it is the first principle upon which all Courts of Equity proceed, that if parties who have entered into definite and distinct terms involving certain legal results - certain penalties or legal forfeiture - afterwards by their own act or with their own consent enter upon a course of negotiation which has the effect of leading one of the parties to suppose that the strict rights arising under the contract will not be enforced, or will be kept in suspense, or held in abeyance, the person who otherwise might have enforced those rights will not be allowed to enforce them where it would be inequitable having regard to the dealings which have thus taken place between the parties".

The doctrine got little attention in the textbooks until it was revived in striking fashion by Mr. Justice Denning (as he then was) in *Central London Property Trust Ltd.* v. *High Trees House Ltd.* [1947] K.B. 130. In that case the landlords had let a block of flats for 99 years at an annual rent of £2,500. The tenant found difficulty in letting them and in 1940 the landlords agreed to reduce the rent to £1,250. There was no consideration given for this nor was any period for the reduction agreed. From then the tenants paid the reduced rent until September, 1945, when the landlords demanded the full amount of £2,500 and the arrears for the period during which the lower rent had been paid.   Mr. Justice Denning held that the rent of £2,500 could not be recovered for any period before September, 1945.   In the course of his judgment he said at p.134 of the report:

> "There has been a series of decisions over the last fifty years which, although they are said to be cases of estoppel are not really such.   They are cases in which a promise was made which intended to create legal relations and which to the knowledge of the person making the promise, was going to be acted on by the person to whom it was made, and which was in fact so acted on.
>
> In such cases the courts have said the promise must be honoured...The courts have not gone so far as to give a cause of action in damages for the breach of such a promise, but they have refused to allow the party making it to act inconsistently with it."

...In *Ajayi* v. *R.T. Briscoe (Nig.) Ltd.* [1964] 1 W.L.R. 1326 the advice of the Privy Council, given by Lord Hodson, was that the doctrine is confined to cases where the representation relates to existing contractual rights...This, if correct, would conclude this case in favour of the plaintiffs as any promissory estoppel arises here because the parent before the deed was signed represented by his conduct and by what he said to his sons that he would not require payment of any part of the "purchase" price.   Until the deed was signed, there were no legal relations to be effected.

In my view there is no reason in principle why the doctrine of promissory estoppel should be confined to cases where the representation related to existing contractual rights.   It includes cases where there is a representation by one person to another that rights which will come into existence under a contract to be entered into will not be enforced.   This is the way in which the doctrine is stated at p. 627 of *Snell's Principles of Equity* (26th ed., 1966) which has the considerable authority of having had Mr. Megarry (as he then was) as one of its co-editors:

> "Where by his words or conduct one party to a transaction makes to the other a promise or assurance which is intended to affect the legal relations between them, and the other party acts upon it, altering his position to his detriment, the party making the promise or assurance will not be permitted to act inconsistently with it."

It seems to me that the parent represented to his sons that he would never seek payment of any part of the consideration of £16,000 and that they acted on this by signing the assignment.   Each of them altered his position to his detriment because by signing each took on a legal liability to pay two-thirds of the consideratrion which they would not otherwise have assumed.   Although they got the benefit of the interest in the joint tenancy, it seems to me to be probable that if they had refused to sign the deed in the form in which it was they would have got this without payment.   The assumption of the legal liability created by the deed was in my opinion sufficient to raise the equity against the parent and the representation has become final because the sons cannot be restored to their original position unless the view is taken that there never was a debt.   This equity does not affect the rights of other parties who would be entitled to rely on the deed, but this does not assist the plaintiffs.

Their claim can succeed only if the parent would have succeeded in a claim against his sons.

Walsh J. (Supreme Court):

In my view, the evidence establishes that the defendants were never indebted at any time to their father in respect of any sum of money arising out of this transaction. The learned trial judge decided this case in favour of the defendants on the basis that the doctrine of promissory estoppel was applicable. It seemed to him that the deceased had represented to his sons, the defendants, that he would never seek payment of any part of the £16,000 and that they acted on this by signing the deed of assignment. The learned trial judge took the view that the defendants had made themselves legally liable to pay the money concerned but that, by reason of the deceased's representations, the trial judge was free to apply this doctrine of promissory estoppel. On this matter I take a different view from that taken in the High Court. The doctrine of promissory estoppel arises in a case such as the present one only when there is a liability in law to pay the money. In the present case it would arise if the sons are, in law and in fact, indebted to the father in the sum mentioned. On the view I have taken of this case on the evidence, I think there was never any indebtedness between the parties and therefore the question of the deceased's representation causing the defendants to enter into such a liability does not arise. I find it, therefore, unnecessary to express any view on the applicability of the doctrine of promissory estoppel to a case such as this if the position in law had been that the defendants were legally indebted to the deceased in the sum claimed.

CHAPTER 5

Contract Terms

The facts of commercial life are that while with a few limited exceptions, such as hire-purchase and sale of land contracts, the law does not demand that contracts be in writing, contracts of any significant value or of long term duration are in practice put in writing. In this Chapter the emphasis is on the extent to which the courts extend their focus of attention to evidence which parties to an agreement attempt to introduce to supplement, for instance, written evidence in the form of a signed document. What amounts to the full picture of a contract is certainly not to be found by excluding such outside evidence. Towards the end of the Chapter, mention will also be made of one problem of interpretation of a particular contract term.

As far as terms actually, or expressly, agreed between parties, the law starts off with the basic proposition that the contract should be deemed to consist of the unvarnished text of the terms agreed in writing, assuming they are dealing with a written document. But this is merely a convenient starting point or presumption and there are many and varied reasons why the courts will be prepared to look outside the confines of the written document to get the full picture of what the parties agreed. This can be seen in the approach of the Supreme Court in *Revenue Commissioners* v. *Moroney* (1971) (Extract 5.1). The courts refer to the outside evidence which they look at as parol or extrinsic evidence and while the law originally talked of a rule against the use of parol evidence, the judgment of Walsh J. in *Moroney* shows how far the courts have departed from that in practice.

As well as looking outside a written document to discover all terms of a contract expressly agreed between parties, courts are prepared to conclude that other terms are implicit in the contract and where implied by the courts these terms have the same value in a court of law as those actually agreed by the parties. Thus, a party who breaks the implied term of a contract will be subject to the same rules regarding the payment of damages as the party who breaks an express term. It is noteworthy, however, that the judges are careful not to imply terms into contracts at the drop of a hat; they will do so only if they are sure that if time was frozen as at the date the parties entered the contract they would concur in having the term included. The courts will not imply a term merely because it would be what a prudent person ought to have inserted; their role is to imply a term which is absolutely necessary to make the contract actually agreed work in practice, not to re-write that agreement. That basic view, exemplified in *Ward* v. *Spivack Ltd.* (1955) (Extract 5.2), has, however, given rise to differences of opinion on how that should be applied in particular instances and in *Ward* the Supreme Court came to a different conclusion as to what was necessary to make that contract work from that reached by the High Court. A more recent case also showed that even experienced judges find difficulty in agreeing on this area: see *Tradax (Irl.) Ltd.* v. *Irish Grain Board Ltd.* [1984] I.L.R.M. 471.

Once terms are deemed part of the agreement, the courts must deal with the consequences which attach to breaking them. In this task, the law recognises that in logic different consequences should follow depending on the seriousness of the particular breach. After years of development a basic distinction emerged between breaking what became known as a condition of a contract on the one hand and breaking what was called a warranty on the other. The Sale of Goods Act, 1893 provided a codification of this development for sale of goods contracts. Breach of a condition, defined as a term which is central to an agreement, for example the description or quality of the goods, would allow the other party to treat the contract as at an end and also claim damages; whereas breach of a warranty, a term peripheral to the main purpose of the agreement, entailed the less drastic consequence that the innocent party must carry on with the contract and is left merely to claim damages for breach of contract. But the rigidity of the distinction drawn in the Act of 1893 led to some anomalies which to some extent were remedied in the Sale of Goods and Supply of Services Act, 1980. In addition, in areas of contract law where the courts were left free to determine the consequences of breach of contract terms they could adopt intermediate solutions. Thus, in the English Court of Appeal decision in *Hongkong Fir Shipping Co. Ltd.* v. *Kawasaki Kisen Kaisha Ltd.* [1962] 2 Q.B. 26, it was held that contract terms can be so complex and the possible breaches of even one term so varied that the consequence of breaking such intermediate or innominate terms should be determined by reference to its importance for the parties themselves and the seriousness of the breach involved. This basic approach is subject to the qualification that in some instances the courts will presume that some terms will be regarded as essential to the contract, as in *Bunge Corp.* v. *Tradax S.A.* [1981] 1 W.L.R. 711, where the Court took this view regarding a time clause in a contract for the carriage of goods by ship. The delicate balancing involved in this amalgam of rules is at work in *Hynes Ltd.* v. *Independent Newspapers Ltd.* (1980) (Extract 5.3). In this case, in the context of time clauses relating to rent reviews in a landlord and tenant contract, while the presumption is quite different the underlying rule is the same.

Finally, an examination of the interpretation of a particular clause which is one the courts run across frequently. In a contract of employment an employer may demand of an employee that if they part company at some future date, the employee must not compete with what would then be the former employer for, perhaps, five years after that. This type of clause in a contract of employment constitutes a clear restriction, or restraint, on the employee's trade. The courts are prepared to regard such restraints as valid if they can be shown to be reasonable. In *European Chemical Industries Ltd.* v. *Bell* (1981) (Extract 5.4), McWilliam J. considered the general approach to restraint of trade as well as the related problem of interpreting the wording of covenants in restraint. If interpreted literally, they may be declared invalid as unreasonable restraints, but if interpreted contextually, within the legitimate commercial interests of the employer, then as the English Court of Appeal did in *Littlewoods Organisation* v. *Harris* [1977] 1 W.L.R. 1472, an appartently unreasonable restraint may be deemed reasonable. While this method of interpretation might be reasonable in relation to most clauses in contracts, it is arguable that to apply this to restraint of trade gives an employer too much leeway in drafting such clauses.

5.1 The Revenue Commissioners v. Moroney [1972] I.R. 372 Supreme Court

[The circumstances of the case are outlined at Extract 4.5 above. The two Moroney sons argued that it was always understood between themselves and their father that he would never look for the amount referred to in the deed of assignment. To support this they wished to introduce the sworn written evidence, that is an affidavit, of the solicitor who had advised on the assignment.

The extract from the Supreme Court judgment of Walsh J. shows the Court agreeing with the High Court decision of Kenny J. on this point in allowing the affidavit in evidence to show whether any consideration had in fact been paid. Walsh J. also notes that for him the evidence was admissible to explain the real intention of the parties.]

Walsh J.:

At the trial in the High Court the plaintiffs objected to the admission of this affidavit and submitted that it was not permissible to adduce evidence of extrinsic circumstances to add to, contradict, vary, or alter the terms of a deed. The learned trial judge admitted the affidavit on a number of grounds one of which, referring to a submission made by the plaintiffs, was to the effect that the statement of the consideration in a deed forms no part of the terms of the deed but is only a statement contained in the deed of an antecedent fact and that, therefore, the evidence was admissible in relation to this matter. The learned trial judge also pointed out with some force that, if no such evidence as to the consideration was admissible, the revenue claim would fail because the deed itself contained a receipt for the payment of the money. The trial judge held that it was permissible to give evidence to the effect that, despite the receipt, consideration had not been paid. Similarly the learned judge held that the evidence was admissible when it was relevant to explain the circumstances in which the deed was executed and to establish that the parties did not intend that the purchase price mentioned in the deed should ever be paid. The plaintiffs took the same objection in this Court but this Court permitted this evidence to be taken into account and decided to receive in evidence the affidavit made by the late Mr. Robinson. In my view, the learned trial judge was correct in admitting the affidavit and, apart from the other reasons given by the learned High Court judge for admitting the evidence, I think it was admissible on the ground that it was relevant to explain the circumstances under which the deed was executed and to establish what in fact was the real intention of the parties. In his affidavit Mr. Robinson stated that there was never any intention on the part of the deceased that the sum of £16,000, or any sum, should be paid to him and that it was clearly understood that no money, or any consideration, was to pass to the deceased from the defendants.

5.2   Ward and Fagan v. Spivack Ltd.
[1957] I.R. 40 Supreme Court

[The plaintiffs were appointed sole agents for the defendant company in a certain area. Their verbal contract provided for payment of commission on orders received by the company from customers introduced by the plaintiffs in their designated area. The company terminated the plaintiffs' agency and the plaintiffs then claimed that they should still be entitled, by virtue of an implied term in their agreement with the company, to a continuing commission on orders from customers which they had introduced to the company.

In dealing with this argument, Maguire C.J., speaking for the Supreme Court, took the view that such an implied term would not reflect the real intention of the parties, but would be making a new agreement entirely. While the judge pointed out this might very well be a reasonable term to insert that was beside the point, thus taking a different view from that of Davitt P. in the High Court. On the terminology used it is useful to compare and contrast the use of the phrase "business efficacy" in the case with its use in the different context of certainty in *Cadbury (Irl.) Ltd.* v. *Kerry Co-Op. Ltd.* (1981) (Extract 4.3) above.]

Maguire C.J.:

It is settled law that a term may be implied in a contract to repair what *Cheshire and Fifoot*, (3rd ed., 1952, at p. 127) calls "an intrinsic failure of expression." Where there has been such a failure the judge may supply the further terms which will implement their (the parties) presumed intention and in a hallowed phrase give "business efficacy" to the contract. "In doing this he purports at least to do merely what the parties would have done themselves had they thought of the matter. The existence of this judicial power was asserted and justified in *The Moorcock* (1889) 14 P.D. 64." In that case Bowen L.J. explained the nature of the implication in all the cases; he says where they were implied "the law is raising an implication from the presumed intention of the parties, with the object of giving to the transaction such efficacy as both parties must have intended that at all events it should have." The test to be applied by the Court has been stated by several judges in much the same language: see Scrutton L.J. in *Reigate* v. *Union Manufacturing Co. Ltd.* [1918] 1 K.B. 592 and MacKinnon L.J. in *Shirlaw* v. *Southern Foundries Ltd.* [1939] 2 K.B. 206.

It will be seen from the language used in so stating the tests that something more is required than the probability of which the President speaks that the parties must have agreed to the term to be implied had the matter been mentioned. There must be something approaching certainty or as put by Jenkins L.J. in *Sethia Ltd.* v. *Partabmull Rameshwar* [1950] 1 All E.R. 51, it must be "clear beyond a peradventure that both parties intended a given term to operate, although they did not include it in so many words."

Can it be said with the degree of confidence required that the parties must, had the matter been raised, have agreed to the continuance of commission on the basis contended for by Mr. Fagan? The President came unhesitatingly to the conclusion that it cannot be so said. With this I am in complete agreement. Whatever view one might take had the agency only related to orders obtained from customers introduced by the plaintiffs the fact that the contract was to pay commission on all orders with the exceptions mentioned suggests that Mr. Spivack was quite unlikely on behalf of his company to agree to the continuance of commission beyond the period of the agency...Furthermore although it might have been a reasonable thing for Mr. Spivack to have agreed to continue to pay commission on orders from customers introduced by the plaintiffs at least for some time after the termination of the agency I am quite unable to hold as the President does that had the matter been raised Mr. Spivack must have agreed. To read such a term into the contract would in my view not be to make clear the intention of the parties unexpressed at the time but would be to make a new contract.

5.3 Hynes Ltd. v. Independent Newspapers Ltd.
[1980] I.R. 204 Supreme Court

[Hynes Ltd. had a tenancy contract for premises owned by Independent Newspapers Ltd. The contract provided that either landlord or tenant could apply to the other for a review of the rent payable, to take effect

66

from the beginning of the eighth year of the lease. The contract also stated that notice was to be given, at the latest, three months before the end of the seventh year of the lease. Independent Newspapers were six weeks over this time limit. Hynes argued that the notice was, therefore, invalid and that Independent Newspapers should not be entitled to a rent review. The Supreme Court disagreed, however, with this argument that the time limits had to be complied with strictly, and it is as well to note the practical importance of this since it was conceded that the annual rent would as a result increase from £42,000 to about £160,000.

The extracts from the judgments of O'Higgins C.J. and Kenny J. show that aside from the presumption that time clauses in leases are generally not regarded as of the essence to the contracts (in other words, need to be complied with strictly) the basic test in all such cases, regardless of the type of contract, is whether the parties showed an intention to make such clauses central to the agreement. The judgment of Kenny J. in particular shows how this can be traced back to the decision in the *Hongkong Fir Shipping* case.]

O'Higgins C.J.:

It is not necessary to examine in any detail the careful, long and detailed speeches of the Law Lords who participated in [*United Scientific Holdings Ltd.* v. *Burnley Borough Council* [1978] A.C. 538.] It is sufficient to say that, with one reservation, they were prepared to regard the inclusion in a lease of a rent review clause as an acceptance by the tenant of an obligation to pay to the landlord a rent so determined and, further, that this acceptance was an inseverable part of the whole consideration for the landlord's grant of the terms of years for the length agreed. The majority view was to this effect even when the right to initiate or to "trigger" the rent review was exclusively that of the landlord. It was recognised that there could be exceptions as where a break-clause was included in the lease entitling the tenant to surrender if the rent were increased.

Viewed in this light, the time-table for the review or determination of the new rent was regarded by the court as subsidiary to an obligation already accepted by the tenant and as mere machinery for carrying into effect the real intention of the parties that periodic increases of rent should take place. In particular, the majority view was that the unilateral right of the landlord to initiate or to commence a rent review was not a right to create a new relationship or contract between landlord and tenant but was merely a power or right to determine the amount of a new rent already agreed to. It merely altered a term in a continuing contract. In this respect it differed from an option under which one party was empowered to create a new and binding contract with the other. Accordingly, the House of Lords adopted and applied to such rent review clauses, when considered in relation to the observance of time limits, the following rule which appears in *Halsbury's Laws of England* (4th ed., vol. 9, para. 481):

"Time will not be considered to be of the essence unless: (1) the parties expressly stipulate that conditions as to time must be strictly complied with; or (2) the nature of the subject matter of the contract or the surrounding circumstances show that time should be considered to be of the essence..."

The result was that, in the absence of any contra indication in the lease itself, the House of Lords in the *Burnley* case ruled that there is a presumption (stemming from the application of equitable principles) that in all rent review clauses time should not be regarded as essential to the initiation or operation of the rent review, even if the right to review is unilateral.

I have considered very carefully the reasoning which led to the decision in the *Burnley* case. It is based on the assertion that such leases for long terms would not be granted or concluded without acceptance by the tenant of rent reviews and that, as a consequence, it would be unfair and inequitable that such a tenant should be allowed to repudiate an obligation he had accepted merely because, in carrying out what was agreed, a time clause was not observed. I find this reasoning compelling. I accept that there may be circumstances in which delay has been extreme or where, because of it, other factors have arisen which alter the equities. However, in the ordinary case where the payment of an increased rent is expressly envisaged and accepted, and where the failure to observe the requirements of a time clause is due to mere inadvertence and is not prolonged and in no way alters obligations already undertaken, I see no reason for saying that the equitable rule as to time in contracts should not apply. This is not to say that failure by the landlord to act in time may not be a breach of contract for which he may be liable in damages, if damage is caused. However, his failure in this respect should not be regarded as such a breach as would entitle the tenant to repudiate obligations which under the contract he has already accepted.

Kenny J.:

Equity was a gloss on or an improvement and reform of the common law and different constructions were placed in the common-law and chancery courts on stipulations in contracts as to time. So it is necessary to deal with the rules applied in the common-law courts as to such stipulations. In the common-law courts, when a contract provided that certain things were to be done within a certain time or on a specified date, the party who sought to sue on the contract had to plead and prove that he had complied with the stipulation as to time and was ready and willing to perform any other parts of the contract which remained unperformed (see the notes to *Cutter* v. *Powell* (1795) 6 Term Rep. 320 in *Smith's Leading Cases*). This rule resulted in such injustice that the common-law judges worked out a number of exceptions to it. The history of these is dealt with in the judgment of Diplock L.J. (as he then was) in *Hongkong Fir Shipping Co. Ltd.* v. *Kawasaki Kisen Kaisha Ltd.* [1962] 2 Q.B. 26. In the courts of equity (where the ideas summarised in the maxim "Equity looks to the intent, not to the form" were applied and developed) relief would be given against failure to comply with a stipulation as to time in a contract, unless time was of the essence of the contract. A plaintiff or defendant who had not complied with a stipulation as to time in a contract could succeed on his claim or defence unless it was established that time was of the essence of the contract.

5.4 European Chemical Industries Ltd. v. Bell
[1981] I.L.R.M. 345   High Court

[The plaintiffs were a company in the chemicals industry who had employed the defendant. His contract of employment with the company stated that if he left the company then, for two years afterwards, he was not to become involved with, directly or indirectly, "any trade or business of a nature similar to or competing or calculated to compete with any business or businesses carried on by the company or any if its subsidiaries". The restraint also provided that it did "not extend to any country in which neither the company or any of its subsidiary or associated companies has or shall have established a place of business." On the extent of its enforceability, the covenant itself provided that if any of it was determined to be partly or wholly unenforceable by reason of the area, duration or type of service covered "then the covenant shall be given effect to in its reduced form." The defendant obtained training with the plaintiff company and learned some of its trade secrets. He then left the company and was employed in another Irish company, which bought machinery to manufacture material which it previously purchased from the plaintiff company. The plaintiff sought an interlocutory injunction preventing the defendant from taking up employment with the other company.

The extract shows that while on an interlocutory application the judge cannot make a final judgment on the issues arising between the parties, he must be concerned with establishing that the plaintiff has a valid claim to make when the case is finally determined. The main issue discussed by McWilliam J., however, was whether, if the restraint involved was unreasonable, the covenant could be pared down, as this one seemed to envisage, to a reasonable meaning. This problem of interpretation is difficult because the judges seem to be at a crossroads in their attitude. Because of the nature of the application in the case, the judge did not make a definite decision on the point, but he was not prepared to throw out completely the new approach set out in the *Littlewoods* case.]

McWilliam J.:

The relevant clauses in the agreement are clearly in restraint of trade and this has not been contested on behalf of the plaintiff. A long line of cases from *Nordenfelt* v. *Maxim Nordenfelt Guns and Amunition Co. Ltd* [1894] A.C. 535 to *Greig* v. *Insole* [1978] 1 W.L.R. 303 appears to establish that a contract in restraint of trade is contrary to public policy and void or unenforceable unless the restraint reasonably protects a valid interest of the person in whose favour it is imposed, is not unreasonable with regard to the person restrained and is not unreasonable as being injurious to the public interest.

On the affidavits before me I am satisfied, notwithstanding the arguments to the contrary on behalf of the defendant, that there is *prima facie*, a valid interest of the plaintiff to be protected, that is to say, the protection of trade secrets, testing techniques and production processes which have come to the knowledge of the defendant. Certainly I cannot accept that there is not, at least, a serious issue to be tried in this respect.

A more substantial objection on behalf of the defendant is that the clause is unreasonable both because it is too wide in the area of its application geographically and as making the period of restraint too long. I was addressed at some length as to the power of the court to modify the agreement should it be considered to be unreasonable in its present form.

The most recent case to which I was referred is that of *Littlewoods Organisation* v. *Harris* [1977] 1 W.L.R. 1472. It has been discussed on behalf of both parties but I find some aspects difficult to follow. It seems to me that the majority of the Court of Appeal, Lord Denning M.R. and Megaw L.J. formed the opinion contrary to the view expressed in the case of *Commercial Plastics Ltd.* v. *Vincent* [1965] 1 Q.B. 623 that the court is entitled to ignore the literal meaning of such a covenant and construe it with regard to the surrounding circumstances existing at the time when the covenant was entered into (see Megaw L.J. at p. 1489) or that the clause should be interpreted as limited to the reasonable objects which the parties to the agreement sought to achieve (see Lord Denning at p. 1483).

It seems to me that a point to be determined is whether a covenant which can be construed as being too wide in some respects and therefore unreasonable in those respects is wholly void in all respects or whether, although including unreasonable provisions which will not be enforced, reasonable provisions which are contained in it may be enforced. This is an aspect discussed by Lord Denning in a different form at pp. 1481-2 of the *Littlewoods* case. He said, at p. 1482: "It has often been said that a covenant in restraint of trade is not to be rendered invalid simply by putting forward unlikely or improbable contingencies in which it might operate unreasonably...If such an unlikely or unusual event should happen, the court would not enforce it so as to work an injustice." The conclusion of the Court of Appeal in the case of *Commercial Plactics Ltd.* v. *Vincent* was that the covenant, being too wide, had to be ruled out and declared void although the actual relief sought was held to be reasonable and proper to be granted. The same view was taken by Browne L.J. in his dissenting judgment in the *Littlewoods* case. He said, at p. 1491: "It seems to me that if the clause is read literally it is much too wide and is void or unenforceable." This was also the view of the Court of Appeal in the case of *Gledhow Autoparts Ltd.* v. *Delaney* [1965] 1 W.L.R. 1366. Sellers L.J. said, at p. 1371:

> "The injunction for which the plaintiffs asked and which they received is admittedly less than clause 6 in its terms would have permitted as regards area, that is, places where the defendant had operated. But when, as is the defendant's contention, the clause is said to be unenforceable because it is in restraint of trade, it must be construed as it stands and not to the extent that the employer seeks to enforce it. The modified request may reveal an apprehension as to the full effects of the clause. Whether this

clause is, as the judge held, enforceable and not in restraint of trade, or whether it is too wide and not to be invoked, is a question of law and has to be decided on the authorities.''

...At the same time, doubts have been cast on the correctness of this strict view and it might be considered that a court of equity is entitled to consider the effect of the contract as the circumstances come before it so as to avoid working an injustice. The entire doctrine that contracts in restraint of trade are void or unenforceable is based on the proposition that such contracts are contrary to public policy or, as was said in a very old case, "against the benefit of the Commonwealth." Can it be said that it is of any advantage to public policy to refuse relief which is held to be reasonable and proper to be granted, as in the *Commercial Plastics* case?

In the case of *McEllistrim* v. *Ballymacelligott Co-operative Agricultural & Dairy Society Ltd.* [1919] A.C. 548 Viscount Finlay, at p. 571, adopted a statement of James V.C. in the case of *Leather Cloth Co.* v. *Lorsont* (1869) L.R. 9 Eq. 345 at p. 353. It is:

"All the cases, when they come to be examined, seem to establish this principle, that all restraints upon trade are bad as being in violation of public policy, unless they are natural, and not unreasonable for the protection of the parties in dealing legally with some subject matter of contract. The principle is this: public policy requires that every man shall be at liberty to work for himself, and shall not be at liberty to deprive himself or the State of his labour, skill or talent, by any contract that he enters into. On the other hand, public policy requires that when a man has by skill or by any other means obtained something which he wants to sell, he should be at liberty to sell it in the most advantageous way in the market; and in order to enable him to sell it advantageously in the market it is necessary that he should be able to preclude himself from entering into competition with the purchaser. In such a case the same public policy that enables him to do that does not restrain him from alienating that which he wants to alienate and, therefore enables him to enter into any stipulation, however restrictive it is, provided that restriction in the judgment of the Court is not unreasonable, having regard to the subject matter of the contract."

I have considered these matters at some length because the present application has been met to a large extent on the basis that it should be refused on the ground that the covenant is void and the plaintiff cannot succeed in its action. I am not satisfied about this as there seems to be a number of arguments open to the plaintiff and it would be improper for me on an interlocutory application to decide the main issue in the case without hearing the evidence which may be adduced and having a full argument on the various aspects to which I have referred. All I have to do on an interlocutory application is to decide whether the plaintiff has established a *prima facie* case in the sense that there is a serious question to be tried and, if so, what is the balance of convenience to the parties between granting and refusing an injunction.

From the facts which are before me and the review which I have made of the decisions, I am satisfied that there is a serious issue to be tried. On the question of the balance of convenience, it seems to me that the defendant can be adequately compensated in damages if he is successful in his defence and that an undertaking by the plaintiff to pay such damages will be met, whereas damages would not be an adequate remedy for the plaintiff and it is doubtful whether any damages could be recovered from the defendant if the plaintiff were to be successful. Accordingly, I am of opinion that the *status quo* should be preserved and that I should grant the interlocutory injunction sought.

CHAPTER 6

The Reality of Contractual Consent

In this Chapter the emphasis will be on the response of the courts to situations where it could be said that one, or both, of the parties to a contract have not given their full consent to the manner in which the contract has been performed. The judges face this dilemma. While in general they require parties to arrive at a consensus about the subject matter and terms of the contract, they are also reluctant to interfere with bargains actually agreed, despite an element of a serious absence of consensus between the parties or even an unfairness in the result.

The extracts show the response to this kind of problem in the context of exemption clauses, mistaken impressions, misrepresentation, undue influence and the frustration of the purpose of a contract.

The first two extracts deal with the much used exemption clause. Such a clause attempts to avoid the usual consequences following on a breach of contract, usually payment of damages. The exemption clause states on the one hand that while the person who inserts it into a contract is willing to perform some part of his side of the bargain, he will not be legally responsible if he fails to meet, perhaps in important respects, the usual standards of performance expected in business agreements. Thus, in a contract for the supply of a service, one party may promise to carry perishable goods to a particular destination, but also insert an exemption clause into the agreement in effect denying responsibility if, when delivered, the goods have deteriorated to an unacceptable level. Because these clauses were in many instances imposed on individuals who had no choice in the matter (see the *Mc Cord* case (1980) (Extract 4.1)) the courts took a stance of interpreting their terms as strictly as possible against the person relying on them - *contra proferentem*. This stance, and the response of, usually, large concerns who employed exemption clauses was summarised by Lord Denning M.R. in *Geo. Mitchell Ltd.* v. *Finney Lock Seeds Ltd.* [1983] Q.B. 284, at p.297: "The big concern could and did not exempt itself from liability in its own interest without regard to the little man. It got away with it time after time. When the courts said to the big concern, 'You must put it in clear words', the big concern had no hesitation in doing so. It knew well that the little man would never read the exemption clauses or understand them." While it is unusual nowadays for the courts to run across unspecific or vague exemption clauses, such clauses do occasionally end up being litigated, and Irish and English courts have a common stance then, as can be seen in the judgment in *Alexander* v. *Irish National Stud Co. Ltd.* (1977) (Extract 6.1). The result there indicates that had the National Stud wished to include an exemption clause in its standard form agreement excluding liability on their part for breaking their agreement as a result of carelessness by their employees they could have done so with a properly worded clause; what they had failed to do was to tailor the clause to meet their particular needs.

Where Irish and English courts have, almost unintentionally, diverged is where they have encountered exemption clauses which companies used to avoid even the most basic core of their contractual commitments, denying responsibility for breaking what courts described as the fundamental term of a contract. This was the type of clause discussed in *Clayton Love & Sons Ltd.* v. *B and I Steampacket Co. Ltd.* (1966) (Extract 6.2). Here was an extremely long and specific exemption clause of the kind referred to by Lord Denning. In *Clayton Love*, the Supreme Court followed the lead of what had been, up to the day before it handed down judgment, the approach of English courts of declaring that such clauses had no legal effect at all. This is quite different from interpreting the clause restrictively so that it has only limited effect. Unknown to the Supreme Court, the English courts had in fact the day before decided that they had no function in declaring such clauses to have no legal effect: the *Suisse Atlantique* case [1967] 1 A.C. 361, reaffirmed in *Photo Production Ltd.* v. *Securicor Transport Ltd.* [1980] A.C. 827. So the English courts fell back on the original stance of interpreting the language of such clauses restrictively but leaving companies free to be specific in excluding almost to vanishing point their liability. The reasons for this change may be that it was unrealistic to adopt the solution taken in the Clayton Love case in contracts made between two hard-nosed commercial concerns and also that the very real problems of "the little man" have to a large degree been resolved for the courts by legislation, in Ireland by the Sale of Goods and Supply of Services Act, 1980 (discussed in Chapter 8, below). There are some indications that, where such reforming legisation does not apply, the Irish courts might be prepared to follow the new (or more accurately the reaffirmed old) approach in England: *Western Meats Ltd.* v. *National Ice and Cold Storage Co. Ltd.* [1982] I.L.R.M. 99.

An equally difficult area for the courts has been deciding what to do where one, or both, of the parties enter into an agreement based on a mistaken impression as to the subject matter of the contract, sometimes given the shorthand description of mistake of fact. The decision in *Lucey* v. *Laurel Construction Ltd.* (1970) (Extract 6.3) points out that courts are reluctant to interfere with, or rectify, agreements which prove to have been based on mistaken impressions where one party is not attempting to benefit by a deception or where the agreement reflects a fair view of the parties' actual intentions at the time. This is even where a refusal by the courts to interfere means upholding a contract where no real consensus exists. The approach is different where one party has made positive steps to induce a misleading impression in the other party. The solution here is known as the rule in *Smith* v. *Hughes* and can be seen applied in the second extract from *Clayton Love & Sons Ltd.* v. *B and I Steampacket Co. Ltd.* (1966) (Extract 6.4). The Supreme Court decided that the party inducing the mistaken belief should be prevented from going back on his promise to perform a contract in a particular way even though the reality is that the promise simply cannot be performed; the contract is in a sense doomed to be broken. The solution is of course a particular form of estoppel.

It is sometimes difficult to draw a clearcut distinction between mistaken impression cases and instances where it is argued that one party has been misleading in giving information which induces the other party to enter into an agreement. As with exemption clauses, legislation has been enacted to protect a party where he enters into a contract on the basis of what the law calls negligent misstatements. This covers a wide field, but one of the most usual is where a professional person gives advice carelessly and another person relying on that advice enters into an agreement and suffers losses as a result. This was the (unsuccessful) claim in *J. Sisk & Son Ltd.* v. *Flinn and Ors.* (1984) (Extract 6.5). While it involved the application of principles going back to *Donoghue* v. *Stevenson* [1932] A.C. 562 (as to which see *Wall* v. *Hegarty and Callnan* (1980) (Extract 1.1)) it is important to remember those principles were applied in a contractual setting. This may mean, as in the *Sisk* case, that some term of the circumstances of the advice indicates it is not of an unconditional kind.

The picture is a lot clearer where the courts look at a situation in which one party through his actions, statements or other surrounding circumstances uses unfair, or undue, influence to persuade another to enter into an agreement. The law says that because of the clear absence of consent in such a situation the contract cannot stand up; this was the conclusion in *O'Flanagan* v. *Ray-Ger Ltd.* (1983) (Extract 6.6). There the judge also reviewed the connected, but more generalised, concept of declaring invalid contracts of an unconscionable kind. It is notable that Costello J. kept these two areas quite separate; this is a view which has since been confirmed in England despite attempts to generalise on this area: *National Westminster Bank Plc.* v. *Morgan* [1985] 2 W.L.R. 588. The approach so far as undue influence is concerned seems to be to ensure that the courts will only intervene where some real loss has been suffered. To this extent, the *Morgan* decision seems to discard the unconscionable bargain idea.

Finally, it is also clear that where parties enter into an agreement but its performance as originally envisaged becomes impossible due to a supervening event between agreement and performance, the contract (by implication in some instances) comes to an end. In the law's eyes, the purpose of the original contract has been frustrated. But, as can be seen from *McGuill* v. *United Airlines Inc.* (1983) (Extract 6.7), the courts will only take this view where the event in question was outside the control of either party and the contract as performed (or not at all performed as in *McGuill*) is fundamentally different in real terms from that originally agreed.

6.1   Alexander v. Irish National Stud Co. Ltd. (1977) High Court

[The plaintiffs owned a mare which was sent to be covered by a stallion in the National Stud. During the covering procedure, the mare reared, plunged forward and was killed when she crashed into a wall.
While normal precautions had been taken, it appeared that human error amounting to negligence had resulted in the mare getting free from her handlers. The plaintiff claimed damages, and the National Stud defended by relying on Condition 1 of its Conditions of Acceptance of Nominations, set out in the extract.

The extract shows the approach of judges to exemption clauses where the causes of possible loss or damage are varied. McMahon J. makes clear the attitude where a clause could only have been intended to deal with particular situations. It was because of this that the National Stud were unable to rely on Condition 1 in the circumstances arising here: a more clearly worded clause might have got around this problem.]

McMahon J.:

The Condition is in the following terms:

> "The Irish National Stud will not be responsible to any owner of any mare or foal in the event of an accident occurring to that mare or foal or in the event of a mare or foal incurring disease".

The Court was not referred to any Irish authorities, and the law in England was, until the decision of the Court of Appeal in *Hollier* v. *Rambler Motors Ltd.* [1972] 2 Q.B. 71, set out in a line of authorities represented by *Rutter* v. *Palmer* [1922] 2 K.B. 87, *Fagan* v. *Green & Edwards Ltd.* [1925] 1 K.B. 102 and *Alderslade* v. *Hendon Laundry Ltd.* [1945] K.B. 189.

The effect of those cases was that a party who wanted to exclude his liability for negligence was required to do so in clear words but if the only liability of the party pleading an exempted clause is a liability for negligence the clause will, to use the expression employed by Scrutton L.J. in *Rutter* v. *Palmer*, "more readily operate to exempt him".

In *Alderslade* v. *Hendon Laundry Ltd.* Greene M.R. went further than the previous decisions when he said (at p.192): "Where the head of damage in respect of which limitation of liability is sought to be imposed is one which rests on negligence and nothing else, the clause must be construed as extending to that head of damage, because it would otherwise lack subject-matter". In the judgment of Greene M.R. there is substituted for Lord Justice Scrutton's "more readily operate" the view that the clause "must be construed as extending" to negligence.

In *Hollier's* case Salmon L.J., with whom Stamp L.J. and Latey J. agreed, held that notwithstanding that negligence is the only ground upon which liability can attach nevertheless an exemption clause in these terms may, but does not necessarily, provide exemption from liability for negligence. The exemption clause may be understood by the other party merely as a warning that damage may occur to his property in the course of the performance of the contract for which the party carrying out the contract will not be liable. The proper test is to consider what the ordinary sensible customer would understand by the words.

It appears to me that the decision of the Court of Appeal in *Hollier's* case corresponds with the reality of the situation where the terms of the contract are negotiated between the parties but are presented by one party to the other as a contract of adhesion which may be accepted or rejected but not modified in its terms. The contract terms may therefore be regarded as a communication from the party offering them to the other party and they are to be construed in the sense which an ordinary sensible person in the relevant circumstances would understand them.

Every breeder knows that accidents may befall a mare at a stud without negligence on the part of anyone. I think a breeder would read these words as a warning that the stud will not be liable for such an accident but he would not understand the words to mean that if his mare were injured in an accident caused by the negligence of the employees of the stud he could not hold the Stud responsible. The fact that the condition includes disease as well as accident reinforces this view because it suggests that the subject matter dealt with is inevitable risks.

I have considered [the] submission that the expression "will not be responsible" suggests that this is something the parties are agreeing to rather than a statement of an existing position but while I appreciate the weight of the point it appears to be not sufficient to outweigh the other considerations.

When as in the case of *Rutter* v. *Palmer* a garage stipulates: "Cars driven by our staff at customers risk" it appears to me that this conveys to the customer a different kind of risk from that which the condition in the present contract would convey. The customer knows that the accidents referred to are accidents involving the negligence of the garage drivers because he would not expect the garage to be responsible for an accident to his car caused by the negligence of some third party. The clause is dealing with risks of damage which in the normal course arise only where some party is negligent. The condition in the present contract is dealing with a state of affairs where injury to a mare may easily occur without negligence on the part of anyone. For these reasons I conclude that the defendants are not exempted from liability by the conditions in question.

6.2   Clayton Love & Sons Ltd. v. B and I Steampacket Co. Ltd. (1966) 104 I.L.T.R. 157 Supreme Court

[The defendants agreed to ship frozen scampi belonging to the plaintiffs from Dublin to Liverpool. Because of the conditions under which the scampi was boarded, as to which see Extract 6.4, the scampi was unfit for eating when it arrived in Liverpool. The plaintiffs sued for the loss they incurred. The defendants denied liability by relying on clauses 3 and 16 of their standard conditions of carriage, which are set out in the Extract below.

The Supreme Court's position in the case was clear: the defendants had made a basic commitment to exercise reasonable care in carrying the plaintiffs' goods and because they broke that core of the agreement they were not entitled to rely on their exemption clauses in any form, no matter how well drafted they were. It is interesting to note that in summarising the judgment of the President of the High Court, Davitt P., the Supreme Court shows that the President felt that even with the exceptional width of clause 3 there was still some contractual content in the agreement between the parties, that is, some remnant of a promise which the defendants were required to keep. By taking the view, that, as a result, B and I could still rely on clause 16 Davitt P. took a view that is very similar to the view in the *Securicor* case in England. This might be worth exploring if *Clayton Love* comes to be re-examined by the Supreme Court itself in the future.]

Ó Dálaigh C.J.:

It will suffice to refer to three clauses in the standard conditions of carriage. In clause 2 the company stipulates that it is not and does not hold itself out as a common carrier. In clause 3 the company exempts itself from liability for any damage howsoever, whensoever or wheresoever the same may have been caused. I quote the main provisions of the clause:

"The Company shall not in any circumstances whatsoever be liable for any damage, loss (including death or sickness or injury to animals), detention, deterioration, delay, misdelivery or non-delivery of or to goods of whatsoever nature they may be howsoever, whensoever or wheresoever the same may have been caused, even though such damage, loss, detention, deterioration, delay, misdelivery or non-delivery, is wholly or partly due to the wrongful act neglect or default of the Company or its servants or agents or of any other person for whom the Company is or may be responsible, and even though any ship or craft in or on which any of the goods may at any time be loaded was unseaworthy at the time of loading or sailing or at any other time."

...Clause 16 requires a claim in respect of goods to be made within three days from the time of arrival: the words of the clause are:

"16. Any claim of whatsoever nature in respect of the goods must be made in writing to the Company in the case of animals within twelve hours and in the case of other goods within three days from the time at which the same arrived, or would in the ordinary course have arrived, at their destination, otherwise all rights of action against the Company shall be absolutely barred".

...Turning next to the clauses of the standard conditions of carriage and, in particular, to clauses 3 and 16 the President held (i) as in his view the service which the plaintiffs got under their contract was something radically different from the service they had contracted for there had been a breach by the defendants of a fundamental term and, accordingly, that they could not avail of clause 3 to escape liability but (ii) that clause 16 did apply in the case of a fundamental breach and could be relied upon. He accordingly entered judgment for the defendants.

The plaintiffs have challenged the President's view of clause 16 and have submitted that equally with clause 3 it is an exempting clause and must fall on breach of a fundamental obligation of the contract being established...[T]he only matter which arises is whether the President was right in his view that clause 16 of the standard conditions could avail the defendants notwithstanding breach of a fundamental obligation of the contract. The terms of the contract as the President found them having been upheld it was not questioned by the defendants that the doctrine of fundamental breach precluded them from relying on the exemptions of clause 3. The President was of opinion that notwithstanding the very wide terms of clause 3 there remained some subject matter upon which clause 16 could operate, and that he should give effect to the clause. In particular, the President pointed out that clause 16 contemplated a sustainable claim being made where the goods never arrive at all at their destination, and this would be a fundamental breach of the contract. Clause 16 he therefore held was intended to apply in case of a claim arising from a fundamental breach of the contract.

It was submitted on behalf of the plaintiff that the correct position in law is that a defendant in breach of a fundamental obligation cannot avail of any exempting clause whatever; and accordingly that clause 16 equally with clause 3 must fall.

As Cheshire and Fifoot in their *Law of Contract* (6th ed. p.17) point out, a primary source of the doctrine of fundamental obligation is to be found in cases of carriage of goods by sea where a ship has deviated from its appointed course; and they instance *Joseph Thorley Ltd.* v. *Orchis S.S. Co. Ltd.* [1907] 1 K.B. 660. Collins M.R., there explained the effect of the doctrine by saying "... it displaces the contract" (p.667). Cozens-Hardy L.J. put it in these words (at p.669) "... the shipowner... cannot claim the benefit of an exception contained in the special contract" and the words of Fletcher Moulton L.J. (at p.669) were, "... he cannot claim the benefit of stipulations in his favour contained in the bill of lading... The most favourable position which he can claim to occupy is that he has carried the goods as a common carrier for the agreed freight".

Lord Sumner in *Atlantic Shipping and Trading Co. Ltd.* v. *Louis Dreyfus & Co. Ltd.* [1922] 2 A.C. 250 at p. 261 uses language similar to Fletcher Moulton L.J.: "The shipowners gain no advantage against the charterer from their neglect to make the ship seaworthy; they merely cannot pray the clause in aid in that case." In this last case the matter in question was the time provision of an arbitration clause.

Devlin J. (as he then was) dealt quite explicitly with this matter in *Smeaton Hanscomb & Co. Ltd.* v. *Sassoon I. Setty Son & Co.* [1953] 2 All E.R. 1471. He said (p.1473): "It is no doubt a principle of construction that exceptions are to be construed as not being applicable for the protection of those for whose benefit they are inserted if the beneficiary has committed a breach of a fundamental term of the contract, and that a clause requiring the claim to be brought within a specified period is to be regarded as an exception for this purpose"- and he refers to the *Atlantic Shipping and Trading Company's* case (*supra*).

In my opinion the basis on which this doctrine rests requires that a party, who like the defendants, has been held to be in breach of a fundamental obligation cannot rely on a time bar in the contract to defeat a claim for damages. Equally with other exempting provisions such a time clause cannot be prayed in aid. In my opinion the President should not have allowed the defendants here to rely on clause 16.

In the result I would allow the plaintiff's appeal and enter judgment for the agreed sum.

6.3   Lucey v. Laurel Construction Ltd.   (1970) High Court

[The plaintiff agreed to purchase a plot of land from the defendants who also agreed to build a house for the plaintiff on the plot. The written agreement between the parties referred to a site plan which described the plot as 170 feet long. The defendants had, prior to signing this agreement, decided that to fit more houses into the site, some individual sites would be either 120 or 140 feet long only. This was not made known to the plaintiff who did not measure the site actually given him but which measured 140 feet in length. When the plaintiff discovered this deficiency, he applied to court for a perpetual injunction restraining the defendants from entering the 170 foot plot which he had by then marked out. Kenny J. granted the injunction.

The extract shows why the judge rejected the defendants claim that the agreement should be rectified to reflect the intention of its director Mr. Casey in providing a 140 foot plot. In this he relies on the comments of Denning L.J. in *F. Rose Ltd.* v. *W. Pim Ltd.* [1953] 2 Q.B.

450 that rectification could only be granted where a written document fails to record accurately what was verbally agreed between parties. While this remains the accepted view, some of Lord Denning's other comments in the case were to some extent doubted in *Joscelyne* v. *Nissen* [1970] 2 Q.B. 86 (decided in 1969) which approved in turn of the *Crane* case mentioned by Lord Denning. It is unlikely, however, that the recent English case would have made any difference to the conclusion of Kenny J. in *Lucey*.]

Kenny J.:

Laurel now contend that .... the site let to Mr. Lucey is 140 feet in length and not 170 feet and that Mr. Lucey has no claim to the extra 30 feet. I am convinced that there was no discussion between Mr. Casey and Mr. Lucey about the length of the site in June 1965 before the agreement for the lease was signed. Mr. Casey had it in his mind that he was giving a lease of a site 120 feet in length but he did not mention this to Mr. Lucey and he did not change the site plan or the agreement for the lease. Mr. Lucey thought that the wall which Mr. Casey built between sites 2 and 3 gave him what he had contracted to take: in this he was in error because the site plan gave him 170 feet.

The next argument was that this is the type of case in which the Court would rectify the agreement of the 5th November 1965 so that Mr. Lucey would get what he knew he was getting when he saw the length of the wall built by Mr. Casey. Throughout, Mr. Lucey believed that he was entitled to get what was shown on the site map which he signed and he assumed that the 120 feet in length which Laurel originally gave him when they built the wall was what was on the map. The Court has jurisdiction to rectify a written agreement made between parties only when either there is a mutual mistake made by the two parties in the drafting of a written agreement which is to give effect to a prior oral agreement or when one party sees a mistake in the written agreement and when he knows that the other party has not seen it and then signs the document knowing that it contains a mistake: see *Monaghan Co. Co.* v. *Vaughan* [1948] I.R. 306, the decision of the Supreme Court in *Lowndes* v. *deCourcy* 1959 No. 92, 7 April 1960 and the following remarks of Denning L.J. in *F. Rose Ltd.* v. *W. Pim Ltd.* [1953] 2 Q.B. 450, at p. 461:

> "Rectification is concerned with contracts and documents, not with intentions. In order to get rectification it is necessary to show that the parties were in complete agreement on the terms of their contract, but by an error wrote them down wrongly; and in this regard, in order to ascertain the terms of their contract, you do not look into the inner minds of the parties - into their intentions - any more than you do in the formation of any other contract. You look at their outward acts, that is, at what they said or wrote to one another in coming to their agreement, and then compare it with the document which they have signed. If you can predicate with certainty what their contract was, and that it is, by a common mistake wrongly expressed in the document, then you rectify the document; but nothing less will suffice...

There is a passage in *Crane* v. *Hegeman-Harris Co. Inc.* [1939] 1 All E.R. 662, 664 which suggests that a continuing common intention alone will suffice, but I am clearly of opinion that a continuing common intention is not sufficient unless it has found expression in outward agreement. There could be no certainty at all in business transactions if a party who had entered into a firm contract could afterwards turn round and claim to have it rectified on the ground that the parties intended something different. He is allowed to prove, if he can, that they agreed something different... but not that they intended something different." [emphasis by Denning L.J.]

In this case however there was not a mutual mistake. Mr. Casey intended to give a site 120 feet in length but did not tell Mr. Lucey this and did not think of the measurements shown on the site plan which Mr. Lucey subsequently signed. Mr. Lucey thought that he was getting what was shown on the site plan. He did not know that the agreement of 1965 or the site plan contained a mistake and he is not making a claim which he knows to be fraudulent.

6.4   Clayton Love & Sons Ltd. v. B and I Steampacket Co. Ltd. (1966) 104 I.L.T.R. 157 Supreme Court

[The essential circumstances are outlined in Extract 6.2. The problem in terms of mistaken impressions revolved around the temperature at which the frozen scampi was to be loaded on to the defendants ship. The plaintiffs, through their Miss Heidorn, believed it would be loaded into a refrigerated hold, based on assurances from the defendants. The defendants, negotiating through Mr. Hailes, did not make it clear to the plaintiffs that this was not possible, since their dockers were not prepared to work in refrigerated holds. The scampi was loaded at atmospheric temperature and as a result had gone off when it reached Liverpool.

The Supreme Court affirming Davitt P. on this point, decided that the defendants were stuck with the terms which they had indicated, by their communication failure, would be part of their agreement. The Court also made its approval of the rule in *Smith* v. *Hughes* (1871) L.R. 6 Q.B. 597, both on legal and policy grounds, quite clear.]

Ó Dálaigh C.J.:

The President believed Miss Heidorn was contracting in the belief that the goods would be loaded into a hold already refrigerated, while Mr. Hailes was contracting on the basis that they would be loaded into a hold at atmospheric temperature. The parties therefore were not ad idem; but it would, he said, nevertheless be wrong to conclude that there was no contractual relationship between the parites as to how the consignments were to be carried. He then cited with approval and as setting out the law applicable in these circumstances the following passage from the judgment of Blackburn J. in *Smith* v. *Hughes* (1871) L.R. 6 Q.B. 597 at p. 607:

> "I apprehend that if one of the parties intends to make a contract on one set of terms and the other intends to make a contract on another set of terms, or, as it is sometimes expressed, if the parties are not ad idem, there is no contract, unless the circumstances are such as to preclude one of the parties from denying that he has agreed to the terms of the other.   The rule of law is that stated in *Freeman* v. *Cooke* (1848) 2 Ex. 654 at page 663.   If, whatever a man's real intention may be, he so conducts himself that a reasonable man would believe that he was assenting to the terms proposed by the other party, and that other party upon that belief enters into the contract with him, the man thus conducting himself would be equally bound as if he had intended to agree to the other party's terms."

The President then continued:

> "I take the view that a reasonable man, who had no knowledge of the circumstances of the defendants in relation to their dockers' refusal to work in refrigerated holds, would infer that the goods would be loaded into a hold which was at the time in fact refrigerated and not at atmospheric temperature.   After all if a person speaks of putting food into a refrigerator he will be normally understood as meaning a refrigerator which is in fact refrigerating and not a receptable at atmospheric temperature.   I take the view, accordingly, that the oral portion of the contract between the parties was that the consignments were to be carried as a very delicate refrigerated cargo and loaded last into the refrigeration holds which would at the time and at all material times be at refrigeration temperature and not at atmospheric temperature".

...The criticism advanced by the defendants on this appeal that Blackburn J.'s proposition is not borne out by *Freeman* v. *Cooke* is in my opinion shown not to be well founded.   I read *Freeman* v. *Cooke* as acknowledging that where the parties are not ad idem there can nevertheless be a contract by estoppel.   Here the position in my judgment was that the stipulations of plaintiff's agent with regard to the carriage of the goods were such that no reasonable person could have misunderstood that she was asking for transfer of the goods on delivery at the port into a refrigerated hold and, consequently, that the defendant's agent had only himself to blame if, faced with such a clear intimation of the plaintiff's requirements, he did nothing to correct her impression that the goods would be loaded into a refrigerated hold...

In between *Freeman* v. *Cooke* and *Smith* v. *Hughes* Pollock C.B., in *Cornish* v. *Abington* (1859) 4 H. & N. 549 at p. 556 stated the law in these terms:

> "If any person, by a course of conduct or by actual expressions, so conducts himself that another may reasonably infer the existence of an agreement...whether the party intends that he should do so or not, it has the effect that the party using that language, or who has so conducted himself, cannot afterwards gainsay the reasonable inferences to be drawn from his words or conduct".

Moreover, cases apart, Blackburn J.'s proposition commends itself on principle and in common sense.

It is my opinion not a valid objection, as the defendants have said, that estoppel is a weapon of defence and therefore cannot afford the plaintiffs here a cause of action. Estoppel enters in only in determining whether there is a contract and what are its terms. The rights the plaintiff seeks to enforce flow from that contract that has been established by the application of the doctrine of estoppel.

6.5   J. Sisk & Son Ltd. v. Flinn and Ors. (1984) High Court

[The plaintiffs claimed damages from the defendants, a firm of accountants, on the basis of the loss they suffered when they bought shares in a company based on accounts of the company prepared by the defendants, who were its auditors. Those accounts contained qualifications as to the sums stated for stock and work in progress on the basis that they were "as certified by management and have not been physically observed by us". After the plaintiffs went into effective control of the company, it emerged that the figure for work in progress had been over stated by about £180,000.

Ultimately, as the extract shows, the case was decided on the basis that although the plaintiffs had suffered loss because the accounts did not give a correct view of the company's financial standing, they had been given a warning about this in the qualifications to the accounts. This is a clear application of the principles set out in *Hedley Byrne & Co. Ltd.* v. *Heller & Partners Ltd.* [1964] A.C. 465, in which the party giving advice had also limited its liability by discreetly disclaiming responsibility.]

Finlay P.:

Legal Principles Applicable

I am prepared to accept as correct the statement of principle contained in the opinion of Lord Reid in *Hedley Byrne & Co. Ltd.* v. *Heller & Partners Ltd.* [1964] A.C. 465 where, at p. 486 speaking of the opinion of Lord Haldane in *Robinson* v. *National Bank of Scotland Ltd.* 1916 S.C. (H.L.) 154, he stated as follows:

> "He speaks of other special relationships and I can see no logical stopping place short of all those relationships where it is plain that the party seeking information or advice was trusting the other to exercise such a degree of care as the circumstances required, where it was reasonable for him to do that, and where the other gave the information or advice when he knew or ought to have known that the inquirer was relying on him."

Applying this statement of principle to the facts of this case as I have found them, I have no doubt that it was in this case plain that the plaintiff, who was the party seeking information from the defendants, was trusting the defendants to exercise such a degrees of care as the circumstances required. Furthermore, though the matter was contended, I have no doubt that in those circumstances it was reasonable for the plaintiff, being the prospective purchaser of shares in the company, to trust the auditors and accountants appointed to the company who had also a function in granting financial advice to the company and were taking an active part in the negotiation for the purchase of shares in it to exercise such care. I cannot see how it would be possible in this case to avoid the further consequential conclusion that the defendants ought to have known that the plaintiff as the inquirer was relying on them to exercise that care. This last conclusion, in my view, necessarily flows from the finding which I have made on the facts that the plaintiff did not, prior to the execution of the agreement on 4 May 1978, have any opportunity of examining the books or accounts of the company except insofar as the abortive investigations in 1977 by Mr. O'Flynn, their building surveyor, involved some access to those books.

The next issue of law which must necessarily arise is as to the standard of care which was required in the circumstances of the facts as I have found them from the defendants in this case.

Hedley Byrne & Co. Ltd. v. *Heller & Partners Ltd.* was, of course, a case of simple inquiry as to the financial stability of a company from the bankers to the company and the facts are significantly different from the facts in this case. Notwithstanding this difference, however, I would adopt with approval the general principle stated by Lord Reid in his opinion at p. 486 as follows:

> "A reasonable man, knowing that he was being trusted or that his skills and judgment were being relied on, would, I think, have three courses open to him. He could keep silent or decline to give the information or advice sought: or he could give an answer with a clear qualification that he accepted no responsibility for it or that it was given without that reflection or inquiry which a careful answer would require: or he could answer without any such qualification.
>
> If he chooses to adopt the last course he must, I think, be held to have accepted some responsibility for his answer being given carefully, or to have accepted a relationship with the inquirer which requires him to exercise such care as the circumstances require."

I am satisfied on the evidence in this case that no case has been made against the defendants of negligence, material to the losses which the plaintiff has suffered other than in respect of the work-in-progress figures. Certain evidence was given critical of the method of the audit and critical of some of the information contained in the working papers leading to the audit which were discovered. None of this, in my view, amounted however to even prima facie evidence of negligence except in respect of the work-in-progress figure.

The evidence of Mr. Blanc ...as to the true interpretation of the qualification contained in the auditor's report on the account to 30 November 1977 to the effect that it means that the auditors have no responsibility for that item, which I accept and which is the evidence on this topic adduced on behalf of the plaintiff, seems to me clearly to put the defendants in the position of having adopted the second course which, in the passage which I have quoted, Lord

Reid states is open to a person knowing that he is being trusted or his skill and judgment is being relied on with regard to an enquiry.

Mr. Blanc did further say in his evidence that, in his opinion as an accountant, the qualification was inadequate and it should have been a qualification in the form of a disclaimer, apparently similar to the qualifications which had been contained in reports attached to the attached accounts to 30 November 1976 and 31 May 1977. I have very carefully considered whether this alteration in the form of qualificaton could found an action by the plaintiff.

As already indicated, I have no doubt on the evidence that the question of the accounts and the financial viability of the company was one which was the prime responsibility of Mr. Headon [Sisk's financial adviser], and that the only other person negotiating on behalf of the plaintiff and making such recommendations both to the parent company Sicon Ltd. and to the plaintiff itself as lead to the decision to execute the agreement, namely Mr. John R. Sisk, left this question and, in particular, left the interpretation of the accounts to Mr. Headon. This is strongly confirmed by the fact that on my findings of fact when the audited accounts to 30 November 1977 complete were received by Mr. Daly, it was to Mr. Headon in Dublin rather than to Mr. Sisk, who was immediately available in Cork, that he brought them for consideration and discussion. Mr. Headon's evidence, as I have already indicated, was that if he had been aware of any qualification to the accounts of 30 November 1977, he would as it is stated "have walked away from the deal". On this evidence, it seems to me impossible to conclude that the entry by the plaintiff into this agreement and the losses which they may have suffered as a result of that step could have flowed from the difference between the qualification contained in the accounts to 30 November 1977 and the qualification contained in the accounts for the previous periods. In these circumstances, I am satisfied that the plaintiff's action fails and that the claim must be dismissed.

6.6   O'Flanagan v. Ray-Ger Ltd.
(1983)   High Court

[Mr. O'Flanagan entered into an agreement with a Mr. Pope, one of the defendants in the case, to form a property-holding company called Ray-Ger Ltd. Part of the company's assests was a shop owned by Mr. O'Flanagan and his wife, who was the plaintiff in the case. Mr. O'Flanagan and Mr. Pope were social friends and frequently drank together. Most of the company's affairs were arranged between them when they met socially. On one such occasion, Mr. Pope persuaded Mr. O'Flanagan to sign a document under which his interest in the shop would be transferred to the company and that "in the event of one of the directors dying, the surviving director shall have the right to acquire all of the remaining unissued ordinary shares of the company". Mr. O'Flanagan had, at the time, been recently discharged from hospital and was suffering from a terminal disease of which he died shortly after. The judge decided that at the date of signing the agreement Mr. Pope knew Mr. O'Flanagan's state of health.

The extract shows that in the circumstances Mr. Pope had exercised excessive influence over Mr. O'Flanagan and so the agreement should be declared invalid under the heading of undue influence. Costello J. also refers to the related area by which courts will set aside unconscionable bargains in which pressure may not have been involved, but does not base his decision on this wider ground. Nonetheless, his acceptance of that ground of invalidation of contracts is in contrast with the views of English courts as in *National Westminster Bank Plc.* v. *Morgan* [1985] 2 W.L.R. 588.]

Costello J.:

In this part of my judgment I will deal with the plaintiff's claim that this written agreement should be set aside because (a) it was obtained by undue influence or (b) it represents an unconscionable bargain. The equitable principles which the plaintiffs call in aid are well established. The cases where a plaintiff seeks to set aside a gift or other transaction on the ground that it was procured by undue influence have been divided into two classes; firstly, those in which it can be expressly proved that undue influence was exercised, in which circumstances the Court intervenes on the principle that no one should be allowed to retain any benefit arising from his own fraud or wrongful act; secondly, those in which the relations between the donor and donee have at or shortly before the execution of a gift been such as to raise a presumption that the donor had influence over the donee. Then, the Court intervenes, not on the ground that any wrongful act has in fact been committed by the donee but on the ground of public policy and to prevent the relations which existed between the parties and the influence arising therefrom being abused. The Court will set aside the gift unless it is proved (and the onus is on the donee in such cases) that in fact the gift was the result of a free exercise of the donor's will: see *Allcard* v. *Skinner* (1887) 36 Ch.D. 145, at p. 171. The courts have not defined the degree of confidence and trust which must exist in a relationship before it can be said that a donee is in a position to exert undue influence. It has been long established that the relationship of parent and child, guardian and ward, doctor and patient, religious adviser and pupil are relationships which give rise to the presumption to which I have referred. But the categories are not closed, and in *Gregg* v. *Kidd* [1956] I.R. 183 Budd J. held that the relationship raised the presumption to which I have referred in a case in which an uncle settled property on his nephew. Recently in England a majority of the Court of Appeal, in *In re Brocklehurst, decd.* [1978] Ch. 14, took the view that the presumption did not arise from the relationship of friendship between an elderly man and a companion from a different class in the social structure, whilst in *In re Craig* [1971] Ch. 95 it was held that the relationship between an elderly man and his secretary gave rise to the presumption. The presumption does not arise in the case of wills: see *In re Kavanagh, decd.* High Court 1975 No. 4631P., 24 October 1978 in which I held that express undue influence was proved.

Just as the courts have declined to define the exact categories of relationship which will give rise to the presumption of undue influence so too they have declined to define exactly what undue influence is. The approach which courts of equity should adopt was suggested by Sir Samuel Romilly (a distinguished chancery lawyer and former Solicitor General) in one of the early leading cases on the matter, *Huguenin* v. *Baseley* (1807) 14 Ves. Jun. 273, an approach which subsequently obtained judicial approval from Lord Cottenham in *Dent* v. *Bennett* (1839) 4 My. & Cr. 269, at p. 277 and from Byrne J. in *Cavendish* v. *Strutt* (1903) 19 T.L.R. 483. The passage to which I refer reads as follows:

> "Where a gift is immoderate, bears no proportion to the circumstances of the giver, where no reason appears, or the reason given is falsified, and the giver is a weak man, liable to be imposed upon, this Court will look upon such a gift with a very jealous eye, and very strictly examine the conduct of the person in whose favour it is made; and if it sees that any arts or stratagems, or any undue influence have been used - if it sees the least speck of imposition at the bottom, or that the donor is in such a situation with respect to the donee as may naturally give an influence over him - if there be the least scintilla of fraud, this Court will and ought to interpose ..."

The plaintiffs do not rely solely on the equitable principles relating to undue influence. They claim in the alternative that the agreement of 15 March 1976 should be set aside on the ground that it is an unconscionable bargain. The principle relied on was stated by Lord Hatherley in a dissenting opinion in *O'Rorke* v. *Bolingbroke* (1877) 2 App. Cas. 814, at p.823, a case dealing with a sale at undervalue by an expectant heir but which enunciated a principle of wider application. The passage reads as follows:

> "It ... appears that the principle on which equity originally proceeded to set aside such transactions was for the protection of family property; but this principle being once established, the Court extended its aid to all cases in which the parties to a contract have not met upon equal terms. In ordinary cases each party to a bargain must take care of his own interest, and it will not be presumed that undue advantage or contrivance has been resorted to on either side; but in the case of the 'expectant heir' or of persons under pressure without adequate protection, and in the case of dealings with uneducated ignorant persons, the burden of showing the fairness of the transaction is thrown on the person who seeks to obtain the benefit of the contract."

This passage was quoted with approval by Gavan Duffy J. in *Grealish* v. *Murphy* [1946] I.R. 35, a case in which the plaintiff was a mentally retarded adult but in which no undue influence was shown to have been exercised. The transaction which he entered into, however, was set aside on the ground that equity comes to the rescue in cases where the parties to a contract have not met on equal terms, the court holding that the deed was an improvident one and the plaintiff's weakness of mind coupled with the inadequacy of the advice he obtained justified the intervention of the Court in that case: see also *Fry* v. *Lane*

(1888) 40 Ch. D. 312, at p. 322.

...Taking into account all the evidence in the case I think there is only one conclusion to be reached in relation to this agreement, namely, that the defendant must have used undue influence to procure it. The defendant has a strong and forceful personality and had obviously exercised considerable influence amounting to domination of the deceased on previous occasions. The deceased was infirm and ill when he signed it. The agreement was egregiously unfair to the deceased's wife and family. The mutual promises it contained were largely illusory in that both parties knew that it was highly probable that the deceased would predecease the defendant. Furthermore the lack of candour of the defendant raises very serious suspicions about the circumstances in which it came to be executed. It is unnecessary for me to decide whether the relationship which existed raises any presumption as to what happened. The evidence satisfies me that I should set the agreement aside.

Because I have concluded that the plaintiffs have been able to establish that the agreement was procured by undue influence it is unnecessary for me to decide whether, apart from undue influence, the Court should by the application of equitable principles to which I have already referred set it aside on the ground that it represented an unconscionable bargain.

6.7   McGuill v. Aer Lingus Teo. and United Airlines Inc. (1983) High Court

[The plaintiff organised flights for over 200 people with United Airlines for a tour through the United States to Hawaii. In November 1978 United confirmed the flight dates for April and May 1979. In March 1979 United's employees began strike action, and regional managers of the airline, including the one dealing with the plaintiff, were told not to issue tickets. Tickets were, however, issued by Aer Lingus in the first week of April when the United representative also hoped that the group could be carried by a management crew. When this became no longer a possibility, the plaintiff and United organised alternative carriers for the group, though at a considerably higher total price. McWilliam J. decided he was satisfied that the plaintiff at all times intended to hold United responsible for the extra cost of the tour and had made this clear to the airline's representative. The major claim brought by the plaintiff was against United for breach of what he claimed was an unconditional contract to carry the group on the tour.

The extract from the judgment deals with United's defence that the contract had become frustrated as a result of the strike action of its employees, a defence which if successful would have allowed United to avoid the claim against it. The judge first sets out the opposing views of the parties as to how they saw the risks when the strike became known to each. This is important for the judge's ultimate decision in favour of the plaintiff, because he viewed as crucial the fact that United had got advance notice of the strike through the "cooling-off" provision in their union agreement. This factor should be seen in the light of his comment at the end of the extract that a strike could, in some circumstances, lead to frustration of a contract, in accordance with the general proposition he sets out earlier.]

McWilliam J.:

The defence of United was made on two grounds. First, that on being informed of the strike, the plaintiff took a calculated risk that United would be able to carry the group and that he should have cancelled the tour immediately. Secondly, that the contract was frustrated by the outbreak of the strike.

For the plaintiff it was argued with regard to frustration that the strike was caused by the employees of United, that the refusal of the employees to operate the planes is a refusal by United and therefore United is liable. It was also argued that United did not, at any time during alternative arrangements to have the group carried, claim that the contract had been frustrated but was holding on in the hope that the strike would be settled.

I was referred to a number of authorities on the question of frustration. They were: *Davis Contractors Ltd.* v. *Fareham U.D.C.* [1956] A.C. 696; *Pioneer Shipping Ltd.* v. *B.T.P. Tioxide Ltd.* [1982] A.C. 724; *Paradine* v. *Jane* (1647) Aleyn 26; and *The Penelope* [1928] P. 180... Although it was not referred to during the hearing I note the following passage in *Chitty on Contracts*, 24th ed., para. 1417: "If one party foresaw the risk but the other did not, it will be difficult for the former to claim that the occurrence of that risk frustrates the contract". The reference given is to *Walton Harvey Ltd.* v. *Walker & Homfrays Ltd.* [1931] 1 Ch. 274. I have also considered this report.

From these authorities, the following principles appear to apply when considering a claim that a contract has been frustrated.

1. A party may bind himself by an absolute contract to perform something which subsequently becomes impossible.
2. Frustration occurs when, without default of either party, a contractual obligation has become incapable of being performed.
3. The circumstances alleged to occasion frustration should be strictly scrutinised and the doctrine is not to be lightly applied.
4. Where the circumstances alleged to cause the frustration have arisen from the act or default of one of the parties, that party cannot rely on the doctrine.
5. All the circumstances of the contract should also be strictly scrutinised.
6. The event must be an unexpected event.
7. If one party anticipated or should have anticipated the possibility of the event which is alleged to cause the frustration and did not incorporate a clause in the contract to deal with it, he should not be permitted to rely on the happening of the event as causing frustration.

It does not appear, from the authorities to which I have been referred, what principle is to apply in considering frustration of a contract in circumstances such as the present so as to establish when a contract comes to an end. No evidence was tendered on behalf of United to indicate that United claimed at any particular time that the contract had come to an end and no submission was made as to the time of the termination of the contract. The suggestion on behalf of United seems to be that, once the parties became aware of the strike, a new agreement must be implied that the contract would continue until it was clear that the strike would not be settled in time to enable United to carry the group. Although the decision in the *Pioneer Shipping* case appears to support this proposition to some extent, I am not satisfied that such a proposition should be extended to the circumstances of the present case.

A significant circumstance in the present case is the fact, stated by two witnesses for United, that there had been a "cooling-off" period of 60 days in operation prior to the strike being declared and taking effect. This must have been within the knowledge of United at all times during that period. It can hardly be suggested that there had not been some threat of industrial action before the "cooling-off" period started to run and that, whatever the dispute was about, there had not previously been negotiations in progress between United and their employees. At no time was any communication about these circumstances made to the plaintiff and I conclude that this was because United felt that, if the plaintiff were made aware of the possibility of a strike, he might try to get another airline to carry the group. In my opinion this means that United, being aware of the threat or possibility of a strike, and the evidence is that United had a somewhat similar strike a few years previously, but being anxious to obtain the business, took the risk of entering into the contract without including a provision to safeguard its position in the event of a strike taking place.

Under these circumstances I am of opinion that United is not entitled to succeed on its defence that the contract was frustrated.

I do not accept the argument made on behalf of the plaintiff that a strike by the employees of a party cannot cause frustration of a contract. In my opinion it depends entirely on the circumstances whether it does or not, but, on the view I have formed as to the position of United, it is not necessary for me to deal with this further.

CHAPTER 7

Agency

In previous chapters, the emphasis has been on the situation where two parties have entered into a contractual relationship (excluding the situation discussed in Extract 4.3). Where a contract of agency is created, however, the position is that a person is given lawful authority to act as middleman, or agent, on behalf of another, referred to as the principal, in negotiating a contract.

In some instances, a case involving an agency agreement may revolve around the rules of contract law, such as whether certain terms ought, by implication, to be incorporated into the parties' agreement: see *Ward* v. *Spivack Ltd.* (1955) (Extract 5.2). But the agency contract also involves special problems. Thus the courts have developed the view that certain persons, such as solicitors or estate agents, ought presumptively to be regarded as agents in the legal sense. This means that where a solicitor signs a letter dealing with the negotiation of a contract, the presumption is that he does not do so in a personal capacity but as some other person's agent; of course, this presumption can be rebutted: see *Lavan* v. *Walsh* [1964] I.R. 87.

The extracts discuss two issues of crucial importance to agency agreements: the problems of authority to act on behalf of the principal, and of the circumstances in which the principal is obliged to remunerate an agent, this being a problem of the terms of the agency agreement.

In *Brennan* v. *O'Connell* (1975) (Extract 7.1), the Supreme Court dealt with the problem of authority on two fronts. The first point to note is that while an agent may not be given express authority to enter into a binding contract on behalf of the principal, subsequent ratification by the principal can validate any agreement concluded by the agent. The second point is that ratification will only be valid where the agent has disclosed to the principal all material facts relevant to the decision whether to ratify. The duty to disclose arises from the special nature of the agency relationship, and crucially the test of materiality is an objective one as the judgment of Henchy J. in the case makes clear. This objective test is similar to the test applied in the context of insurance contracts (see Extract 9.1).

In *Galvin (Estates) Ltd.* v. *Hedigan* (1984) (Extract 7.2.), Costello J. dealt with a fairly common problem of interpreting the terms of an estate agency agreement. This revolves round whether an estate agent who is the "sole selling" agent may be entitled to his commission where the principal has in fact arranged the sale. The answer in most instances seems to be "no", although in *Galvin* the fact that the agent there was providing the additional services of lobbyist complicated the matter a little.

7.1 Brennan v. O'Connell
[1980] I.R. 13 Supreme Court (1975)

[The defendants appointed a Mr. Byrne as agent to obtain a purchaser for their farm for £25,000. The plaintiff offered this sum to Mr. Byrne who passed this on to the defendants and they accepted this.

However, they subsequently refused to complete the contract on the ground that Mr. Byrne had not disclosed information relating to another potential purchaser, a Mr. Moloney. Moloney had made an offer of £24,000 on certain conditions, and when informed of this the defendants turned it down. Then came the £25,000 offer from the plaintiff and, before Mr. Byrne passed this on to the defendants, Mr. Moloney inquired whether the defendants would sell the farm together with another, for which Mr. Byrne was also their agent. Mr. Byrne said that they would for £45,000. Mr. Moloney replied that that was a lot of money. It was this inquiry which was not passed on to the defendants.

The extract from the judgment of Henchy J. for a unanimous Supreme Court pointed out that ratification of the contract concluded with the plaintiff could only be negatived if the undisclosed information would have altered the deliberations of a vendor who examined matters based on ordinary business standards. As far as the Court was concerned, the inquiry from Mr. Moloney in this instance was not concrete enough to have the essential objective element of materiality required to negate the ratification.]

Henchy J.:

It is common case that when the defendants appointed Mr. Byrne as their agent for the purpose of procuring a purchaser of the home farm for £25,000, Mr. Byrne did not thereby acquire any authority to enter into a contract on the defendants' behalf for the sale of the home farm for £25,000. His contract of agency merely authorised him to pass on to the defendants for their further instructions an offer to purchase for £25,000, if he obtained such an offer.

Consequently, when the plaintiff made an offer to Mr. Byrne of £25,000 for the home farm, Mr. Byrne was not competent to bind the defendants when on that date he entered into a written contract purporting on their behalf to sell the home farm to the plaintiff for £25,000. It is also common case that the contract could not become enforceable against the defendants unless they subsequently ratified it and that, if ratification took place, it would operate retroactively so that the contract would then become the defendants' contract just as if they had authorised it when Mr. Byrne entered into it: see *Sheridan* v. *Higgins* [1971] I.R. 291.

...The central point in this appeal is whether the failure of Mr. Byrne to inform the defendants of Mr. Moloney's telephone conversation was a non-disclosure which prevented the defendants' assent to a sale to the plaintiff from being a ratification of the written contract entered into by Mr. Byrne and the plaintiff...

Before a principal can be held to have ratified a contract made on his behalf by his agent, the principal must be made aware of all the material facts on which the contract is founded; that is well-established law. This stands to reason, for clearly it would be unfair to hold a man bound by the obligations of a contract made on his behalf if he was debarred by lack of factual information from being able to assess what a ratification would let him in for. The nature of the information that must be made available to the principal depends on the circumstances of the particular case. In the instance of a vendor and an estate agent, the vendor should not be held to have ratified a contract for sale which the estate agent has purported to make on his behalf unless the vendor is made aware of all facts in the knowledge of the estate agent which, in the particular circumstances and without the benefit of hindsight, could objectively be said to have been necessary to enable the vendor to decide if he should assent to the sale. Applying that test to the present case, the question at issue reduces itself to this. Before the defendants could be said to have been able to decide if they should approve of the sale to the plaintiff of the home farm for £25,000, should they have been told (a) that on the day after the purported sale Mr. Moloney had inquired of Mr. Byrne if the two farms might be sold together and, if so, at what price, and (b) that, on being told that the two farms could be bought together for £45,000, Mr. Moloney had merely replied that that was a lot of money?

In my opinion it was not necessary for the defendants to be given that information before they could be said to have been in a position to ratify the sale to the plaintiff for £25,000. Mr. Moloney was a person who had made a qualified offer of £24,000 for the home farm a few days previously; that offer was rejected and he had made no further offer. His inquiry about the possibility of a sale of the two farms as one lot was no more than an inquiry.

The evidence does not disclose that there was at the time any reason to expect that Mr. Moloney's inquiry would lead to an offer from him for either or both farms. The inquiry was in character indistinguishable from the usual inquiries about properties on their books which it is the business of estate agents to elicit and to answer. In the absence of special terms in the contract of agency between a vendor and an estate agent, and so long as they remain mere inquiries, disclosure of such inquiries to the vendor could not be said to be necessary to enable him to decide whether or not to accept a particular offer. They would be objectively immaterial. So much so, that the estate agent and his staff might not even think it necessary to keep a record of them. Only facts which are material to the decision of acceptance or non-acceptance have to be disclosed for the purpose of ratification...

The defendants insist that they would not have approved of the sale to the plaintiff if they had been told of Mr. Moloney's inquiry. They point to the fact that after they learned of that inquiry they sought, and still seek, to avoid being bound to sell to the plaintiff; they say that this shows that it was a material fact that was essential for a valid ratification by them. Viewed in the light of the subjective requirements of the defendants, that may be so; but an objective test of materiality must be applied. If information which, by the subjective standards of a particular vendor, is thought necessary to be disclosed before a sale can be approved, the contract of agency should provide for such disclosure. If that were not the law, a vendor could avoid an otherwise valid ratification, on which the estate agent may have acted, by claiming that the estate agent had withheld from him information which he (the vendor), for private and unpredictable reasons, considered necessary - such as the identity of the purchaser; or the nature of his race, religion or politics; or the way in which the property is to be used by the purchaser; or other purely personal or idiosyncratic considerations which would not reasonably be expected to be material to a decision to reject or to accept an offer to purchase.

The contract of agency should expressly, or by necessary implication, authorise the property owner to do so before he can avoid an otherwise valid ratification by relying on non-disclosure of a circumstance which, according to ordinary business standards, could not be said to be material to a decision to accept or reject a particular offer. No such term can be read into the agency here. As the mere fact that someone had made an inquiry about the terms on which the property might be sold could not, without more, be held to be a consideration which might be expected in the ordinary course of business to affect a decision to assent to an otherwise acceptable offer, the non-disclosure of that inquiry cannot be held to avoid the ratification.

The effect of the ratification is that Mr. Byrne is to be deemed to have had authority to make on behalf of the defendants the open contract in writing which he made: see *Law* v. *Robert Roberts & Co. Ltd.* [1964] I.R. 292. The plaintiff is entitled to specific performance of the contract.

7.2 Galvin (Estates) Ltd. v. Hedigan
[1985] I.L.R.M. 295 High Court

[In 1980, the defendants entered into a written agreement with the plaintiffs giving them the "sole selling agency" for the sale of their land. The plaintiffs also agreed to act as lobbyists, the parties hoping that Dublin County Council would rezone the land for industrial purposes. The agreement stated that the defendants intended "to market these lands at the earliest possible date after the hoped for rezoning", this being made "subject to the land being and remaining rezoned 'industrial'." In 1982 the defendants sold their land without any assistance from the plaintiffs. In 1983, the Council provisionally decided to rezone the land in question for industrial use, but this was never formally confirmed by a second motion of the Council.

In the extract, Costello J. explains why the plaintiffs were not entitled to a commission on the sale which had taken place. While the plaintiffs were to be sole selling agents, the agency was not to arise until after the Council had considered the rezoning issue, and applying the decision in *Murphy Buckley and Keogh Ltd.* v. *Pye (Ireland) Ltd.* [1971] I.R. 57 the defendants were entitled to look for a purchaser themselves. And while the defendants were not entitled to obtain the lobbying service for nothing if it brought about a sale, there was no term implicit in the 1980 agreement which made this extra factor in the case a crucial point of departure from the ordinary estate agency contract.]

Costello J.:

I conclude... that the parties agreed (a) that the plaintiffs would be granted a sole selling agency if and when a motion was adopted that a proposal for their rezoning be included in the draft variations which were to be made available for public inspection and (b) that the sole agency would cease if the rezoning proposals were not included in the variations as finally adopted and (c) that the plaintiffs would be entitled to commission at 3% on any sale which took place after the first motion was passed provided the rezoning proposals were later formally adopted.

There still remains for consideration the meaning of the phrase "sole selling agency" employed in the contract, for it has been urged on the defendants' behalf that if and when the plaintiffs' employment as sole selling agent arose this would not have precluded the defendants themselves from selling the land without any obligation to pay the plaintiffs 3%, or any, commission.

I was referred to *Murphy Buckley and Keogh Ltd.* v. *Pye (Ireland) Ltd.* [1971] I.R. 57 which was a case in which it was held the plaintiffs appointment as sole selling agent did not confer on them exclusive selling right so as to prohibit the landowner from selling themselves. But Mr. Justice Henchy's judgment in the matter quoted with approval certain observations in *Luxor (Eastbourne) Ltd.* v. *Cooper* [1941] A.C. 108 to the effect that it is dangerous to formulate general propositions as to contracts with agents for commission and I do not consider that this decision constrains me to find in the defendants favour merely because the phrase "sole selling agency" (and not "exclusive selling rights") was used by the parties. I have to determine the parties' intention when using this phrase. I agree with [the plaintiffs'] submission that this is by no means the ordinary case of the auctioneer being given exclusive rights to auction or sell his clients lands - here the auctioneers were employed to do different and additional work as lobbyists before their agency would arise. And it seems to me that the parties must have intended that if the plaintiffs efforts (along, of course with those of the defendants themselves who were also active in canvassing support from local representatives) were successful to the extent of getting the first motion adopted that then they would be entitled to commission even if they did not introduce the purchaser. I conclude, therefore, that if and when the plaintiffs' sole agency arose by the adoption of the first motion by the Council the parties intended that the defendants could not defeat the plaintiffs claim to commission by themselves selling the lands.

The conclusions which I have reached on the meaning of the express terms of the contract do not, of course, help the plaintiffs, because the parties expectations in March 1980 were not realised, and no motion in relation to the defendants' land was considered by the Council for over two years. Before that happened, that is, before the plaintiffs' sole agency arose, the defendants themselves sold the lands. The contract is silent as to what the parties rights were if a delay occurred in the adoption of the rezoning motion and in particular whether in the event of such a delay the defendants were free to sell their lands without reference to the plaintiffs' contingent rights. The plaintiffs' contention (which I will now examine) is that the contract should be construed as containing an implied term protecting their interests.

Having concluded that the express terms of the contract meant that the sole agency was to arise when and if the first motion to which I have referred was adopted, I cannot imply a term inconsistent with that to the effect that the sole agency was to commence immediately the letter of 7 March 1980 was signed.

But the plaintiffs suggest that I can imply a term to the effect that pending the adoption of the proposed rezoning motion the defendants would not take any steps to prejudice the plaintiffs' rights to earn 3% commission under the contract - in effect, that the defendants were not free to sell their land in the interval between the contract and the consideration of the motion by the Council without the plaintiffs' consent.

Whether or not it would be proper to imply the suggested term depends on the intention of the parties to be collected from the words of the written agreement and the surrounding circumstances. This is a case in which the parties did not address their minds to the eventuality which in fact occurred but it is not one in which it is necessary to imply the suggested term in order to give business efficacy to the parties' agreement - the contract is a perfectly effective one (albeit one less favourable to the plaintiff in the absence of the suggested term) as it stands. Applying the officious bystander test and imagining an inquiry as to the parties views on the possibility of a two year delay before consideration of the rezoning issue by the Council, I think it is extremely unlikely that the defendant would have agreed either readily or at all that during the intervening period he and his family would be precluded from selling without the plaintiffs' consent - he was obviously aware that a sale might be necessary to meet estate duty demands; and, further, the knowledge that a sale at the insistence of one of the family entitled to a distributive share in their father's estate might well be required would render his agreement for the suggested term highly improbable.

In the light of the views I have expressed on the parties' contract I conclude that the defendants did not breach it.

CHAPTER 8

Regulation of Sales, Services and Credit

For a variety of reasons, the legislature has from time to time intervened to codify and regulate particular areas of contract law relating to the sale of goods, the supply of services and agreements based on credit facilities. At least two different strands of thought were at work in formulating these pieces of legislation.

In enacting the Sale of Goods Act, 1893 the main intention was to provide a convenient source setting out the most important specialised rules of contract law as developed by judges in case law. At the same time the Act reflected the prevailing view of the time that parties should be free to arrive at a contract of sale on their own terms if they so wished, free from any legislatively imposed implied terms. So the Sale of Goods Act, 1893 reflects the hands-off *laissez-faire* of the 19th Century, as to which see the comments of Henchy J. in *McCord* v. *Electricity Supply Board* (1980) (Extract 4.1).

By the end of World War II, however, the climate regarding law reform had changed significantly. Where, in particular, parties to contracts of sale and the by now popular hybrid agreement of hire-purchase, had met on unequal terms, the legislature decided to intervene to protect what Lord Denning would call "the little man" (see his comments in the *Mitchell* case referred to in the Introduction to Chapter 6). Thus, in the Hire-Purchase Act, 1946 a prescribed form for hire-purchase contracts was specified as mandatory for enforceability in a court of law. The information which must be set out in such agreements was clearly intended by the Oireachtas to protect the hirer of goods. But such protection was available to all hirers and subsequent experience indicated the need for further protection for those individuals who could be legislatively defined as "consumers", whose bargaining powers were restricted when entering into contracts with carefully advised companies. This protection was ultimately provided in Ireland through the Sale of Goods and Supply of Services Act, 1980, which reflected similar earlier enactments in the United Kingdom. The law in the United Kingdom and Ireland in this area is now, in broad terms, similar, though crucial differences of detail exist with the Irish law in some instances forging ahead of developments on the other side of the Irish Sea: see Whincup, (1981)

Journ. Bus. L. 478, Gill, (1983) 18 *Ir. Jur.* (n.s.) 378 and Grogan, King and Donelan, *Sale of Goods and Supply of Services: A Guide to the Legislation* (Dublin, 1983) (hereinafter *Guide*).

The extracts in this Chapter may be divided into two broad categories. Extracts 1 to 5 deal with the regulation, principally by legislation, of the circumstances in which sales are conducted in commerce untouched by what might be described as consumer oriented considerations. They centre around issues such as when ownership in goods is either deemed by law, or intended by the parties, to have been transferred from the seller to buyer. And the provision of credit facilities in its many guises is of crucial importance here. Extracts 6 and 7 deal with the concern of the legislature to protect "the little man", in particular by rendering it virtually impossible for one party with the whip hand in negotiations to exclude the operation of important legislatively imposed terms.

In *Flynn* v. *Mackin* (1974) (Extract 8.1), the Supreme Court had to determine who was owner of a car when it was involved in a crash in which the plaintiff was injured. Who was the plaintiff to sue, the car dealer driving the car at the time of the crash or the person who agreed to trade in his old car for it and to whom the dealer was driving it at the time? Ownership in this instance involved particularly critical legal issues of some nicety. The Court addressed two points. The first was whether the contract between the car dealer and this customer amounted to a sale to which the provisions of the Sale of Goods Act, 1893 would apply, or was a contract of barter to be governed by common law, that is judge-made, contract law rules. An interesting, and mildly critical, discussion of this aspect of the case is Canton, (1976) 29 M.L.R. 589. The second matter was, assuming the contract to be a sale, which statutorily ordained rule for the determination of ownership ought to be applied? As it happened both points resolved the ownership issue in the same way, ownership remaining with the dealer at the time of the crash.

The courts take seriously the provisions of s.17 of the Sale of Goods Act, 1893 which allow parties to such a contract to decide for themselves when ownership is to be transferred, rather than having statutory rules, as in the *Flynn* case, imposed on them. This emerges from such English cases as *R.V. Ward Ltd.* v. *Bignall* [1967] 1 Q.B. 534. The point has also been made in this jurisdiction in the context of contracts for the sale of goods on credit terms in which a party supplying goods reserves or retains ownership over them until it has been paid in full in accordance with the credit terms: see *Frigoscandia (Contracting) Ltd.* v. *Continental Irish Meat Ltd.* [1982] I.L.R.M. 396. The extent to which such reservation (or retention) of title clauses have legal effect is reviewed in Byrne and Pierce, (1985) 3 I.L.T. 25

(Supplement) and by Carroll J. in *Somers* v. *J. Allen Ltd.* (1983) (Extract 8.2). One of the crucial legal points in recognising the validity of such clauses at least in some areas is that parties to a contract for the sale of goods can enter into an agreement to transfer ownership in goods at some future date. This is what the Sale of Goods Act, 1893 calls an agreement to sell: clearly the contractual and ownership-transfer elements are separable legal events.

The concept of the agreement to sell and the ownership of goods also arises where goods have been removed from the possession of the true owner by some confidence trickster (sometimes referred to in the cases as a rogue) who has then entered into a contract of sale with an innocent buyer. Who should bear the loss resulting from the con man's activities, the true owner or the innocent buyer? While the general rule *nemo dat quod non habet* indicates that the con man does not have anything in terms of legal title to pass to the innocent buyer, since he has no lawful authority to possess the goods for the purpose of sale, the Sale of Goods Act, 1893 codified a number of already recognised exceptions to that rule. The general principles in this area are discussed in *Anderson* v. *Ryan* (1967) (Extract 8.3), which illustrates that the overall thrust of the law favours the innocent buyer.

Many sales and commercial contracts in general are dependent on the provision of some form of credit or security arrangement. In international sales in particular, the documentary credit, involving a commitment of funds to the seller by the buyer through his bank, is a common mode of operation. The nature of these credits was discussed by the Supreme Court in *Tradax (Irl.) Ltd.* v. *Irish Grain Board Ltd.* (1983) (Extract 8.4). The decision illustrates (as do the cases in Chapter 5) the importance not only simply of understanding contract terms but also tailoring negotiated terms to the particular requirements of an individual agreement.

If the line between sales and other forms of contracts relating to goods based on credit seems blurred in practice, as can be seen in Extracts 2 and 4, the legislature has recognised this by imposing similar terms into sale of goods and hire-purchase contracts. Historically, of course, hire-purchase emerged as a form of contract from the problems created for true owners by the provisions of the Sale of Goods Act, 1893, discussed in Extract 3. In *Butterly* v. *U.D.T. (Commercial) Ltd.* (1960) (Extract 8.5) the judge points out the similarity between these imposed terms. As the *Butterly* case shows, it is artificial to mention these statutorily imposed terms in isolation, since it is vital to remember that stiff penalties (some in the criminal sphere) attach to a failure by a seller, or owner in a hire-purchase agreement, to match the legislated standards. In the crucially important "consumer" transaction, full protection against any attempt to exclude such implied terms as to title, fitness for purpose, correspondence with description and the provision of spare parts and servicing, is given in the Sale of Goods and Supply of Services Act, 1980 by making completely void any clause attempting to prevent them operating in a sale or hire-purchase contract. It is of great importance, therefore, to understand precisely how the legislature has defined a consumer transaction, for two reasons. The first is that in relation to exemption clauses, in sale and hire-purchase contracts, any attempt to exclude the implied terms mentioned is regarded as having no legal effect when done in a consumer transaction context, while exclusion is possible in a non-consumer sale and hire-purchase if shown to be "fair and reasonable". (In contracts for the supply of services exclusion of similar statutorily imposed terms is permissible in all instances, the only restriction being that in consumer transactions the exclusion must be "fair and reasonable"). The second reason is that in certain situations, third parties, such as finance houses, may be sued under the Sale of Goods and Supply of Services Act, 1980 but only where the contract concerned is a consumer transaction. This was the point at issue in *O'Callaghan* v. *Hamilton Leasing Ltd.* (1983) (Extract 8.6), but the decision of McWilliam J. on the exact scope of the definition of a consumer transaction in s.3 of the 1980 Act is vital in the related exemption clause context.

While it is important to emphasise the impact of the new legislative tests regarding exemption clauses, there are two limitations to note also. First, they apply only to those contracts to which the 1980 Act extends, namely, contracts for the sale of goods, of hire-purchase, for the supply of services, credit sales, and leases in a consumer setting. It is an extensive list but not all encompassing. Secondly, common law rules may still be relevant (as to which see Extracts 5.1 and 5.2), in determining whether in fact a particular clause attempted to exclude the operation of a statutory term in the category of contracts to which the 1980 Act applies. Such common law rules will, of course, continue to hold sway where the Act does not apply.

One final matter of importance is the strictness which applies to compliance with statutory formality, particularly regarding legislative provisions intended to protect against the rigours of freedom of contract. This is clear in *B.W. Credit Ltd.* v. *Henebry* (1962) (Extract 8.7) where the judge pointed out that much of the recent legislation was designed to clarify, with legal sanctions as back-up, contractual formalities.

8.1 Flynn v. Mackin and Mahon
[1974] I.R. 101 Supreme Court

[Mr. Flynn was involved in an accident in which his car collided with a blue Vauxhall Viva being driven by Mr. Mahon. Mr. Mahon was a car dealer and was driving the car from Athlone to Kinnegad where he was due to hand it over to his customer Fr. Mackin. Mahon and Mackin had agreed that in return for a new blue Vauxhall Viva, Fr. Mackin would trade-in his old car and also pay over £250. The crucial issue for Mr. Flynn was who of the two defendants owned the blue Vauxhall at the time of the accident.

The extract from the judgment of Walsh J. for the Supreme Court shows that on any view of the case Mr. Mahon was still legal owner at the time of the accident. Viewing the contract as a barter and applying general rules as to when ownership would pass, delivery would be required. And even assuming that the contract was a sale, in the absence of a contrary intention, the Court applied the fixed rules for passing of property in s.18 of the Sale of Goods Act, 1893. The crucial issue here was whether the car had been "unconditionally appropriated" to the contract; the Supreme Court held it had not. This reflects the view of Pearson J. in *Carlos Federspiel & Co. S.A.* v. *Charles Twigg & Co. Ltd.* [1957] 1 Lloyd's Rep. 240 that the quoted phrase requires that ownership only passes when the seller carries out the last act expected of him. This case was cited in argument to the Supreme Court.]

Walsh J.:

S. 1(1) of the Sale of Goods Act, 1893 provides as follows:

> "A contract of sale of goods is a contract whereby the seller transfer or agrees to transfer the property in goods to the buyer for a money consideration, called the price..."

[Counsel] has submitted that the transaction in this case did not amount to a sale within the meaning of the Act of 1893 as it was partly a barter. In my view, this submission is correct. There is no evidence in the case of an agreement to buy the motor car for an agreed price. The question of the price of the motor car, if it arose, is not referred to at all in the evidence. The terms of the transaction, as given in evidence, are that the new motor car was to be obtained by Fr. Mackin in exchange for the motor car which he possessed plus a sum of £250. If the transaction had been that the new motor car was to be a particular price but that in lieu of part of that price the vendor would take the existing motor car and cash for the balance then, in my view, the contract would have been a contract for sale because it would have been an agreement to buy a new car for an agreed price. That was not the case here. Therefore, the provisions of s.18 of the Act of 1893 are not applicable to the transaction under review. The particular transaction was one which, on the evidence, was an agreement to transfer the Vauxhall Viva in consideration of a particular sum of money together with another chattel which was not valued; this transaction was one of exchange or barter. In such a case the ownership of the new Vauxhall Viva would only have been transferred when it was handed over to Fr. Mackin with the intention of transferring ownership. That point was never reached in the present case.

[Assuming the Act applied:]

The "contract for sale" between Mr. Mahon and Fr. Mackin was made before Mr. Mahon acquired the motor car from Athlone Motors. Therefore, the motor car constituted future goods within the meaning of s.62 of the Sale of Goods Act, 1893. The motor was ordered by description, namely, that it was to be a blue Vauxhall Viva car. Each side of this present appeal has relied upon the provisions of s.18, rule 5 of the Act of 1893 which provides as follows:

> "18. Unless a different intention appears, the following are rules for ascertaining the intention of the parties as to the time as to which the property in the goods is to pass to the buyer...
>
> Rule 5-(1) Where there is a contract for the sale of unascertained or future goods by description, and goods of that description and in a deliverable state are unconditionally appropriated to the contract, either by the seller with the assent of the buyer, or by the buyer with the assent of the seller, the property in the goods thereupon passes to the buyer. Such assent may be express or implied and may be given either before or after the appropriation is made..."

...In my view, on the facts as given in evidence, there was no unconditional appropriation of the motor car to the contract by Mr. Mahon. He undoubtedly collected a blue Vauxhall Viva which he intended to use for the purpose of fulfilling his contract with Fr. Mackin. However, Mr. Mahon's contract was to sell a blue Vauxhall Viva and, in collecting this one, he was preparing to appropriate the motor car to the contract. However, there was nothing in the contract between himself and Fr. Mackin which would have in any way prevented his selling that car to another party anywhere between Athlone and Kinnegad or at any time before he came to conclude the transaction with Fr. Mackin. His obligation was to sell Fr. Mackin a blue Vauxhall Viva and any blue Vauxhall Viva would have satisfied his side of the bargain. He was not under an obligaton to sell this particular one. Therefore, in my view the motor car had not been unconditionally appropriated to the contract. When Mr. Mahon collected the motor car in Athlone he was not acting as an agent for Fr. Mackin, but was a principal in the contract to which Fr. Mackin was the other principal. If the original plan had been carried out, namely, the plan of having Fr. Mackin go to Athlone with Mr. Mahon and the car had been delivered to Fr. Mackin in Athlone, even directly by Athlone Motors, it would have been a constructive delivery on behalf of Mr. Mahon because he was the vendor and the property would have passed at that stage with delivery provided that Fr. Mackin, having seen the car, was satisfied to accept it. However, in the events which happened, I am satisfied that as there was no unconditional appropriation of the motor car to the contract the property in the motor car did not pass to Fr. Mackin, apart altogether from any question of a different intention appearing within the meaning of s.18 of the Act of 1893. In view of the conclusion which I have reached, it is unnecessary for me to decide whether or not the parties had intended that the property in the motor car was not to pass in the event of an unconditional appropriation of the motor car to the contract.

8.2 Somers v. J. Allen Ltd.
[1984] I.L.R.M. 437 High Court

[Mr. Somers was the receiver appointed to a company in the business of the manufacture and sale of animal feed. The company was supplied by J. Allen Ltd. with soya bean meal, herring meal and cereal replacement pellets. The contract of sale between the companies relating to these raw materials included a reservation of title clause, clause 9: "The transfer of title to [the buyer] of the goods as detailed in this contract shall not occur until the invoice covering same has been paid in full and, accordingly, the goods wherever situated shall be thereupon at [the buyer's] risk". At the date of the case the raw materials supplied had not become involved in the process of manufacturing animal feed. The issue for the court was whether the intention evident from the contract was legally effective in preventing the passing of ownership to the buyer.

In the extract from her judgment, Carroll J. explains why the simple clause used in this instance was legally effective. In most part, this turned on the fact that the claim made by J. Allen Ltd. was in respect of goods which remained in the form they had been supplied. This explains the judge's ability to contrast this case with the *Borden* and *Kruppstahl* decisions. Underlying this is the basic proposition that only where goods do not become irretrievably mixed in a manufacturing process can the company being suppied be under the special duty to account to the supplier for what happens to the goods: only then does the supplier retain ownership in law.]

Carroll J.:

In this case I am not concerned with whether the reservation of title clause was effective to create or reserve an interest in the goods to be manufactured. I am concerned only with goods which still exist in the same state as they were supplied by the respondent. They have not been mixed with similar goods or transmuted into a manufactured product. The question therefore is whether a simple reservation of title clause is effective to reserve title in the goods in the same state as they were supplied.

In *Borden (U.K.) Ltd.* v. *Scottish Timber Products Ltd.* [1981] Ch. 25 Bridge L.J. was prepared to admit this. At p. 35, while he says that he is attracted by the view that the beneficial interest in the resin passed to the buyers and the sellers retained bare legal title, he goes on to say:

"But I am quite content to assume that this is wrong and to suppose that up to the moment when the resin was used in manufacture it was held by the [buyer] in trust for the [seller] in the same sense in which a bailee or a factor or an agent holds goods in trust for his bailor or his principal. If that was the position then there is no doubt that as soon as the resin was used in the manufacturing process it ceased to exist as resin, and accordingly the title to the resin simply disappeared."

... In my opinion, the simplicity of the provision in the contract does not *per se* prevent its being an effective reservation of title of the goods as supplied to the company and still existing in that state. *Prima facie* title is not to be transferred until payment in full. That title has not been extinguished by manufacture. It still exists, and because payment has not been made, that title has not been transferred.

The [next] proposition is that s.8 of the Bills of Sale (Ireland) Act, 1879 applies to the contract because an immediate beneficial interest passes to the buyer. The Act applies to bills of sale of personal chattels, whether absolute or subject to a trust, whereby the holder or grantee has power, with or without notice, either immediately or at any future time, to take possession of such chattels. There must be a maker or giver of the bill of sale and a holder or grantee of the bill. The purpose of the Act was to prevent the owner of chattels defeating the claims of his creditors by making or giving a bill of sale which would entitle the holder or grantee to seize or take possession of chattels where those chattels remained in the possession or apparent possession of the giver.

In the case of a contract for sale, the goods belong initially to the seller. If he contracts to sell goods and is paid by the buyer and then becomes insolvent, not having delivered the goods within seven days, the contract for sale unless registered within seven days under the Bills of Sale Act is void against the seller's creditors.

If the goods are delivered to the buyer who has not paid for them, on terms that title remains with the seller until he is paid, the buyer's creditors cannot seize the goods. Even though the goods are in the apparent possession of the buyer, he is not the maker or giver of the bill of sale. He is the holder or grantee under the bill.

However, if a contract deals with the future title of the buyer in the goods to be manufactured from the goods supplied, then, as regards that future title, the contract would be a bill of sale in which the buyer is the maker or giver and the seller is grantee.

This point also arose in *Kruppstahl A.G.* v. *Quitmann Products Ltd.* [1982] I.L.R.M. 551. That case involved a detailed retention of title clause which dealt with inter alia handling, processing, blending and mixing the goods, which were steel. The contract was to be construed according to German law but that does not affect the basic issue at stake here.

Gannon J. held that as between Quitmann (the buyer) and other parties, including a debenture holder or other creditors, the unworked steel in the possession of Quitmann in respect of which payment was more than one month overdue was not the property of Quitmann.

In considering the position regarding the steel used in the manufacturing process, he held that the interest created was in the nature of a floating charge. The realisation of such security granted by way of charge was not permitted unless the particulars were registered pursuant to s. 100 of the Companies Act, 1963. Therefore any claims by Krupps against Quitmann for overdue payments for any steel used in the manufacturing process were deferred to the claims of the debenture holder and receiver.

This case therefore illustrates that a seller can make an effective reservation of title to goods prior to manufacture but if he requires security over the manufactured goods the buyer will have to grant him this and this would require registration as a bill of sale.

In this case the clause in question is not complex enough to create a charge over future manufactured goods, the title to which cannot exist at the date of the contract. The contract deals only with the present title to the goods sold and not with future title of goods to be manufactured.

The Sale of Goods Act, 1893 allows the parties to decide when the property in the goods is to be transferred to the buyer: s.17. Here the parties have agreed by a simple condition to reserve title and risk to the seller until payment. The goods were to be used in manufacture. It follows, therefore, that the unpaid seller intended to retain title as long as those goods existed, as supplied. When those goods were manufactured into another product, the seller's title disappeared.

I do not accept [the] submission that the parties intended to split the legal and equitable title to the goods or that such split occurred as a necessary consequence of their contract. I do not see it as an impossible legal concept that the seller of goods to be used in a manufacturing process can retain title as long as the goods exist in the state they were supplied. Therefore, in my opinion, the clause is an effective reservation of title clause for the goods in that state. Accordingly, s.8 of the Bills of Sale (Ireland) Act, 1879 does not apply to this contract.

8.3   Anderson v. Ryan
[1967] I.R. 34 High Court

[The plaintiff agreed to buy a Mini from the defendant for £225 plus £22 for panel repairs to it, which the defendant proceeded to do. The plaintiff paid the defendant and took possession of the car. It turned out, however, that the Mini had been obtained from its real owner by a group of con men who had swopped it for another car (an Austin-Healey Sprite) which they had earlier stolen, pretending that they were the car's owner. They then approached the defendant with the Mini claiming they were its owners and looking for £200 for it; it was in these circumstances that the defendant agreed to sell it to the plaintiff. The problem for the plaintiff was that the Mini was then impounded by the Gardai who, after it was used in criminal proceedings, returned it to its real owner. The plaintiff sued the defendant on the basis that he was in breach of the implied term in s.12 of the Sale of Goods Act, 1893 that as seller he would have title to pass to the buyer.

In the extract, Henchy J. explains why, whoever else the plaintiff might have a claim against, it was not the defendant. This was for the simple reason that the defendant had at the time of sale obtained title to the goods from the con men because they had a voidable title under s. 23 of the Act as a result of their exchange agreement with the real owner.]

Henchy J.:

The plaintiff rests his case on ss. 12 and 21 of the Sale of Goods Act, 1893. In support of his contention that he is entitled to recover the £247 as money paid upon a consideration that has wholly failed, he relies upon sub-s. 1 of s. 21 which is as follows: "Subject to the provisions of this Act, where goods are sold by a person who is not the owner thereof, and who does not sell them under the authority or with the consent of the owner, the buyer acquires no better title to the goods than the seller had, unless the owner of the goods is by his conduct precluded from denying the seller's authority to sell."

In the present case, it is clear that, if the defendant was not the owner of the Mini at the time he sold it to the plaintiff, the plaintiff got nothing for his money and he would be entitled to recover the £247 as money paid upon a consideration that had wholly failed. Counsel for the plaintiff says that the car was sold on the 15th January, 1965, when the plaintiff inspected it, agreed on the price and gave a cheque for £244 10s. Od.; and that the defendant then had no title.

In my view, the flaw in that argument is that it confuses an agreement to sell with a sale. The distinction is made clear in s. 1 of the Act of 1893, which is in the following terms:...

> "(3) Where under a contract of sale the property in the goods is transferred from the seller to the buyer the contract is called a sale; but where the transfer of the property in the goods is to take place at a future time or subject to some condition thereafter to be fulfilled the contract is called an agreement to sell. (4) An agreement to sell becomes a sale when the time elapses or the conditions are fulfilled subject to which the property in the goods is to be transferred."

The transaction between the plaintiff and the defendant on the 15th January, 1965, was no more than an agreement to sell. The property in the car did not pass. It was plainly the intention of the parties that the property would not pass until the panel beating had been done by the defendant and the balance of £22 had been paid; until that had happened the agreement to sell would not have merged into a sale. S. 21(1) has reference only to a case "where goods are sold," i.e. where there has been a sale of goods. It matters not for the purposes of the sub-section if the seller is not the owner at the time of the agreement to sell. He may mend his hand between then and the sale. But if at the time of the sale (i.e. when the property passes or is due to pass) the seller is neither the owner nor a person selling under the authority or with the consent of the owner, and in fact has no title whatsoever, the buyer would be entitled to claim the purchase money back on the ground that he had paid it on a consideration that has totally failed, subject to the proviso that the owner may be estopped by his conduct from denying the seller's authority to sell. S.21(1) is applicable in the present case only if I hold that the defendant had no title to transfer ownership when he handed over the car.

...Therefore, the central question which decides the points raised...is: "Did the defendant have a good title to the car when he sold and delivered it to the plaintiff?" To decide this question one must go back to the circumstances under which the original owner, Mr. Davis, parted with possession of the car.

As I have said, he exchanged it for the Sprite. The inducement for him to do so was not alone the desirability to him of the exchange but also the representation by the other party that the Sprite was his property. That was a false and fraudulent representation as to an existing fact. The contract of exchange was, therefore, a voidable contract. Since Mr. Davis intended to pass the ownership of the Mini, the person who got the car in exchange acquired a title to it, but it was a voidable title, that is, voidable at the option of Mr. Davis. It would have been different if Mr. Davis had parted with the Mini as a result of larceny by a trick, for then no title would have passed. Authority for the conclusion that what passed on the exchange was a voidable title is to be found in *Cundy* v. *Lindsay* (1878) 3 App. Cas. 459, 464; *Robin & Rambler Coaches Ltd.* v. *Turner* [1947] 2 All E.R. 284; *Central Newbury Car Auctions Limited* v. *Unity Finance Ltd.* [1957] 1 Q.B. 371, 382 and *Archbold on Criminal Pleading* (36th ed.) para. 1497.

There is no evidence that there was any intermediate sale of the Mini between the fraudulent exchange and the sale to the defendant. In fact, all the likelihood is that the car was sold to the defendant by or on behalf of the person who effected the fraudulent exchange. One looks then to see what title, if any, such person conveyed to the defendant. The answer is to be found in s. 23 of the Act, which is as follows: "When the seller of goods has a voidable title thereto, but his title has not been avoided at the time of the sale, the buyer acquires a good title to the goods, provided he buys them in good faith and without notice of the seller's defect of title." It is clear from the evidence that Mr. Davis had not avoided the title of the person who sold the car to the defendant at the time of that sale, and it has not been suggested that the defendant bought otherwise than in good faith and without notice of the seller's defect of title.

I am satisfied, therefore, that the defendant acquired a good title to the car and that he in turn passed a good title to the plaintiff. It is unfortunate that the plaintiff has been deprived of a car of which he was the rightful owner, but the fault for that does not lie with the defendant. As the plaintiff may wish to recoup his loss in other proceedings, I express no view on the legal interpretation to be put on the events that led to him being permanently deprived of a car that was lawfully his. I go no further than saying that no liability attaches to the defendant for the plaintiff's loss and that the plaintiff's claim must be dismissed.

8.4   Tradax (Ireland) Ltd. v. Irish Grain Board Ltd.
[1984] I.L.R.M. 471 Supreme Court

[The defendant company agreed to sell a large quantity of grain to the plaintiff company.   The grain was to be collected by the plaintiff from the defendant company's stores.   It was agreed between the parties that the plaintiff would guarantee payment for the grain by drawing a letter of credit on its bank in favour of the defendant.   The grain was to be collected by the plaintiff during the months April, May and June, and the parties also agreed that the letter of credit was to be available for the defendant to call on by 1 May.   About a third of the grain had been taken up by the plaintiff by the third week in April when the defendant decided to repudiate the agreement on the ground that the letter of credit had not been made available at that stage.   The plaintiffs refused to accept this repudiation and proceeded to draw on its bank a letter of credit which was available for calling on by 1 May. The plaintiffs then sued for breach of contract.

The extract from the judgment of O'Higgins C.J. in the Supreme Court indicates clearly why the parties had decided that Tradax should be allowed to take up part of the agreed amount of grain before the letter of credit was in place.   By distinguishing this situation from the arrangements in the English cases discussed in the judgment, the Chief Justice concluded that the defendants had wrongly repudiated the contract.   This indicates that the promise to provide a letter of credit was a condition of the contractual obligations continuing to exist between the parties; it was not a condition precedent to the coming into existence of a contract between the parties.]

O'Higgins C.J.:

What is a letter of credit?
A letter of credit is a form of documentary credit commonly used in international trading, particularly in relation to goods being shipped by a seller in one country to a buyer in another.   It involves a guarantee to the seller from a bank acceptable to him that having shipped or delivered the goods he has contracted to sell he will be paid.   [Counsel] has directed the court's attention to the definition of documentary credits set out in para. 2133 of the 2nd edition of *Benjamin's Sale of Goods* (1981).   It is in the following terms:

> "The definition of documentary credits which is currently accepted by the banking world is that of General Provision *b* of the Uniform Customs and Practice for Documentary Credits.   According to this definition a documentary credit is 'any arrangement....whereby a bank (the issuing bank), acting at the request and in accordance with the instructions of a customer (the applicant for the credit), (i) is to make payment to or to the order of a third party (the beneficiary), or is to pay, accept or negotiate

bills of exchange (drafts) drawn by the beneficiary, or (ii) authorises such payments to be made or such drafts to be paid, accepted or negotiated by another bank, against stipulated documents, provided that the terms and conditions of the credit are complied with.' "

It cannot be doubted that in this case some such arrangement was intended by the parties. While no bank was specified it could fairly be inferred that the credit was to be provided through the plaintiffs' bank of which the defendants were also customers. Again, while the nature of the credit, whether irrevocable or not, was not specified, this does not appear material since it was to be such as would mature and result in payment to the defendants of the entire purchase price on the named day.

The contract did not provide that the opening of the letter of credit be confirmed to the seller. The absence of such a stipulation may be of some significance in assessing the weight to be attached to the submissions made by the defendants in this case. In fact, however, on 24 April an irrevocable letter of credit was opened by the plaintiffs and notification thereof given to the defendants. This letter of credit provided for the payment of the full purchase price against invoices from the defendants in respect of the goods answering the description contained in the contract as found by the learned trial judge. However, three days before, on 21 April, by letter and telex of that date, the defendants purported to cancel the contract. The question which now arises is whether they were entitled to do so.

Defendants' submission

It is submitted on behalf of the defendants that they were entitled to cancel the contract because the plaintiffs were in breach of a fundamental term thereof in that they failed to have established or opened the agreed letter of credit prior to the commencement of the contractual shipment or drawing period which was 1 April 1978. The defendants submit that this fundamental term must necessarily be implied into the contract made on 23 March 1978 because it represents the presumed intention of the parties. It is clear that this submission has been so framed having regard to what was decided in three English cases upon which considerable reliance was placed by counsel for the defendants. These cases are *Pavia & Co. SPA* v. *Thurmann-Neilsen* [1952] 2 Q.B. 84; *Sinason-Teicher Inter-American Grain Corp.* v. *Oilcakes and Oilseeds Trading Co. Ltd.* [1954] 1 W.L.R. 935 (Q.B.), 1394 (C.A.) and *Ian Stach Ltd.* v. *Baker Bosley Ltd.* [1958] 2 Q.B. 130. In these cases which related to the shipment of goods over a particular period, with payment in respect of each shipment to be by letter of credit with no date provided in the contract for the opening of the credit, terms were implied as to the latest date on which credit should have been opened. In the first two cases, which concern c.i.f. contracts, it was held to be an implied term that the credit be opened a reasonable time before the first date for shipment. In the third case which concerned a classic f.o.b. contract, it was held to be an implied term that the credit be opened, at the latest, on the first day of the shipping period. The defendants' submission is that a similar term should be implied into the contract in this case and that the plaintiffs should be held to have been bound by a condition which required them to open the necessary letter of credit at the

110

latest, by the first day of the drawing or shipment period, which was 1 April 1978.

...In the *Sinason-Teicher* case payment was to be cash against documents on the buyers' bankers' guarantee. In the *Pavia* case the contract provided for payment "by opening of a confirmed, irrevocable, divisible, transmissible and transferable credit opened in favour of the sellers and utilisable by them against delivery of the following documents". The documents were then specified.

In the *Ian Stach* case payment was to be "by confirmed, irrevocable, transferable and divisible letter of credit in favour or our [the sellers] nominees". In none of these cases was there a fixed date for payment. Payment was to be made against presentation of documents which in turn came into existence according to shipments. In each case a shipment period was provided for in the contract. As indicated in the first two cases, it was held in effect that the necessary guarantee or credit should be made available before the commencement of the shipment period and, in the *Ian Stach* case, at the latest, by the first day of that period. An examination of the basis for the decisions indicates that it was the availability of the machinery for payment and not the date of the actual shipments effected by the seller which were regarded as crucial...

Authorities relied on not in point.

I cannot see that any of these three cases are of much assistance in deciding the issue which arises on this appeal. We are concerned with two companies, both operating in Dublin, both being customers of the same bank, that contract in relation to Irish feeding barley already available in the hands of the seller. The contract, an oral one, provides for a delivery and shipment period stretching over the three months, April, May and June. It provides for the payment of the entire of the contract price on 1 May by letter of credit maturing on that date. The nature of the letter of credit is not described nor is any provision made that it is to be confirmed - it is merely to mature for payment on the named day. Under this contract the seller has the advantage of two months' payment in advance of delivery, with payment then being effected, not by the buyer, who may have limited resources, but by the buyer's bank. Here the machinery for payment operates on a single day with a single payment and it is specifically recognised that it cannot operate for the first month of the delivery or shipping period. I cannot see how decisions which were arrived at on facts quite different and in relation to a payment machinery intended to operate over the whole of a shipping period can be of any relevance to a case of this kind.

Here neither of the contracting parties had any experience of the working of a letter of credit. This necessarily involved consultation and co-operation between them as to what was to be done...

It appears...that in the first place Mr. Kyne was concerned that his company would be paid on 1 May not by Tradax but by the bank, so that no risk of inability to pay would arise. He went on further to say that in considering the prudence of asking for a bank guaranteed payment on 1 May he had in mind that this would ensure that the risk he was exposed to for the previous month of April would be covered. In other parts of his evidence Mr. Kyne explained that the arrangement he had made of two months' payment in advance of the entire purchase price of £2.4 million to the bank would have an important bearing on his own company's liquidity position.

8.5   Butterly v. U.D.T. (Commercial) Ltd.
[1963] I.R. 56 High Court (1960)

[The plaintiff entered into a contract of hire-purchase with the defendant for the purchase of a new Opel car.   After he took delivery of the car, various defects which are referred to in the extract and included the breakdown of the crown wheel and pinion became apparent.   He then issued proceedings claiming he was entitled to repudiate the contract on the ground of breach of the implied conditions as to merchantable quality and fitness for purpose contained in s.9 of the Hire-Purchase Act, 1946.   As to the consequences of breach of a condition see Extract 5.3.

The extract from the judgment of Davitt P. deals with two issues. First, the extent of the plaintiff's statutory remedies available under s.9 of the Act.   In determining this the judge placed reliance on the clearly analogous provisions in the Sale of Goods Act, 1893, and concluded that merchantable quality and fitness for purpose are not always mutually exclusive ideas.   Secondly, the judge examines the old question of how far one party may exclude the operation of statutorily implied terms by inserting an exemption clause into a contract.   As is evident from the provisions of s.9(3) of the Hire-Purchase Act, 1946 the legislature was already aware of the importance of preventing the operation of exemption clauses in this context.   That awareness came to fuller fruition, of course, in the provisions of the Sale of Goods and Supply of Services Act, 1980, ss 26-31 of which strengthened the value of the terms imposed by the now repealed s.9: see Grogan, King and Donelan, *Guide.*, *op.cit.*, at p. 77].

Davitt P.:

The first matter I have to consider is one arising on the interpretation of s.9 of the Hire-Purchase Act, 1946.   [Counsel] has submitted that sub-s. (1) (d) and sub-s. (2) are mutually exclusive, and do not "overlap," as he said, in the sense that a hirer who gets goods which are not of merchantable quality is confined for remedy to the provisions of sub-s. (1) (d); and that, where the goods have normally only one useful purpose, that he cannot, by making that purpose known, bring himself within sub-s. (2), as sub-s. (2) is designed to cover the case where the goods are required for a particular purpose in the literal sense, as distinct from a general purpose.   For instance, where a person buys a car and does not specify any particular purpose for which he requires it, but merely intimates that he requires it to drive about in, then s.9(2), has no application. That was [counsel's] submission.   If the car is not of merchantable quality and is therefore not fit for his purpose, his remedy lies under s.9(1) (d), and not under s.9 (2).   If, by reason of the qualifications contained in s.9(1) (d), he is precluded from any remedy thereunder, he cannot then turn for relief to the other sub-section.   Accordingly, in [counsel's] submission it would be illogical and unreasonable that where a car had defects of which the owner could not reasonably be aware, which made it unmerchantable, that he should nevertheless become liable under s.9(2) because it was not reasonably fit for use as a car. It would also be illogical and unreasonable that where a hirer on examination could have discovered defects which made the car unmerchantable, but did not do so, that he should then be able to have his remedy under the second sub-section. He said if this were so, then the protection afforded to owners by the qualification contained in s.9(1) (d) was illusory and useless...

Now, I think it is reasonably clear that s.9 of the Hire-Purchase Act was modelled upon certain provisions of the Sale of Goods Act, 1893. Sub-s.(1) (a) corresponds word for word with s.12(2) of the Sale of Goods Act. Sub-s.(1) (b) corresponds closely with s.12(1) Sub-s.(1)(c) corresponds closely with s.12(3). Sub-s.(1) (d) corresponds with s.14(2). In each case there is to be an implied condition that the goods shall be of merchantable quality.

In the case of sub-s.(1) (d) of the Hire-Purchase Act, goods expressly stated to be second-hand are excluded; and no condition is to be implied as regards defects of which the owner could not reasonably have been aware, or as regards defects which an examination in fact carried out by the hirer should have revealed.

In the case of s.14(2), of the Sale of Goods Act there is to be a condition that the goods shall be of merchantable quality limited to cases where the goods (a) are bought by description, and (b) are bought from a seller who deals in goods of that description; and there is a similar provision as to examination of the goods. S.9(2) corresponds to s.14(1) of the Sale of Goods Act. S.9(2) provides that where the hirer expressly or by implication makes known the particular purpose for which the goods are required there shall be an implied condition that the goods shall be reasonably fit for that purpose. S.14(1) contains an exactly similar provision...

It will be seen, although there are significant differences, that s.9 (1) is modelled closely on these provisions of the Sale of Goods Act, and, in my opinion, was an attempt by the Legislature to place the hirer, in the case of a hire-purchase transaction, in much the same position as a buyer in the case of a sale of goods, subject to certain essential differences on account of the difference in the nature of the transaction. Now, I do think that the corresponding sections can be reasonably said to be *in pari materia*. When we find the Legislature using the same words in s.9 of the Hire-Purchase Act as in s.14 of the Sale of Goods Act it is to be presumed that they intend the same meanings to be applied to them as have been consistently applied for over half a century by the courts interpreting the Sale of Goods Act. Now, it is well settled... that s.14 (1) and (2) of the Sale of Goods Act are not mutually exclusive; and that the words "particular purpose" as used in s.14(1) do not mean a particular purpose as distinct from a general purpose, but mean a specified purpose, that is, the purpose which is either expressly or impliedly made known to the seller by the buyer. I think it is unnecessary to refer to reported cases on that point. One that comes to my mind at once is the famous "sale of crabs" case in which this section was analysed and dealt with quite exhaustively by Chief Baron Palles [*Wallis* v. *Russell* [1902] 2 I.R. 585].

Now, a situation can arise under s. 14 which is parallel to the unreasonable and illogical situation which [counsel] envisages as arising under s.9 if his interpretation is not correct. For instance, a buyer purchases goods by description from a seller who deals in goods of that description. They can normally be used for only one purpose - as, for instance, food for human consumption or a motor car for driving around in - and the seller knows from what the buyer says that he requires the goods for that purpose and is relying on the seller's skill and judgment. The buyer examines the goods but fails to ascertain that they are not of merchantable quality, though his examination should have revealed the fact. He accepts them and they turn out not to be suitable for his purpose. He has no remedy under the provisions of s.14(2) but, on the decided cases he appears to have a remedy under s.14 (1). That is the parallel illogicality.

I take the view that s.9 (1) (d) and s.9 (2) are not mutually exclusive in the sense for which [counsel] has contended; and that the section gives the hirer the double-barrelled remedy. If he fails with the first barrel under s.9 (1) (d), he may hit with the second under s.9 (2).

The next matter to be determined is whether the application of either sub-section is excluded by the terms of the hire-purchase agreement. Term 2 of the agreement provides:

> "The hirer's acceptance of delivery of the goods shall be conclusive that he has examined the goods and found them complete and satisfactory. Except as provided in section 9(1) of the Hire-Purchase Act, 1946, the owner gives no warranty as to the state or quality of the goods; and save as aforesaid any warranty as to description, repair, quality or fitness for any purpose is hereby excluded."

As was held in *Baldry* v. *Marshall* [1925] 1 K.B. 260 these words are apt to exclude warranties only, and are not apt to exclude conditions; they have not the effect in this case of excluding the conditions implied by s. 9(1)(d) or s. 9(2). Moreover, the provision that acceptance by the hirer is to be conclusive that he has examined the goods is a modification and, to that extent, a part exclusion of the condition implied by s.9(1)(d), of the Act; and is in my opinion contrary to the first provision in sub-s.(3). Sub-s.(3) reads:

> "(3) The warranties and conditions set out in subsection (1) of this section shall be implied notwithstanding any agreement to the contrary and the owner shall not be entitled to rely on any provision in the agreement excluding or modifying the condition set out in subsection (2) of this section unless he proves that before the agreement was made the provision was brought to the notice of the hirer and its effect made clear to him." [This provision has been replaced by much-strengthened prohibitions on exemption clauses in s.31 of the 1980 Act: see Grogan, King and Donelan, *Guide...*pp. 76-77]

It seems to me that when term 2 is read in connection with that section, it is clearly an attempt to evade the provisions of the statute and therefore invalid and ineffective.

The next matter to be considered is whether there has been any breach of

114

either of these conditions. I have no intention of reviewing the evidence as to the alleged defects in the car in question in this case. We have heard a vast lot of evidence, expert and otherwise. I take the view that the car was not of merchantable quality. The breakdown of the crown wheel and pinion is conclusive upon the point. Nobody is going to accept a car that cannot run on the road. The complete breakdown interrupted the flow of power from the engine to the wheels, and simply meant that the car could not go. Obviously, it was not of merchantable quality. In addition to this major defect there are several minor defects which undoubtedly existed; though there is a great conflict of evidence as to their extent, and as to the existence of some of them. The bonnet cover did not fit properly. There were some defects in the paint-work. The steering required adjustment; the braking was uneven; and there was also a defect in the spring-lock to the glove compartment or "cubby-hole," as it has been called. There were other minor matters which I do not propose to deal with specifically. Finally, there is the complaint as to the excessive consumption of oil which is the subject of conflicting expert evidence and has occupied a very great deal of my time, and other people's time at considerable expense. I have come to the conclusion that the consumption was not excessive, in all the circumstances, mainly for this reason, that the onus of showing that the consumption was excessive rests on the plaintiff. I have had a vast amount of expert evidence which is absolutely contradictory; I cannot say that the plaintiff has succeeded in discharging that onus and I have to hold that point against him. All these matters taken together contribute to make the car unmerchantable.

8.6 O'Callaghan v. Hamilton Leasing Ltd and Anor.
[1984] I.L.R.M. 146 High Court

[The plaintiff owned a shop in which he sold food on a take away basis. He entered into an agreement with the second defendant, Access Refrigeration Ltd., to buy an iced drinks dispensing machine which the plaintiff operated in his shop. Finance for the purchase was provided by Hamilton Leasing Ltd. through a leasing agreement with the plaintiff. The plaintiff made two payments to Hamilton Leasing under this agreement, but defects in the machine then became apparent. He brought proceedings claiming repayment of the instalments from Hamilton Leasing as well as consequential damages. The only issue for the High Court was whether Hamilton Leasing should be liable in these circumstances. S.14 of the 1980 Act provides that a finance house is liable for breaches of contract by a seller if the contract of sale is made with a buyer "dealing as consumer". This term is defined in S.3(1) of the 1980 Act as referring to a contract (a) where one party "neither makes the contract in the course of a business nor holds himself out as doing so", and (b) "the other party does make the contract in the course of a business" and (c) the goods or services supplied "are of a type ordinarily supplied for private use or consumption".

The extract shows that, against this legislative background, the judge was clearly obliged to conclude that Mr. O'Callaghan was not dealing as consumer in this instance so that Hamilton Leasing could not be successfully sued.]

McWilliam J.:

The defendant, Hamilton Leasing (Ireland) Ltd. can only be liable to the plaintiff under s.14 of the Sale of Goods and Supply of Services Act, 1980 if the plaintiff was a buyer dealing as a consumer within the meaning of subs.(1) of s.3 of the Act.

It seems to me that this contract was made in the course of the plaintiff's business. It was certainly made for the purposes of his business although I appreciate the point made on behalf of the plaintiff that this business does not in any way include a re-sale or further dealing with the goods dealt with by the contract before me.

In order to interpret the words of s.3 otherwise I would have to amend paragraph (a) of subs.(1) by reading it as though it provided "in the course of a business which includes a further dealing with the goods" or some words of that sort.

I cannot depart from the clear words of a statute and try to construe it in accordance with my view of an unexpressed intention of the legislature although I suspect the legislature was more concerned with the business of engaging in further dealings with the goods.

With regard to paragraph (c) of the subsection, I am of opinion that the expression "ordinarily supplied for private use or consumption" should be contrasted with use for the purposes of a business rather than contrasted with use for the purpose of re-sale of or further dealings with the goods. These goods were supplied for the purpose of a business and it has not been suggested that they would ever be supplied for use other than for the purpose of a business.

Accordingly, although these goods were supplied for the personal use of the plaintiff and he is the consumer in the ordinarily accepted meaning of the word, I must hold that, in this transaction, he did not "deal as consumer" within the meaning of the Act.

8.7   B.W. Credit Co. Ltd. v. Henebry
(1962) 97 I.L.T.R. 123 High Court

[The defendant entered into a contract for the hire-purchase of a second hand tractor, the finance being provided by the plaintiffs. The tractor turned out to defective. Ultimately, the defendant refused to continue paying instalments under the contract and the plaintiffs then commenced proceedings claiming the arrears. The hire-purchase agreement produced in court appeared to have the details regarding the hire-purchase price, initial deposit and the instalment amounts inserted after the defendant had signed the agreement. S.3(2) of the Hire-Purchase Act, 1946 requires that such details be included in the contract at the time of entering into the contract for the agreement to be enforceable, subject to the proviso referred to in the extract.

In his judgment, Murnaghan J. points out the purpose of the strict requirements of the legislation in protecting the hirer of goods. The contrast with the apparently similar provisions of the Statute of Frauds (which have been interpreted more flexibly by the courts) is important. The judge repeated his remarks in similar vein just one day later in *U.D.T. (Commercial) Ltd.* v. *Nestor* [1962] I.R. 140.]

Murnaghan J.:

There is a proviso to sub-section (2) that if the Court is satisfied in any action that a failure to comply with the requirement specified in paragraphs (b) or (c) of this sub-section has not prejudiced the hirer, and that it would be just and equitable to dispense with the requirement, the Court may - not shall - subject to any conditions it thinks fit to impose, dispense with that requirement for the purposes of the action.

Now, dealing first with this proviso it is quite clear that the requirements of subsection (2) remain unless compliance therewith is dispensed with by the Court in a given case. There must be a note or memorandum which has been made and signed by the hirer and by or on behalf of all other parties to the agreement. Some difficulty arises as to the matters which this memorandum is to contain. It is clear that it must contain in addition to those items set out in paragraph (b) of s. 3(2), the names and description of the parties sufficient to identify them. What is to be found here? I have no direct evidence that this hire-purchase agreement was made and signed by the defendant. A signature "John Henebry" appears upon the hire-purchase agreement, the proposal form and the delivery receipt. But the signature of a witness to the hirer's signature appears on the hire-purchase agreement. The normal way of proving a party's signature upon a document is to call the person who was present when it was signed by him; and when I say "the document" I mean the document in the form in which it was presented to him for signature. Alternatively, the party who is alleged to have signed the document may himself be called and asked in the witness box to acknowledge his signature. In this case, however, neither of these modes of proof was adopted. But there is still a third mode of proving signature-circumstantial evidence of signature will suffice if it is such as to satisfy the Court. Having regard to the history of this case, and the evidence adduced, I am satisfied that this was Henebry's signature.

In my view, the onus is on the hire-purchase company to establish to the satisfaction of the Court that a note or memorandum was made and signed according to the requirements of the sub-section and that it contains the items required by the sub-section unless compliance therewith is dispensed with. If the plaintiffs have discharged this onus in so far as the signature on the note or memorandum is concerned, the onus still rests on them to prove the existence of a sufficient note or memorandum at the time of the signature by the hirer.

They have produced documents, which are now complete and as such would be a sufficient note or memorandum and [counsel] submits that I should hold that these documents in that form are sufficient. I will not make any presumption of regularity with respect to the state of the documents when presented to the defendant for his signuture. I doubt if the maxim *omnia praesumuntur rite esse acta* does apply in a case of this kind. It does not, in my opinion, apply if there are apparent irregularities in the completion of the documents such as there are for example here as to the filling in of one of the essential matters, the hire-purchase price, after Mr. Henebry had signed the proposal form and the hire-purchase agreement. It has been urged upon me that the requirements of s.3 of the Hire-Purchase Act, 1946 are analogous to those of s.4 of the Statute of Frauds and that the requirements of this latter section are sufficiently complied with if a note or memorandum is shown to have been made before action brought. I do not think that any such analogy exists - there is a clear distinction. There is in the Hire-Purchase Act the requirement that a note or memorandum of the agreement is made and signed by the hirer; this is of real significance and it appears that the note or memorandum should be made at the time of the agreement. This is clear from the Act and from the requirements respecting the statutory notice which, it is provided, shall be at least as prominent as the other part of the agreement. Then there is another provision which requires that a copy of the note or memorandum shall be sent to the hirer by the owner within seven days of the making of the agreement. That provision would make no sense if the hire-purchase company could, by delaying its signature, make the date of its signature the date of the agreement. I do not decide, however, this question, but I would have some doubt that the date of the agreement was the ultimate date upon which the signature of the hire-purchase company was affixed to the agreement. I am not satisfied on the evidence that there was a sufficient note or memorandum signed by Henebry. That being so the plaintiffs must fail in this action.

CHAPTER 9

Insurance

Two issues of importance mark out the contract of insurance as meriting particular attention separately from the general rules relating to contracts. One relates to the special obligation to disclose information at the time a contract of insurance is being formed and performed; the other to the nature of the contract as one of indemnity.

A contract of insurance is formed through the completion, by a person seeking insurance cover, of a proposal from the insurance company. When completed the proposal constitutes an offer in the ordinary way. The crucial point is that the information contained in the proposal, when completed, forms the basis for the decision by the insurance company whether to take on a particular risk and the premium it will charge if it does. Because of the risks inherent in the insurance contract the law has required the person seeking insurance cover to disclose all information known to him which would be material to the insurance company's decisions. Failure to disclose such information will make the insurance contract void. As *Chariot Inns Ltd.* v. *Assicurazioni Generali S.p.a.* (1981) (Extract 9.1) shows, the test of materiality is of necessity an objective one and only information which would have been of importance to the prudent insurer will be relevant. This means, for instance, that an insurance claim can still be successfully made by an insured person who failed to disclose information which, in the opinion of a court, would not have altered the decisions made by the insurance company.

In most instances, a contract of insurance is one of indemnity, by which the insurance company agrees to compensate an insured person for the loss suffered by him on the happening of the event insured against. But the contract document may specify a sum of money as the amount up to which cover is to be given. This was the situation in *St. Albans Investment Co.* v. *Sun Alliance and London Insurance Ltd.* (1983) (Extract 9.2). The Supreme Court stated clearly that the agreement to indemnify is one to compensate for actual loss suffered, and that for good policy reasons the insured person is not to be allowed make a windfall profit from a claim.

9.1 Chariot Inns Ltd. v. Assicurazioni
Generali S.p.a. [1981] I.R. 199 Supreme Court

[The plaintiff company was the owner of a premises known as the Chariot Inn, and requested fire insurance for it from the defendants.

In the proposal form, the plaintiff company was asked to "give claims experience for loss over the last five years...If none in any class say so." The answer given, after consultation with an insurance broker, was "None". In fact, the principal director in the plaintiff company, Mr. Wootton, was also director of a company which owned premises where some furniture from the Chariot Inn had been stored and burned and in respect of which the plaintiff company had been paid a sum of money on foot of an insurance policy. When the Chariot Inn was subsequently badly damaged in a fire, the defendants repudiated liability because of the non-disclosure of the fire in the other premises.

The extract discusses the basis on which the test of materiality of information not disclosed operates, and why in this instance the insurance company was entitled to repudiate. On another aspect of the case, it is of interest to note that the plaintiffs, while unsuccessful against the insurers, made a successful claim in negligence against its insurance broker in respect of the loss involved in the advice not to disclose the relevant information.]

Kenny J.:

A contract of insurance requires the highest standard of accuracy, good faith, candour and disclosure by the insured when making a proposal for insurance to an insurance company. It has become usual for an insurance company to whom a proposal for insurance is made to ask the proposed insured to answer a number of questions. Any misstatement in the answers given, when they relate to a material matter affecting the insurance, entitles the insurance company to avoid the policy and to repudiate liability if the event insured against happens. But the correct answering of the questions asked is not the entire obligation of the person seeking insurance: he is bound, in addition, to disclose to the insurance company every matter which is material to the risk against which he is seeking indemnity.

What is to be regarded as material to the risk against which the insurance is sought? It is not what the person seeking insurance regards as material, nor is it what the insurance company regards as material. It is a matter or circumstance which would reasonably influence the judgment of a prudent insurer in deciding whether he would take the risk and, if so, in determining the premium which he would demand. The standard by which materiality is to be determined is objective and not subjective. In the last resort the matter has to be determined by the court: the parties to the litigation may call experts in insurance matters as witnesses to give evidence of what they would have regarded as material, but the question of materiality is not to be determined by such witnesses.

The test of materiality which is generally accepted in all forms of insurance against risks when property of any kind is involved is stated in s. 18(2) of the Marine Insurance Act, 1906:

> "Every circumstance is material which would influence the judgment of a prudent insurer in fixing the premium, or determining whether he will take the risk."

Although that test is stated in an Act which deals with marine insurance, it has been accepted as a correct guide to the law relating to insurance against damage to property or goods of all types.

The rule to determine the materiality of a fact which has not been disclosed to an insurer was expressed by MacKinnon L.J. with his customary pungency in *Zurich General Accident and Liability Insurance Co. Ltd.* v. *Morrison* [1942] 2 K.B. 53 at p.60 of the report:

> "Under the general law of insurance an insurer can avoid a policy if he proves that there has been misrepresentation or concealment of a material fact by the assured. What is material is that which would influence the mind of a prudent insurer in deciding whether to accept the risk or fix the premium, and if this be proved it is not necessary further to prove that the mind of the actual insurer was so affected. In other words, the assured could not rebut the claim to avoid the policy because of a material misrepresentation by a plea that the particular insurer concerned was so stupid, ignorant, or reckless, that he could not exercise the judgment of a prudent insurer and was in fact unaffected by anything the assured had represented or concealed."

...Three experts on insurance business gave evidence. Their unanimous view was that the fire at Leeson Street and the damage to the plaintiffs' goods were matters that were material to the risk which the defendant insurers were asked to insure. Their opinions were not conclusive on this matter. The question whether any of these matters were material is essentially an inference from facts established by evidence.

The circumstances that Mr. Wootton was a director of the plaintiff company and of Consolidated Investment would not, of itself, make a fire on property owned by Consolidated Investment a fact which was material to the risk undertaken by the defendant insurers when they insured the plaintiff company against fire on its premises. However, I think that it was material to the insurance effected by the plaintiffs with the defendant insurers that goods belonging to the plaintiffs were damaged by fire in premises owned by Consolidated Investment. The answer to the query about claims made by the plaintiffs for loss over the previous five years was literally correct but, though the plaintiffs had no claim against Sun Alliance (who issued the policy in respect of the Leeson Street premises), the plaintiffs were paid by Sun Alliance the sum negotiated in respect of their stored furnishings. The circumstances in which the plaintiffs' goods were stored in the Leeson Street premises and the fact that the plaintiffs ultimately got payment in respect of them were, in my view, matters which would reasonably have affected the judgment of a prudent insurer in deciding whether to take the risk or in fixing the premium, particularly as Mr. Wootton was a director of, and managed and controlled, the plaintiff company and Consolidated Investment.

It was contended strenuously by counsel for the defendant brokers that the onus of establishing that the matter not disclosed was material to the risk undertaken lay on the defendant insurers and that, in order to discharge this onus, the defendant insurers had to establish that the matter not disclosed did affect (and not merely might have affected) their judgment. I accept the first part of this proposition but not the second part. It is necessary to establish that the fact which was not disclosed would have reasonably affected the judgment of a prudent insurer if it had been disclosed. The second part of counsel's proposition contains the error which MacKinnon L.J. condemned.

9.2   St. Albans Investment Co. v. Sun Alliance and London Insurance Ltd. [1983] I.R. 362 Supreme Court

[The plaintiff company insured a premises which had been bought for £16,000 with two insurance companies for sums totalling £300,000. The premises were destroyed in a fire. The director dealing with the matter, Mr. O'Hara, entered a claim for the full sum for which the premises were insured, on the basis that he intended to rebuild a comparable building on the site. The insurance companies offered to compensate on the lower basis of a sum representing the market value of the premises at the time they were destroyed.

The Supreme Court's approach was to ask what sum would put the plaintiff in the position, so far as money could do so, he was before the building was destroyed. The choice was between the plaintiff's and defendants' arguments: either solution would fit into the general scheme of indemnifying against loss suffered. In the end, the solution depended on the intention of Mr. O'Hara: since he had not brought forward convincing evidence to support his assertion of an intention to rebuild the premises, the insurance companies arguments were upheld.]

Griffin J.:

The learned trial judge held that there was no agreement to grant reinstatement cover, and I agree with the Chief Justice that, on the facts, [he] was fully justified in so holding. Indeed, in view of the evidence given at the trial, it is difficult to see how he could have come to any other conclusion.

However, the plaintiffs claim that, even if there was no reinstatement clause in the contract, they are entitled under the terms of the policy to the cost of rebuilding the premises, as that is the only way, they allege, in which they can be paid the value of the property.

Under the policies issued respectively by Sun Alliance and Provincial Insurance, each defendant agreed that, if the property insured or any part of such property should be destroyed or damaged by fire (*inter alia*), each defendant would pay to the plaintiffs the value of the property at the time of the happening of its destruction or the amount of such damage (or, at its option, reinstate or replace such property, or any part thereof), subject to a limit of £250,000 in the case of Sun Alliance, and to £50,000 in the case of Provincial Insurance. Each of these two policies was a standard fire insurance policy.

It is well settled for upwards of one hundred years that such a policy is a contract of indemnity under which an insured may recover his actual loss, not exceeding the maximum amount specified in the policy...In the case of such a policy, therefore, what the insurer agrees to do is to indemnify the insured in respect of loss or damage caused by fire, and the insured is entitled to be paid his actual loss - no more and no less. The net issue in this appeal is the basis on which the amount of that loss is to be ascertained. The plaintiffs claim that they can be compensated properly only by the cost of rebuilding, whilst the defendant insurers say that, on the facts of the case the correct basis should be that of market value at the time of the destruction of the premises...

In *Munnelly* v. *Calcon Ltd.* [1978] I.R. 387, in which the plaintiff's premises had been demolished as a result of the wrongful act of the defendants, Henchy J. put the matter thus at p.399 of the report:

> "I do not consider that reinstatement damages, which may vastly exceed damages based on diminished value, are to be awarded as a prima facie right or, even if they are, that the plaintiff's intention as to reinstatement should be the determining factor. I do not think the authorities establish that there is a prima facie right to this measure of damages in any given case. In my view, the particular measure of damages allowed should be objectively chosen by the court as being that which is best calculated, in all the circumstances of the particular case, to put the plaintiff fairly and reasonably in the position in which he was before the damage occurred, so far as a pecuniary award can do so."

...Mr. O'Hara acquired a number of textbooks on fire insurance and some articles written in professional periodicals on the principle of indemnity. From his reading of that material he concluded that, as he was insured for £250,000, he was entitled to that sum and not a penny less, and that he was entitled to settlement on a rebuilding basis regardless of whether he rebuilt or not...That was a misconception by him of the law on the question.

In my view, the correct legal position is stated in the joint judgment of Kitto, Taylor and Owen JJ. in the High Court of Australia in *British Traders' Insurance Co. Ltd.* v. *Monson* (1964) 111 C.L.R. 86. At p. 92 of the report of that case they said:

> "It is far too late to doubt that by the common understanding of businessmen and lawyers alike the nature of such a policy controls its obligation, implying conclusively that its statement of the amount which the insurer promises to pay merely fixes the maximum amount which in any event he may have to pay, and having as its sole purpose, and therefore imposing as its only obligation, the indemnification of the insured, up to the amount of the insurance, against loss from the accepted risk."

CHAPTER 10

Negotiable Instruments and Banking

Given that money makes the commercial world go around, it is important to note that money is not usually seen by commercial people in terms of what the ordinary person would call cash. In most instances, commercial transactions are financed on some kind of credit terms. Three such forms have already been discussed in Chapter 8, namely, reservation of title (see Extract 8.2) documentary credits (see Extract 8.4) and hire-purchase (see Extract 8.7). Such forms of credit arrangements are fairly straightforward, but the world of high finance, involving a continuous stream of interconnected contracts, required the development of a more sophisticated form of money-document which would be recognised as having the same value as, for instance, a herd of cattle or the equally unwieldy bar of gold. In this climate of convenience, the answer was found in the negotiable instrument.

The essential characteristic of an instrument in law is that it is a document which creates rights or liabilities which may be sued on in court. To that extent, it has a special legal life over and above the piece of paper of which it consists. The element of negotiability is of crucial importance to commercial people. It involves the idea that the instrument, in the hands of its present holder, will normally entitle that holder, so long as he has in good faith provided value for possessing the negotiable instrument, claim the full value of that document, in other words its money's worth.

So the negotiable instrument is a document of recognised worth which can be used to finance transactions and which is ultimately redeemable for what the ordinary person might regard as the most important form of money, cash in the pocket.

Where a business person wishes to buy goods but does not have the money to pay for them immediately, he might arrange with the seller that the seller will be paid in, say, 90 days time by somebody who already owes the buyer a sum which will cover the amount due to the seller. If this arrangement is put in writing, then the document created is the negotiable instrument known as a bill of exchange, the buyer being designated the drawer of the bill, his creditor is called the drawee (the acceptor if he actually agrees to pay when the bill when drawn up is presented to him) and the seller, quite properly because he has to be paid, the payee. If this is slightly confusing, it might be easier to think in terms of a more familiar negotiable instrument, the cheque, a bill of exchange which is drawn on a bank. Here, the drawer is the person who owns the cheque book, the drawee is the bank, and the payee the person to whom the cheque is made out. The bill of exchange and its particular form the cheque both have in common a legally enforceable request of the drawee, primarily, to pay a certain sum of money to the payee. The time lag between drawing and payment is, clearly, usually longer with the bill of exchange than the cheque.

The third common form of negotiable instrument is the promissory note, which involves a legally enforceable promise to pay a sum of money. Some bank notes still issue as promises to pay the holder (or bearer) a certain sum, though no doubt to the ordinary person this appears a pointless exercise as one bank note is as good as another, there being a certain futility in taking such notes literally by requesting the bank to hand you one bank note in exchange for the same note you hand across the teller's counter, as to which, see s.45 of the Central Bank Act, 1971. One related point worth noting by negotiable instrument watchers is that an I.O.U. is not a negotiable instrument, but merely an acknowledgment of a debt. This is, no doubt, of little consolation to the unfortunate gambler whose marks have been acquired by the local loan shark, who then moves in for the dramatic blackmail kill.

One of the most important features of a negotiable instrument is that it consists either of a definite order requesting payment of a certain sum (in the case of bills of exchange and cheques) or of a definite order promising payment (in the case of a promissory note). This problem is analysed and resolved in a practical manner by Pringle J. in *Creative Press Ltd.* v. *Harman* (1972) (Extract 10.1).

In many instances, negotiable instrument problems arise in the context of their being processed for payment through a bank. In this respect, it is relevant to examine two matters, firstly, precisely what constitutes a banker, and secondly what duties are owed in law by banks.

The courts have been reluctant to lay down precise rules as to what constitutes the carrying on of a banking business, but in more recent years legislative guidelines have assisted in providing a clearer picture. The question usually arose where it was argued that a particular institution was carrying on business as an unlicensed moneylender, the institution's defence being that it was in fact a bank. This was the problem addressed in *Commercial Banking Co. Ltd.* v. *Hartigan* (1951) (Extract 10.2) where the limited regulatory provisions of the Central Bank Act, 1942 were used by the judge to conclude that the plaintiff company was carrying on a banking business. Since then, Lord Denning M.R. described a bank as having the characteristics that it (i) accepted money from, and collected cheques for, its customers and placed them to their credit, (ii) borrowed cheques or orders drawn on the bank by its customers when presented for payment and debited its customers accordingly, and (iii) kept current accounts in its books in which the credits and debits are entered: *U.D.T. Ltd.* v. *Kirkwood* [1966] 2 Q.B. 431. Finally, in Ireland, the Central Bank Act, 1971 provides a comprehensive code for the licensing of banks. Under the Act, the Central Bank is given power (subject in particular respects to the Minister for Finance) to grant or refuse licences, and banking may not be carried on without such a licence. The Act sets out some matters which give guidance as to what constitutes a banking business, but the decision whether to grant a licence is also partly based on the Central Bank's own guidelines, many of which are policy-based. Of course, the deliberations of the Bank must be carried out in a procedurally fair manner (see, for example, Extract 1.2).

The characteristics of a bank described by Lord Denning M.R., above, point up that, as between banker and customer, the legal duties arise in the context of a contract between two parties. A fairly complete list of the duties was compiled by Atkin L.J. in *Joachimson* v. *Swiss Bank Corp.* [1921] 3 K.B. 110. These duties are most commonly at issue where the transmission of, for example, a cheque through the banking clearing system has resulted in a loss to either the drawer or payee. While the Cheques Act, 1959 provides substantial protection to a bank where such loss arises in relation to the problem of irregular cheques, important areas of responsibility and liability remain. The duty owed by a bank in the manner it decides to honour cheques presented for payment is discussed in *Dublin Port and Docks Board* v. *Bank of Ireland* (1976) (Extract 10.3), where, apart from the contractual duties owed by a bank to its customers, the Supreme Court raised the general duty of care by bankers as professional business persons to persons they ought reasonably foresee might be affected by their activities as bankers (see also Extract 6.5).

Finally, *Town and County Advance Co.* v. *Provincial Bank of Ireland* (1917) (Extract 10.4) deals with a particular issue relating to whether a cheque is payable to bearer and in that context whether payment should be made on presentation.

10.1 Creative Press Ltd. v. Harman
[1973] I.R. 313 High Court

[The defendants signed the following document: "We, George S. Harman and Annette Harman jointly and severally promise to pay the

Creative Press Limited on or before the 1st day of November 1970, the sum of £2,000.00 for value received."

As the extract shows, the main issue in the case was whether this was a promise to pay the specified sum at a fixed future date. In coming to the conclusion that it was, and was therefore a promissory note as defined in s.83(1) of the Bills of Exchange Act, 1882, Pringle J. got around the English case *Williamson* v. *Rider* [1963] 1 Q.B. 89 by adopting the minority view in that decision. The important point is that while the defendants had an option to pay before the specified date, they could not be forced to do so.]

Pringle J.:

The first point raised is that this is not a promissory note as defined in s.83 (1) of the Bills of Exchange Act, 1882, because it is not "an unconditional promise in writing....signed by the maker, engaging to pay on demand or at a fixed or determinable future time, a sum certain in money, to, or to the order of, a specified person or to bearer." The document is clearly an unconditional promise in writing signed by the defendants engaging to pay a sum certan in money to a specified person, namely, the plaintiffs; but it is argued that, by reason of the words "on or before the 1st day of November, 1970" it is not a promise to pay the money either on demand or at a fixed or determinable future time and that, therefore, it does not comply with the definition in the Act. Mr. McCarthy relied upon the decision of the Court of Appeal in England in *Williamson* v. *Rider* [1963] 1 Q.B. 89 which is directly in point as it was there decided by the majority of the Court of Appeal (Willmer and Danckwerts L.JJ., Ormerod L.J. dissenting) that the use of the words "on or before December 31st, 1956", which gave the maker of the document an option to discharge his obligation by paying the amount at a date earlier than the date named, created an uncertainty and contingency in the time of payment, and that therefore the document was not a promissory note within the meaning of s.83 of the Act.

At p. 97 of the report Danckwerts L.J. referred to *Dagger* v. *Shepherd* [1946] K.B. 215 in which a notice to quit "on or before" a fixed date was held to be an effective notice. In delivering the judgment of the Court of Appeal in *Dagger* v. *Shepherd*, Evershed J. said at p. 223 of the report:

> "The use of the phrase 'on or before' some fixed date is today by no means uncommon, particularly in covenants or demands for payment of money, and in such a context it cannot, in our judgment, be open to serious doubt that it means, and would be understood to mean, that the covenantor or debtor is under obligation to pay the debt on (but not earlier than) the date fixed but has the option of discharging it at any earlier time selected by him: see per Parker J. in *In re Tewkesbury Gas Co.* [1911] 2 Ch. 279, 284."

Danckwerts L.J. then goes on to say that he did not think that *Dagger* v. *Shepherd* was of much relevance because a promissory note is a very different thing from a notice to quit, but he did say that the case was special because it expressed exactly what he thought to be the proper construction of the words "or on before December 31st, 1956", that is to say, that no action could be brought to enforce payment by the maker before the 31st December but that he had an option to discharge the debt at an earlier date selected by him. His obligation was to pay on the 31st December and could arise at no earlier date.

Danckwerts L.J. then seemed to indicate that his view was that the conferring of an option of payment at an earlier date should not prevent the document from being a promissory note, but that he found it difficult to maintain that view consistently with the view expressed by the three judges of the Court of Queens Bench in *Crouch* v. *Credit Foncier of England Ltd.* (1873) L.R. 8 Q.B. 374. In that case debentures were issued repayable at a certain date, but subject to a condition which permitted redemption by drawings by lot.

Danckwerts L.J. said that the decision in *Crouch's* case showed that the element of uncertainty introduced by a term of the contract may be fatal, and he said that he had come to the conclusion that the option reserved by the instrument in *Williamson* v. *Rider* created an uncertainty and a contingency as to the time for payment and, therefore, that it was not a promissory note. Willmer L.J. agreed with this view, stating that it was largely a matter of first impression and that he found it difficult to resist the conclusion that the introduction of the words "on or before" did introduce a contingency.

On the other hand Ormerod L.J. said that he could not agree with the opinion of the other judges in *Williamson's* case. He agreed with the view of Danckwerts L.J. that the meaning of the words "on or before December 31st" was that the promisor bound himself to pay on that date, but that, if he chose to pay at an earlier date, then the holder was under an obligation to accept that payment; but he did not agree that the *Crouch* case was on all fours with the case before the court. He pointed out that in that case, if the holder of a debenture was sufficiently fortunate to hold one with a number that turned up in the draw, the holder was then entitled to have his money back at a much earlier date than if he had not been so fortunate. He said that it appeared to him that there was a very clear distinction between the two cases. In the case before him the promisor could not be sued for the amount due until the 31st December, whereas in the *Crouch* case there was a legal obligation on the part of the company to pay at an earlier date if the particular condition were fulfilled. I must say that I entirely agree with this distinction between the two cases, and I prefer the reasoning of Ormerod L.J. to that of the other two learned judges.

I am reinforced in this view by the decision of the five judges of the Supreme Court of Canada in *John Burrows Ltd.* v. *Subsurface Surveys Ltd.* [1968] S.C.R. 607 in which the same point was argued...At p.614 Ritchie J. said:

> "The instrument here in question is an unconditional promise in writing made by the respondent to pay the appellant or order the sum of £42,000 at a fixed and determinable future time,... and the fact that the maker was accorded the privilege of making payments on account of principal from time to time did not alter the nature of his unconditional promise to pay at the time fixed by the instrument, but merely gave him an option to make earlier payment."

128

In my opinion the fact that the defendants in the present case had an option to pay the sum of £2,000 before the 1st November, 1970, and that the plaintiffs would have had to accept such payment, does not mean that the defendants did not engage to pay the money at a fixed future time. They could not be made to pay on any date prior to the 1st November 1970, and this in my opinion is the all-important factor. Therefore, I hold that the document is a promissory note.

10.2   Commercial Banking Co. Ltd. v. Hartigan
(1951) 86 I.L.T.R. 109 Circuit Court

[The defendant signed a promissory note payable to the plaintiff company, and when there was default in payment the plaintiff sued.
The defence made to the claim was that the plaintiff was a moneylender, and that since it had no moneylending licence, as required by the Moneylenders Act, 1900, the promissory note was invalid.   This defence was rejected.
The extract shows that Judge Fawsitt, in following the approach in *In re Shields' Estate* [1901] 1 I.R. 172 was also influenced by the compliance of the plaintiff company with the provisions of the Central Bank Act, 1942]

Judge Fawsitt:

I have had handed to me today and, verified on oath, a list of the company's activities all such matters as a bona fide bank would concern itself with.   I have also had evidence from Mr. O'Reilly [a branch manager] of the compliance by the company with the statutes passed by our Parliament to regulate the business of banking, and in particular with the Central Bank Act, 1942.

By s.47(6) of that Act, power was given to the Central Bank to recognise banks other than what the Act terms the "associated banks".   Such banks must be authorised by licence of the Revenue Commissioners granted pursuant to s.47(3) of the Act to carry on a banking business.   Section 47 (1) the section defining the expression "banking business" runs as follows:

"In this section, the expression "banking business" means a business which consists of or includes the acceptance of deposits payable on demand or on not more than seven days' notice, but the acceptance by a trader of deposits from persons employed by him in his trading business or deposits from persons who are customers of that trading business or the acceptance by a trader of both these classes of deposits shall not of itself make the trading business of such trader banking business for the purposes of this section."

Here, the company is carrying on no business which is not either its main business or subsidiary to the business of banking, and its business does include the acceptance of deposits payable on demand or on not more than seven day's notice.

The company have made application for and have obtained the licence from the Revenue Commissioners required by s.47 (2) of the Central Bank Act, 1942 and granted pursuant to s.47(3) of that Act. I have also been given evidence that the company has made the deposits in the High Court required under the relevant section of the Central Bank Act - s.42 - from persons and companies carrying on banking business.

I have been told by Mr. O'Reilly that the company's accounts are published in accordance with the requirements of the Central Bank Act from licenced banks.

[Counsel for the defendants] relies on the Moneylenders Act, 1900, and on the fact that the company is not registered as a moneylender in pursuance of that Act. The relevant section of that Act is s.6 which runs as follows:

"The expression 'money-lender' in this Act shall include every person whose business is that of money-lending or who advertises or announces himself or holds himself out in any way as carrying on that business."

Undoubtedly the company do advertise and announce themselves and hold themselves out as carrying on the business of moneylenders. S.6, however, continues-

"but shall not include.....(d) any person bona fide carrying on the business of banking or insurance, or bona fide carrying on any business not having for its primary object the lending of money, in the course of which and for the purposes whereof he lends money"

It is a question of fact whether the company is in fact carrying on the business of banking in addition to that of moneylending.

The facts of this case are not unlike those of *In re Shields' Estate* [1901] 1 I.R. 172, a decision of the Court of Appeal in Ireland allowing an appeal from Ross J. ...The history of banking in Ireland was gone into in the judgments both of Ross J. and of the Court of Appeal, and it was decided by the Court of Appeal that as Shields was carrying on the business of money-lending with money received by him on deposit from customers, he was in fact carrying on a banking business.

In this case we have the additional fact that the plaintiffs are carrying on banking business under a licence from the Revenue Commissioners pursuant to s.47 (3) of the Central Bank Act, 1942.

I am satisfied that the company is a bank, and not merely a moneylending establishment, and shall give judgment for the plaintiffs for the amount of their claim...

10.3 Dublin Port and Docks Board v. Bank of Ireland [1976] I.R. 118 Supreme Court

[The plaintiffs were payees of a cheque for over £18,000 drawn by a company Palgrave Murphy Ltd., on that company's account in a branch of the defendant bank. The cheque was presented for payment by the plaintiffs, who were also customers of the bank, on 1 April 1970, when the drawer company's account was sufficient to meet demands.

However, the cheque was not paid because at that time the bank's employees were operating a go-slow which had led to a backlog of cheques for clearing through the banking system. The bank closed for business completely on 30 April 1970, and the dispute did not end until 21 October 1970 when the bank started to deal with the backlog.
At this stage the drawer company's account was not sufficient to meet all claims on it, and the branch dealing with the account decided to select cheques for payment by lot. The plaintiffs cheque was not selected in this process. They commenced proceedings against the bank.

The extract shows that the Supreme Court rejected the plaintiffs' claim that the bank was in breach of contract to them by pointing out that in selecting the cheques for payment, the defendant was acting purely as a paying bank on behalf of its drawer customer. But, as the extract from the judgment of Griffin J. shows, the Court was not altogether satisfied with the method chosen, viz-a-viz its duty to its drawer customer had it been a party to the case.]

Henchy J.:

Put shortly, the plaintiffs' claim is for damages for breach of an implied term in the contract that existed between them and the defendant bank; the implied term being to the effect that the defendant bank would show reasonable skill, care and diligence in the exercise of its function as a collecting bank. Counsel for the plaintiffs argue that the defendant bank defaulted in that duty in coming by a process of lottery to a decision not to pay the cheque for £18,129 18s.7d.; it should have decided on the merits whether to pay that cheque; and that, if it had exercised its discretion on the question of payment, it could not but have honoured that cheque which was drawn as far back as the 26th March, 1970, on an account which was then sufficiently in credit to meet it.

I do not understand counsel for the defendant bank to seek to controvert the submission that there was a contractual duty owed by the defendant bank to the plaintiffs to show reasonable skill, care and diligence in carrying out its duties as a collecting bank towards them as a customer. What counsel do say, however, is that, in deciding not to honour this cheque, the defendant bank was not acting as a collecting bank for the plaintiffs but was acting as a paying bank for the drawer of the cheque (Palgrave Murphy Ltd.); counsel submit that the only duty the defendant bank owed when thus acting as a paying bank was a duty to Palgrave Murphy Ltd. Counsel repudiate the suggestion that any duty was owed by the defendant bank to the plaintiffs when deciding whether to pay that cheque; they submit that the plaintiffs were simply the payees of the cheque and that the coincidence of being customers in another branch of the bank did not prefer them into a contractual relationship in respect of the decision to dishonour the cheque.

It is important not to allow the exaggerated scale of banking activity after the end of the shut-down (artificially based on the 1st May, 1970, as the notional banking day to which all outstanding transactions were to be referred) to deflect attention from the essential nature of the functions of each branch in dealing with cheques drawn by the customers of the branch on their accounts in the branch, according as those cheques arrived in the branch from the central clearing house.

The duty of the defendants, acting through their O'Connell Street branch, was to honour cheques drawn on that branch provided that the presented cheques were in legal form and provided that the customer's account was in sufficient and available credit to meet the amount of the cheques; and, if more cheques had been drawn by the customer than his account was able to meet, to use a discretion, having regard to the interests of the customer, as to which cheques should be paid. This function was essentially a paying function which was part of the contractual relationship between the defendants and the customer who had drawn the cheques.

The submission made on behalf of the plaintiffs means that in regard to the decision as to payment of this cheque, it should be held that there was superimposed on the contractual relationshp between the defendants as paying bankers and Palgrave Murphy Ltd. a further contractual relationship between the defendants and the plaintiffs arising from the fact that, as payees of the cheque, the plaintiffs happened to be customers of the defendants - albeit in another branch. Such contractual relationship, it is submitted, required the defendants, acting as a collecting bank, to exercise reasonable skill, care and diligence towards the plaintiffs, and it is said that, if the defendants had so conducted themselves, this cheque would have been paid.

In my judgment the contractual relationship for which the plaintiffs contended did not exist. Under our law and our system of banking, when cheques drawn by a customer on a particular branch arrive in that branch from the central clearing house, the bank, in deciding whether to pay those cheques acts entirely as a paying bank and, apart from statute, is bound only by the contract between it and the drawer of the cheque. I find no authority - judicial, text-book or otherwise - to support the proposition that in such circumstances the bank has a contractual duty to a payee of one of those cheques who happens to be a customer in another branch of the bank. The existence of such a contractual duty would run counter to both legal principle and sound banking practice. It would confuse and bring into possible conflict the paying and collecting functions of the bank, it would make it impossible on occasion for the bank to act with the required propriety to both drawer and payee of a cheque, and also on occasion it would result in the unfair preferment of a payee who happened to be a customer in another branch of the bank over a payee who happened not to be a customer. In terms of practical operation, the number of branches a bank may have (the defendant bank has 75 in Dublin alone) would make it impossible to process cheques received from the central clearing house by ascertaining the identity and considering the interests of customers in other branches who happen to be payees of those cheques. For instance, if the cheque in question here had been drawn in favour of (say) "P. Murphy" rather than the plaintiffs, it is difficult to see how the officials in the O'Connell Street branch of the defendant bank could have ascertained if that "P. Murphy" had an account in another branch of the bank. And even if they ascertained that he had, neither legal principle nor sound and fair banking practice would indicate that he should be accorded a special or preferential treatment when deciding whether the cheques should be paid, on the ground that his position as a customer of the bank gave him a contractual standing not available to payees of cheques who happened not to be customers of the bank.

The trial judge found in favour of the plaintiffs on the ground that the defendant bank was in breach of its contractual duty to the plaintiff as paying banker. However, counsel for the plaintiffs did not seek to uphold the conclusion thereby implied that, in deciding whether or not to pay this cheque, the bank was acting as paying banker vis-a-vis the plaintiffs. Instead, they rest their case entirely on the proposition that in deciding not to pay the cheque, the defendant bank was acting as a collecting bank vis-a-vis the plaintiffs and that, in that capacity, it owed a contractual duty to the plaintiffs. For the reasons I have given, I must reject that submission. In my opinion, the defendant bank was not then acting as a collecting bank for the plaintiffs so the contractual duty which was relied on did not arise. I consider the defendants to have been acting solely as paying bankers for the drawer of the cheques that were being considered for payment.

Griffin J.:

Although the point has not been fully argued, and while I reserve my decision on the point in case it should arise in an action the subject of an appeal to this Court, it seems to me that a banker should pay his customers' cheques in the order in which they were presented, subject to the interest of the customer being taken into account. The fact that the manager should take the interest of the customer into account was accepted by Mr. Fitzpatrick in evidence. He gave the example of a customer, being the owner of a public-house, whose cheque to a brewery would be paid in priority to other cheques where the customer had insufficient funds in his account to pay all outstanding cheques, as payment of this cheque would enable the customer to stay in business since it would be presumed that the brewer would cut off the customer's supplies if the brewer's cheque was dishonoured. The order in which cheques should be paid is, however, of no advantage to the plaintiffs in this case, as it is settled also that the payee of a cheque cannot enforce payment from the paying banker if he dishonours the cheques, and that a bank owes no duty of care to a payee.

In my view, the method adopted by the O'Connell Street branch for selecting the Palgrave Murphy cheques to be paid (i.e. by holding a lottery) was not the correct one either at law or by the usage and practice of bankers. From the evidence, it appears that 42 separate draws were made before a reasonably satisfactory result was obtained and that the plaintiffs were unfortunate in not having any luck in the draw, or at any rate in the last draw as no information was available on the result of the earlier draws. Indeed, if Palgrave Murphy Ltd. had not become wholly insolvent, and if their interests were to be taken into account by the manager of the paying bank, it seems likely that the plaintiffs would have been one of the first payees to be paid in order to keep Palgrave Murphy Ltd. in business.

However, as there was no privity of contract between the plaintiffs and the O'Connell Street branch, the fact that an incorrect method of selecting the cheques to be paid was used can be of no avail to the plaintiffs.

10.4 Town and County Advance Co. v. Provincial Bank of Ireland [1917] 2 I.R. 421 King's Bench

[The plaintiffs, a loan company, received a request for a loan from a man called Philip Patrick Higgins (who lived with his father Michael) and representing himself to them as a person called Michael P. Higgins. He supplied them with documents, on the front of which was the name Michael Higgins, which seemed to indicate he owned certain lands. On the strength of these, the plaintiffs sent a cheque for £50 to their correspondent, on the security of a promissory note which was purportedly signed by Michael P. Higgins. The cheque was made out to Michael P. Higgins. It was presented for payment to the defendant bank in the circumstances set out in the extract.

In his judgment, Campbell C.J. discusses whether the bank should have paid out on foot of the cheque presented to it. This revolved around whether the cheque was made out to either a fictitious or a non-existing person within the meaning of s.7(3) of the Bills of Exchange Act, 1882. In concluding it was not, the court held in favour of the plaintiffs whose argument was that they intended to have the cheque paid to Michael Higgins and that this intention had not been carried through by the bank.]

Campbell C.J.:

On the strength of the documents which I have mentioned, and of course on the strength of this promissory note, the plaintiffs agreed to lend £50; and accordingly they sent a cheque for the amount, less an agreed deduction, to the address with which they had been corresponding. The payee named in the cheque is Michael P. Higgins. Philip Patrick Higgins having intercepted the cheque when it came to the house where he lived with his father, brought it to the branch of the Provincial Bank of Ireland at Dungarvan, having indorsed it, first as "Michael P. Higgins," and next as "Philip P. Higgins", and on the strength of these two indorsements the bank paid him the amount. The Provincial Bank negotiated the cheque in good faith and in the ordinary course of business, and the question for us to determine is which of two innocent parties is to suffer.

In support of the defendants' case we were referred to sub-s. 3 of s. 7 of the Bills of Exchange Act, 1882, which says: "Where the payee is a fictitious or non-existing person the bill may be treated as payable to bearer." In [*Bank of England* v. *Vagliano Bros Ltd.*] [1891] A.C. 107 the question came up in the House of Lords as to whether the Act made any change in the pre-existing law. In that case it was argued on behalf of the Bank of England that, in as much as the Act was a codifying Act, s. 7 did not extend the law as previously existing. The House of Lords did not accept that view, and the law must now be taken to have been altered by that section, which applies whether the drawer was or was not aware that the payee was a fictitious or non-existing person.

[Counsel for the Provincial] argued that *Vagliano's* case decided the present case, but the very concise and able argument which we have heard from [counsel for the Town and County] has satisfied us that the decision in that case does not apply to the facts before us.

The subsequent cases seem to establish this, that in order to have a fictitious payee within the meaning of the section you must always find that the drawer knew and intended that the payee was to be an unreality, but that if his intenton was to have a real payee and a real transaction there cannot be a fictitious payee so far as the drawer is concerned.

I adopt and follow the decision of Warrington J. in *Vinden* v. *Hughes* [1905] 1 K. B. 795 and more particularly the judgment of Buckley L.J in [*North and South Wales Bank Ltd.* v. *Macbeth*] [1908] 1 K.B.13 at p.22 from which it would follow that the question of a "fictitious person" cannot arise in the case before us because the drawer intended the cheque to be for a real payee, and it represented a bona fide and a real commercial transaction upon his part.

...There only remains the question, was the payee named in the cheque a "non-existing" person? That is a question of fact, and Dodd J., who tried the case, seems to have come to the conclusion that as a matter of fact the payee was Michael Higgins, the father of the borrower, because in his report the learned judge says that the so-called fictitious and non-existing person appeared in the witness-box before him. It was proved that Philip Patrick Higgins had before the trial of this action left his native land as a fugitive from justice. I am unable to agree with the view of Mr. Justice Dodd in this respect, or to hold as a question of fact that Michael Higgins, the father, was the payee; for I think that the borrower and payee was an existing person, namely, Philip Patrick Higgins, who had induced the plaintiffs to represent and describe him as Michael P. Higgins. But that did not enable him to alter and kill his identity any more than he could alter his sex by masquerading in female attire. I put several cases to Mr. Phelps [counsel for the Provincial] in which a creditor for some purpose of his own might ask his debtor to describe him by a wrong name in a cheque, as, for instance, a person engaged in betting transactions might ask his bookmaker to draw any cheques payable to him in a wrong name. Mr. Phelps did not contend that in such a case the payee would be non-existent, but he pointed out that in the present case the consideration for the cheque was a promissory note which purported to be signed by Michael P. Higgins and two other persons. Mr. Phelps put his view of the case very neatly by saying that Philip Patrick Higgins manufactured a ghost and got a cheque made payable to that ghost.

On the whole, however, I have come to the clear conclusion that the facts in evidence demonstrate that the payee named in the cheque was an existing person, namely, Philip Higgins, whose Christian name was at his request and for his fraudulent purpose innocently misdescribed by the plaintiffs as "Michael P." but that this misdescription never caused the payee to cease to exist or become a non-existing person, and that from the first to the last he was, in fact, and in the intention of the drawer, an existing person, namely, Philip Patrick Higgins.

CHAPTER 11

Restrictions on Unfair Competition

The law recognises that through running a business over a period of time, a business person may accumulate certain rights and entitlements in relation to the business which may not be unfairly taken away by a competitor. In *European Chemical Industries Ltd.* v. *Bell* (1981) (Extract 5.4), the extent to which a business person may place a restraint on trade of his former employees to prevent unfair competition was discussed. Ireland's membership of the European Communities has also impacted on Irish commercial law, since the thrust of, for example, Articles 30, 31, 36, 85 and 86 of the Treaty of Rome (which established the European Economic Community) is against restraints on competition. It is not intended to discuss the European provisions in this chapter, but discussion of some of the tensions in this area may be gleaned from *Cadbury (Irl.) Ltd.* v. *Kerry Co-Op Ltd.* [1982] I.L.R.M. 77, at pp. 87-90 (noted by Schuster, (1981) 3 D.U.L.J. (n.s.) 94) and Case 72/83 *Campus Oil Ltd. and Ors.* v. *Minister for Industry and Energy and Ors.* [1984] 3 C.M.L.R. 544. It is also of note that certain areas of what would be regarded as restraint of trade, namely exclusive dealing contracts, are now governed by European Commission Regulations: Reg. 1983/83 and Reg. 1984/83 (Official Journal No. L, 30 June 1983).

This chapter concentrates on the extent to which Irish law has recognised the accretion of property rights to a business in particular circumstances.

The first such example is where the courts are prepared to prevent a business person passing off as his own an identical or similar name to the extent that the public would be confused as to the business concerned. This common law concept of passing off is discussed in *C. & A. Modes* v. *C. & A. (Waterford) Ltd.* (1975) (Extract 11.1). In this case the Supreme Court protected a business from the unfair competition of another business which intended to use an established name (and associated goodwill) as a springboard to business success.

The important point to establish is the intention to deceive the public on the part of the competitor. One point of interest here is that while it is possible to register a name to be associated with a business under the Registration of Business Names Act, 1963, registration does not on its own establish the proprietary interest required to succeed in a passing off action. The essential element is the intention to deceive allied to public confusion: this involves the business having established some kind of image in the public eye.

In many instances, cases involving unfair competition problems revolve around a number of matters. It might be the use by a former employee of a similar business name, so that restraint of trade and passing off may both be involved. The position was equally complex in *House of Spring Gardens Ltd.* v. *Point Blank Ltd.* [1983] F.S.R. 213; [1983] F.S.R. 489. (H.C.); Supreme Court 1984 No. 184, 11 January 1985. In that case former employees of the plaintiff company had used confidential information obtained while employed by the plaintiff to secure a contract in a new business they had started up. Misuse of confidential information is another recognised head of claim in the area of unfair competition. But in the *House of Spring Gardens* case, there was the extra element that the confidential information related to the design of a bullet-proof vest which had in turn been registered under the terms of the Copyright Act, 1963. This Act is one of a number of pieces of legislation which regulate the manner in which business items which are of potentially great value may be protected in a structured system.

The Trade Marks Act, 1963 and the Patents Act, 1964 along with the Copyright Act prevent registered business works (copyright), business marks or names (trade marks) and business inventions (patents) from being copied without suitable compensation to the originator of the various items. In the *House of Spring Gardens* case, damages were awarded on the basis of breach of copyright, breach of contract and also misuse of confidential information. The important point is to recognise the overlap between the common law and statutory remedies.

The remaining extracts deal with the scope and extent of the three areas of statutory regulation.

In *Application of Mothercare Ltd.* (1968) (Extract 11.2), Kenny J. dealt with the alternative possible modes of protecting trade marks provided for in the Trade Marks Act, 1963. The register of trade marks provided for under the Act, is divided into Part A and Part B. The basis for this division is explored by O'Higgins C.J. in *Waterford Glass Ltd.* v. *Controller of Patents Designs and Trade Marks* [1984] I.L.R.M. 565. The essence of the division relates to the nature of the mark concerned. Registration in Part A is reserved for marks which, in the words of s.17 of the Act, have no direct reference to the character or quality of the goods with which they are connected and are distinctive, in the sense of having been adapted to distinguish them from any other goods. Part B registration was introduced to provide protection for those marks which although not adapted to distinguish, were capable of distinguishing the goods concerned from other goods: s.18 of the Act. Thus, in the *Mothercare* case, although registration under Part A was not possible, Kenny J. felt the mark was registrable under Part B. This is an area where judges can frequently disagree, as the *Waterford Glass* case shows, when the Supreme Court, by a majority, upheld the application to have the "Waterford" motif registered under Part B.

In *Allibert S.A.* v. *O'Connor* (1981) (Extract 11.3) Costello J. dealt with problems relating to copyright, which centered around whether particular works or products were original, and to what extent similar works or products were unauthorised copies.

And in *Ranks Hovis McDougall Ltd.* v. *Controller of Patents, Designs and Trade Marks* (1978) (Extract 11.4), McWilliam J. deals with the problem that whereas the development of a new product might be regarded by ordinary people as an invention, the Patents Act only allows registration of manufactured matter. Clearly, this has policy implications for the legislature in terms of what is deemed to be important areas of research in the future.

11.1   C. & A. Modes and C. & A. Ireland v. C. & A. (Waterford) Ltd. [1976] I.R. 198 High Court & Supreme Court

[The plaintiffs were companies running a number of retail outlets in Great Britain, including Belfast, under the banner and symbol "C & A". The first plaintiff advertised its goods extensively in the Republic but did not have any retail outlets here at the time of these proceedings. The defendant company began business in 1972 and the plaintiffs applied for injunctions preventing it from using the motif "C & A" or any other name closely resembling it which would be calculated to lead to its business being confused with the plaintiffs'.

The High Court and Supreme Court agreed that the plaintiffs were entitled to succeed. The judges, in the extracts, deal firstly with the definition of what constitutes passing off. The other issue was whether the fact that the plaintiff had no outlet in the Republic should prevent them from obtaining relief. In answering "no", the courts clearly took account of the reality of modern everyday communication between Britain and Ireland.]

Finlay P. (High Court):

In my opinion, it becomes necessary to consider whether there is a distinction in principle which justifies the grant of relief to a person or firm who, though providing a service such as the Sheraton hotels entirely outside the jurisdiction of the Court, has maintained within the jurisdiction an office for securing orders and bookings for that service but which compels the refusal of relief to a firm that maintains a retail shop outside the jurisdiction (which shop, on the evidence, is substantially frequented and used by persons travelling from within the jurisdiction) and advertises that retail shop and products sold in it in a manner which reaches a substantial number of members of the public within the jurisdiction of the court but which does not have a selling or booking agency within the jurisdiction.

To answer this question it is necessary to consider the fundamental principles applicable to the action of passing-off. On the authorities, the fundamental ingredients of the action for passing-off are that the plaintiff has a name applicable to his goods or business which is known to the public in the area in which the defendant seeks to carry on his business to an extent that the name, brand or mark proposed to be used or being used by the defendant is likely to deceive and to cause confusion. If that be an adequate general statement of the fundamental ingredients of the action of passing-off, then it does not appear to me to imply necessarily the recognition of territorial boundaries. In an age when the purchase of ordinary consumer goods by members of the public outside the territorial boundaries of their own State is a common and increasing activity, and in the particular situation of the Republic of Ireland where, as has been proved to my satisfaction in this particular case, the purchase of goods in Northern Ireland by residents and citizens of the Republic of Ireland is a usual and frequent occurrence, I can see no sound reason why the Court should absolve itself from the responsibility to prevent deception and what, in effect, is dishonest trading merely upon the grounds that the attraction to persons of the name and business and reputation of the plaintiff company operating in Belfast has occurred through advertisements in papers and magazines and through the broadcasting media and not through a booking or selling agency operating within the Republic of Ireland.

Furthermore, apart from the existing retail store of the plaintiffs in Belfast, I am satisfied that there is in this context relevence to be attached to the possibility of the plaintiff company opening a retail store within the Republic of Ireland in Dublin. In the *Sheraton* case [1964] R.P.C. 202 part of the evidence on behalf of the plaintiff was that, in addition to maintaining a booking office in Great Britain for their existing hotels which were located outside Great Britain, they had a project consisting of a tentative agreement with a Government department to erect a hotel at Prestwick Airport and that they had in contemplation or under negotiation projects for building hotels elsewhere in Great Britain and in Ireland as well...

It seems to me that, once - and only once - the plaintiffs have established that their name and reputation are known within the Republic of Ireland and generally well known as an established name, the plaintiffs are entitled to retain the possibility of opening a retail shop using that name, and any brand associated with it, for their goods within the Republic of Ireland without interference by the defendant companies arising from the use by them of a name or brand which is likely to deceive and lead to confusion.

Henchy J. (Supreme Court):

Here it is contended that there was no reach of the plaintiffs' goodwill which could be affected by the defendants' conduct. The plaintiffs have no shop or place of trading within the State and it is urged that the evidence fell short of showing that the orbit of their trading activities outside the State was capable of carrying with it a public awareness within the State of the import of C & A as a business name or symbol, and that, consequently, the defendants' conduct was incapable of invading their goodwill.

Consider this submission in the light of the evidence. Sixty-five shops throughout the United Kingdom, including the one in Belfast, purvey the distinctive C & A wearing apparel. It would be remarkable, considering the movement of people between this State and the United Kingdom, if there were not a significant number of at least intermittent C & A customers in this State. The evidence also showed that there has been massive advertising of C & A goods on television and in some of the most widely read British newspapers and magazines circulating in the Republic of Ireland, as well as in Northern Ireland newspapers. The Belfast shop draws a not inconsiderable number of its customers from the Republic. The C & A organization recruits staff from the Republic. In 1975, one factory in Cork manufactured 850,000 items which were sold in the C & A shops.

Can it be said in these circumstances that, because the plaintiffs have no direct retailing outlets in the Republic, they have no protectable goodwill in the Republic? In my opinion the answer is "No". Goodwill does not necessarily stop at a frontier. Whether in a particular area a plaintiff has a goodwill which is liable to be damaged by the unlawful competition resulting from passing off is a question of fact and of degree. What has to be established for the success of a plaintiff's claim in an action such as this is that by his business activities - be they by direct selling within the State or otherwise - he has generated within the State a property right in a goodwill which will be violated by the passing-off. It is true that there is authority for the proposition that a plaintiff's reputation which owes nothing to user in this State is not sufficient to support a passing-off action (*Alain Bernardin et Cie* v. *Pavilion Properties Ltd.* [1967] R.P.C. 581) but, as is stated in *Kerly's Law of Trade Marks and Trade Names* (10th ed. p. 386), it is difficult to see any rational basis for this distinction. If there are in this State sufficient customers of a plaintiff's business to justify his claim to have a vested right to retain and expand that custom, then there is ample authority in principle and in the decided cases for the conclusion that, no matter where the plaintiff's business is based, he is entitled to be protected against its being taken away or dissipated by someone whose deceptive conduct is calculated to create a confusion of identity in the minds of existing or potential customers.

I consider that the evidence in this case amply satisfies the test. The nature and spread of the C & A trade throughout the United Kingdom, the extent to which the shop in Belfast draws its custom from this State, the advertising campaign in papers and magazines circulating here, the distinctive nature of C & A goods in their labelling and packaging and in the C & A symbol, all these in combination point to a goodwill in this State. If there were any doubt that the first plaintiffs enjoy in this State "the attractive force which brings in custom" (per Lord Macnaghten in *Commissioners of Inland Revenue* v. *Muller & Co.'s Margarine Ltd.* [1901] A.C. 217, 224) one might ask why did the individual defendants purloin the name and symbol of the C & A ? The answer is that they did so to gain commercial advantage from the resulting confusion in the public mind between their trading activities and those of the first plaintiffs. Their passing-off was calculated to operate to the detriment of the goodwill in this State of the first plaintiffs. It is to prevent unfair competition of that kind that the action for passing-off lies.

Kenny J.:

The legal wrong known as passing-off includes the incorporation in the Republic of Ireland of a company with a name likely to give the impression to the public that it is a subsidiary or branch of or is associated or connected with another company which has an established goodwill, whether the latter company is incorporated in the Republic or outside it. The incorporation with the name selected may have been with the intention of creating that impression (*Lloyds & Dawson Bros.* v. *Lloyds (Southampton) Ltd.* (1912) 29 R.P.C. 433; *Harrods Ltd.* v. *R. Harrod Ltd.* (1924) 41 R.P.C. 74) or innocently without knowledge of the existence of the well-known company: *Ewing* v. *Buttercup Margarine Co. Ltd.* [1917] 2 Ch. 1. In either event, the wrong of passing-off may be restrained by the company with the established goodwill.

The defendants urged that this principle should be limited to cases where the well-known company had acquired some of its goodwill in the Republic by user or trading in this country. I do not see any reason why this limitation on the general principle should be imposed today when extensive advertising can be carried out by television, radio and newspapers all of which go into almost every home in this State. Programmes broadcast by B.B.C. 1, B.B.C.2 and U.T.V. are regularly looked at on television sets in this State. I suspect that the idea that some of the goodwill must be acquired by user or trading in the country where it is sought to protect it comes from the days when television and radio were unknown and when international trade in domestic goods was not as extensive as it is today. It is not an appropriate rule for this age and as no authority binds me to accept it, I refuse to do so.

11.2   Application of Mothercare Ltd.
[1968] I.R.359 High Court

[The applicant company applied for registration of the mark "Mothercare" under the Trade Marks Act, 1963 in either Part A or Part B of the register of trade marks. The relevant provisions of ss.17 and 18 of the Act have been summarised in the Introduction.

In the extract, Kenny J. examines the issues in turn, by asking, firstly, whether the word concerned bears a "direct reference" to the character or quality of the goods with which it is connected. Having decided it did not, the second matter was whether it was a word which was adapted to distinguish so as to qualify for Part A registration; in this instance the judge felt the word failed this test. But the third issue, whether the word was capable of distinguishing was answered in its favour, thus making it registrable under Part B; and in this respect the two Irish cases mentioned by Kenny J. towards the end of the extract are highly relevant.]

Kenny J.:

Has the word "Mothercare" a direct reference to the character or quality of the goods in respect of which its registration is now sought? In the Patents, Designs, and Trade Marks Act, 1883, the corresponding clause had the words "having no reference to the character or quality of the goods". The word "direct" was introduced by the Trade Marks Act, 1905. This shows, I think, that a word is not disqualified under s.17, sub-s. (1)(d), of the Act of 1963 because it contains some element of reference to the character or quality of the goods. It has been decided that "Motorine" has not a direct reference to any character or quality of lubricating oils though it had a reference to motors in which lubricating oils are used: see *In re Compagnie Industrielle des Petroles' Application* [1907] 2 Ch. 435. "Mothercare" has at least two meanings. One is the care which a mother gives to her children but, as these may range in age from one month to sixty years, any reference to character or quality implied in the word would be as appropriate to perambulators as it would be to a racing car for a man of forty. The other meaning is care for mothers, and in this sense the reference to character or quality includes everything that makes the lives of mothers enjoyable or comfortable; it would include electric fires and clothing. [Counsel for Mothercare] said that the word could not have a direct reference to the character or quality of any goods because it has these two meanings.

In my opinion "Mothercare" is a word having no direct reference to either the character or quality of the goods in respect of which its registration is sought in these two applications. It was argued that the test to be applied was to ask whether the word was descriptive, in which event it would not qualify as a trade mark under s.17 sub-s. 1(d), or whether the word was distinctive; but this suggested dichotomy is fallacious for the two words are not mutually exclusive - see the judgment of Fletcher Moulton L.J. in *Re Joseph Crosfield & Sons Ltd.* [1910] 1 Ch. 130, 145. There is some element of descriptiveness in the word, but it would apply to so many domestic goods that I think that the word must be regarded as having no direct reference to the character or quality of the goods...

But although "Mothercare" has no direct reference to the character or quality of the goods in respect of which its registration is sought, it cannot be registered in part A unless it is distinctive in the sense that it is adapted to distinguish. The words "any other distinctive mark" in s.17, sub-s. 1 (e), of the Act of 1963 show that a word which falls within paras. (a) to (d) should not be registered in Part A unless it is distinctive: see the application of the *Minnesota Mining & Manufacturing Co.* (1948) 65 R.P.C. This issue was not considered by the Controller because he held that the word could not be distinctive as it had a direct reference to the character of the goods. I agree that a word which has a direct reference to the character of the goods cannot be distinctive in the absence of evidence of its distinctiveness; but if the word has not this reference, and if there is no evidence of user, the issue arises whether it is "adapted to distinguish" and, if it is not, the further issue arises whether it is "capable of distinguishing." The difference between these two phrases was not discussed in the argument, and the cases decided before 1919 do not assist because registration in Part B and "capable of distinguishing" (as opposed to

142

"adapted to distinguish") first appeared in our law in that year. Sects. 17 and 18 of the Act of 1963 show that there is a distinction between a mark which is inherently adapted to distinguish and one which is inherently capable of distinguishing, though the original basis for the distinction (two years user) has been abolished. What then is the distinction?

The decided cases show that there are some words which can be adapted to or capable of distinguishing, but the grounds on which these words have been rejected for registration have varied. Some judges have said that the words proposed were not adapted to distinguish, some have said that the same words were not capable of distinguishing, while others have said that the Controller and the Court should, in the exercise of discretion refuse to register them. Examples are the word "Liverpool" applied to electric cables which, despite strong evidence of distinctiveness, was held to be incapable of registration in the application of *Liverpool Electric Cable Co. Ltd.* (1929) 46 R.P.C. 99; and the word "Glastonburys" which, despite similar evidence, was held not to be adapted to distinguish in *Baily & Co. Ltd.* v. *Clark, Son & Morland Ltd.* [1938] A.C. 557...

In my opinion "Mothercare" is not a word which is inherently incapable, when used as a trade mark, of distinguishing the goods of the proprietor of that mark. It is not a laudatory epithet, like "Perfection," nor is it a word which the Court should, in its discretion, refuse to allow to be on the register because it would interfere with the rights of other traders.

Is the word, however, in the absence of evidence of user producing distinctiveness, adapted to distinguish? I think that this must mean that there is some feature of the word which makes it suitable to distinguish the goods of one trader from another. "The Act meant that the trader may take a word which from something in the word itself - say the fact that no one had ever heard the word before, that it was an invented word, or that it indicated the particular trader as distinguished from another trader, but always from something found in the word itself as distinguished from the way in which it is used - is such as to answer the description of being adapted to distinguish the goods": per Lord Justice Buckley in *Re Leopold Cassella & Co.* [1910] 2 Ch. 240, 245.

"Mothercare" consists of two words which are frequently used in English and which, when used as a trade mark, are inherently ambiguous. It is not, in my opinion, adapted to distinguish for it is not a new word, it is not an invented word, it does not point to any particular trader and it does not indicate anything remarkable in the wide range of goods to which it may be applied. There is nothing in the word itself which makes it adapted to distinguish the goods of one trader from those of another.

It is, however, capable of distinguishing. I have read the judgment of Mr. Justice Meredith in *Richardson* v. *Weiner* [1936] I.R. 32 in which there is a closely-reasoned analysis of the distinction between "adapted to distinguish" and "capable of distinguishing." He expressed the view that the words "capable of distinguishing" were used in s. 86 of the Act of 1927 because two years user was then necessary for registration in Part B. At p. 42 of the report he sought to express the distinction in this way: "If, however, the Controller is to reject on the ground that a mark that has in fact been used by the applicant for two years for the purpose of distinguishing his goods is not capable of distinguishing them, then the mark must continue incapable with any amount of user, and it is difficult to see how the Controller could satisfy himself on the question unless the mark had a positive incapacity for becoming distinctive by user - i.e. unless it was in itself so inapt for distinguishing that it could not by user acquire *de facto* distinctiveness. And that I regard as the meaning. The difference involved in the change of expression from 'adapted to distinguish' and 'capable of distinguishing' is brought out when the expressions are used in the negative. It is the difference between not being adapted to distinguish and being unadapted for distinguishing. Only where there is such positive unadaption could the Controller be unable to satisfy himself that a mark that had been used for two years for the purpose of distinguishing was not capable of distinguishing; for *prima facie*, such user will always procure de facto distinctiveness eventually." The repeal of the provisions for two years user for registration in Part B by the Act of 1963 makes much of the reasoning of Mr. Justice Meredith inapplicable, but the passage is a useful discussion of the difference between the two expressions.

This question was also discussed by Mr. Justice Gavan Duffy in *British Colloids Ltd.* v. *Controller of Industrial Property* [1943] I.R. 56 in which he held that the words "Crookes' Lacto-Callamine" were capable of distinguishing the applicant's goods in an application for registration in Part B. He said at p.67 of the report: "The tests of capacity to distinguish defy any rule of thumb, but they should not be difficult tests for a mark to pass, unless the mark belongs to a type that obviously cannot be recognised, as involving an invasion of common right or similar impropriety; it is not much to exact of a mark that it shall be usable in actual business to assure a purchaser that the article he buys comes from the particular trader he knows, and is therefore up to that trader's accustomed standard; and, where, as in the present instances, the mark to be registered has already been registered in the country of origin upon a similar register, for the like classes and under a virtually identical law, the applicant is naturally dismayed if he finds himself precluded from proceeding with his application on a priori grounds." The last matter relied on by Mr. Justice Gavan Duffy seems to me to be very relevant, for this mark has been registered in its country of origin under a system of trade-mark law which is now, in almost all aspects, identical with ours.

In my opinion "Mothercare" is a word which is capable of distinguishing the applicants' goods of the types for which its registration is sought: this is corroborated by the fact that it has already been registered on the Irish register in Part B for some goods.

11.3   Allibert S.A. v. O'Connor and Can-Am Containers Ltd. [1981] F.S.R. 613 High Court

[The plaintiff company claimed copyright ownership over two drawings of plastic fish boxes. The second defendant, Can-Am, began manufacturing plastic fish boxes and attempted to sell them on the Irish market; the first defendant was the distributor.   The defendants claimed that the drawings were not "original" because at least one of them, drawing No. 00334, seemed to have been based on an earlier 1963 drawing. S.9 of the Copyright Act, 1963 states that copyright may be claimed for "original artistic work".

This is the first issue dealt with by Costello J. in the extract, and he explains by reference to the *L.B. (Plastics)* case why copyright protection can exist in some instances, as here, even where a product drawing is based on an earlier one. The other issue dealt with in the extract is the extent to which "designs" are capable of copyright protection. This turns on the connection between the Copyright Act, 1963 and the provisions of Part III of the Industrial and Commercial Property (Protection) Act, 1927 which gives protection to "designs" outside the scope of copyright protection. If an article amounts to a "mere mechanical device", then only copyright protection is possible, as the discussion by Costello J. of s.3 of the 1927 Act shows.]

Costello J.:

Counsel for the defendants referred me to *L.B. (Plastics) Ltd.* v. *Swish Products Ltd.* [1979] R.P.C. 551. This was a case which concerned artistic copyright in a product drawing, the drawings in the case being of a plastic knock-down drawer system. A number of points were raised in the case which eventually were determined by the House of Lords. The question of the originality of the drawings in dispute was raised in the High Court and decided by Whitford J., whose judgment in this respect was accepted by both parties and was not the subject of appeal. Referring to the defendants' plea that copyright did not exist because the product drawings were not "original", Whitford J. stated:

"There is another aspect of originality which must be dealt with, and conveniently dealt with, at this stage, that is the question as to whether there can be copyright in a copy. Here again it must be in my judgment a question of degree. It arises in this case because of a suggestion that some of the drawings relied upon by the plaintiffs may have been made from models first produced in three dimensions, which models not being works of artistic craftsmanship would not attract copyright.... There is the further point to be considered that some of the drawings, undoubtedly, derive in part from earlier drawings, but on the evidence I am still of the opinion that each work relied upon can claim to be a separate original artistic work attracting copyright and, indeed, Counsel for the defendant, if against his assumption copyright were to be found to reside in these drawings at all, was specifically concerned to assert that one drawing must be considered as being a separate copyright work although it was in some not inconsiderable measure a redrawing of an earlier drawing. The draughtsmen called on both sides made it quite plain that even where there has been a previous drawing or some sketches have been made which are in part redrawn, the making of any drawing of the kind I have to consider is a skilled business involving hours of labour, although the end result may seem relatively simple."

...So, copyright protection can exist in a product drawing even though it is based on an earlier product drawing. What the court has to determine in a disputed case is whether the designer has performed sufficient independent labour to justify copyright protection for the drawing he has produced (see *Copinger on Copyright*, 10th ed., para. 126). Because of the loss of the original 1963 product drawing in this case, it is not possible to be certain as to the extent of the labour and skill involved in the production of the 1967 drawing No. 00334. But I am satisfied on the balance of probability that the labour and skill involved was significant. It is quite clear from examining the drawing that it could only have been produced by a skilled draughtsman. It contains four different plans and five cross sections with the detailed measurements and information which would be required for the production of the finished article. To produce such a drawing, in my view, involves the application of a considerable degree of skill and a considerable amount of time. I am satisfied that it is an "original" artistic work.

The situation in relation to M. 127 is clearer. The name of the designer, M. Bourgneuf, appears on the drawing. It cannot be a copy or a tracing of the 1963 drawing as I think it is highly unlikely that M. Bourgneuf would have used the 1963 drawing as a basis for the design of the 70-litre box - if he consulted any drawing the 1967 drawing, which incorporated all up-to-date improvements, would have been the obvious drawing to choose. When the 1974 drawing is compared with the 1967 drawing it is clear that it is an "original" work within the principles of copyright law. It is quite clearly a different drawing. There are three plans and two cross sections shown and the measurements and information given are different from those shown on the 1967 drawing. It seems to me that a considerable degree of original skill and labour was required to produce this drawing and that it, too, is an "original" artistic work.

But even if the drawings are "original" drawings the plaintiffs may not enjoy copyright in them because of the provisions of s.172 of the 1927 Act. This is the next issue in the case which I should consider.

Are the plaintiffs drawings "designs" capable of being registered under the 1927 Act?
S.172 of the Industrial and Commercial Property (Protection) Act 1927 (a section which occurs in that Part of the Act which confers copyright protection) provides that "this Part of this Act shall not apply to designs capable of being registered under Part III of this Act." Part III referred to is that Part dealing with the registration of designs. The effect of this section, combined with s.3(11) of the 1963 Act,is that if the drawings on which the plaintiffs rely in these proceedings are capable of being registered as "Designs" under the provisions of Part III of the 1927 Act then they have no copyright protection and this action fails.

S.64 of the 1927 Act allows the controller to register "any new or original design" which had not been previously published as set out in the section. But the Act does not provide that every new and original design is capable of being registered - only those which come within the definition of "Design" contained in s.3 of the 1927 Act can be registered. This section defines

"Designs" as meaning:

"only the features of shape, configuration, pattern, or ornament applied to any article by any industrial process or means, whether manual, mechanical or chemical, separate or combined, which in the finished article appeal to and are judged solely by the eye, but does not include any mode or principle of construction, or anything which is in substance a mere mechanical device."

It will be noted that the definition falls into two parts. The first provides that the word "design" means inter alia those features of the shape and configuration of the finished article, which appeal to and are judged solely by the eye. The second part excludes from the definition anything which is "in substance a mere mechanical device". This definition is the same as that which was contained in s.19 of the British Patents and Designs Act 1919 whose meaning and effect has been helpfully explained by Luxmore J. in *Kestos Ltd.* v. *Kempat Ltd.* (1936) 53 R.P.C. 139 when he said at p. 151:

"The first part of the definition is directed to describing what may be the subject matter of registration while the latter part of it is directed to excluding from that definition the possibility of any claim to monopoly by reason of registration for any mode or principle of construction , or for any mere mechanical device. A mere mechanical device is a shape in which all the features are dictated solely by the function or functions which the article has to peform (see: *Tecalemit Ltd.* v. *Ewarts Ltd. (No. 2)* (1927) 44 R.P.C. 503). In other words, if a person produces an article for a particular purpose though that person may obtain the grant of letters patent for it, the producer cannot obtain a monopoly of that article by registration of a design for it. The only protection given by the registration is for the particular form of the article shown in the design registered. Moreover, a particular form must possess some features beyond those necessary to enable the article to fulfil the particular purpose, but the fact that some advantage is derived from the adoption of a particular shape does not exclude it from registration as a design".

... Accordingly, if I come to the conclusion that the design with which I am concerned in this case is a shape in which all the features are dictated solely by the function which is to be performed by the article to which the shape is applied and that this shape possesses no features beyond those necessary to enable the article to fulfil its functions then the drawings with which I am concerned cannot be regarded as "designs" within the meaning of s.3 of the 1927 Act. It would follow that they would not then be capable of being registered under the provisions of that Act, and that the plaintiffs may claim copyright protection for them...

I am satisfied that all the features of shape which I have just described are dictated by the functions which the box was required to perform and I cannot find any feature on the box which was there for any other purpose. In reaching this conclusion I have been greatly assisted by the evidence of Mr. Patrick Lavell, an independent expert in this particular field of design with whose view I find myself in agreement.

The defendants were unable to point to any feature of the plaintiffs box which had a purpose other than a functional one or which could be regarded as an embellishment. Their case rested on two submissions. First they urged that the plaintiffs' evidence, in particular that of Mr. Ward the managing director of the plaintiffs' English subsidiary company was to the effect that the plaintiffs' boxes were readily identifiable and that they could be and were in fact distinguished from the boxes of other suppliers by their users. This argument, it seems to me, emphasised the first part of the definition of "design" in the 1927 Act but failed to have proper regard to the words of exclusion in the second part of the definition. I have no doubt that the plaintiffs' boxes appear to the eyes of a customer of these products as different from those of their competitors. But it does not follow from this that the design of these boxes is capable of being registered under the 1927 Act, because a distinctive design which results from features which have been dictated by the functions which the box is required to perform cannot be registered. The second submission is based on the fact that designs of these boxes were in fact registered under the 1927 Act and it is urged that this is at least *prima facie* evidence that they are capable of being registered. This may be true. But the Controller had not the benefit of the expert evidence which was available to this court, and I do not think that the fact of registration requires me to reach a conclusion different from that which the evidence before me and my own examination of the exhibits in the case suggested.

I conclude therefore that neither Drawing 00334 or Drawing M 127 is capable of being registered as a design under the 1927 Act. It follows, then, that the plaintiffs can claim copyright protection for them.

11.4   Ranks Hovis McDougall Ltd. v. Controller of Patents, Designs and Trade Marks [1979] I.R. 142 High Court

[The plaintiff company applied for a patent from the Controller in respect of the invention of a new type of micro-organism which provided edible protein. The micro-organism did not occur naturally and had to be treated in laboratory conditions and provided with certain nutrients before it produced the edible protein. The Controller allowed the plaintiff a patent in relation to the process leading to production of the micro-organism, but refused it as far as the micro-organism itself was concerned. S.2 of the Patents Act, 1964 defines "invention" as including "any new and useful art, process, machine, manufacture or composition of matter."

The extract shows that McWilliam J. drew a clear distinction between products which are manufactured (they can be patented) and those which are grown (they cannot be patented). The judge made it clear also that while policy, or even science-fiction, considerations might make it desirable to provide for patenting grown products, this was not a function to be performed by the courts, and so the application

148

in this case could not succeed.]

McWilliam J.:

I have been referred to several dictionaries for the meaning of the word "manufacture." Some of these refer to "things manufactured" and the process of "manufacturing", which is not very helpful. In *Collins New English Dictionary* "manufacture" is described as (1) the process of making goods either by hand or machine; (2) anything produced from raw materials; and (3) to make from raw materials, to fabricate. In a small school dictionary published by the Educational Company of Ireland the word is described as "the making of articles or materials" and "to produce (articles), to work up (materials) into finished articles." With regard to the expression "composition of matter," I suppose that, in the general sense, everything is composed of matter of some sort but, in the present context, I think it is the word "composition" which must be considered. The *English Oxford Dictionary*, to which I was referred, describes it as the act of putting together, formation, construction.

Having considered these dictionary meanings, I return to a consideration of the definition of "invention" in s.2 of the Act and it seems to me that, in the context of the Act, the words "manufacture" and "composition" must be distinguished from the word "grow" which, amongst other things, means "cause to grow". This latter meaning appears to me to apply whether the products grown are grown naturally or are artificially assisted to grow. Were it not for the large body of authority to which I have been referred, I would have accepted this distinction as conclusive in the present case because these micro-organisms appear to me to be wholly composed of living cells which have been grown, admittedly under very special and complicated conditions, and not to have been "made" or "put together" or "constructed".

Although the distinction between "manufacture" and "grow" appears clear to me, I have some hesitation about basing my decision on it because this distinction does not appear to have been considered in the various cases to which I have been referred. Indeed, the American cases, which were so strongly relied upon by the plaintiffs, do not explain satisfactorily for me what is understood to be the meaning of the words "manufacture" and "composition".

In *Bergy, Coats and Malik's Application* [1977] C.C.P.A. which was decided in October 1977, an application for a patent for micro-organisms had been rejected by the Board of Appeals of the United States Patent and Trademark Office on the ground that a living organism does not fall within the provisions of the American statute. The relevant American provision states:- "Whoever invents or discovers any new or useful process, machine, manufacture, or composition of matter, or any new and useful improvement thereof, may obtain a patent therefor, subject to the conditions and requirements of this title." It will be seen that this provision is almost identical with the relevant part of the definition of "invention" in the Irish statute. On appeal to the United States Court of Customs and Patent Appeals, it was held by a majority that micro-organisms could be patented. In the judgments the entire discussion centered around the question whether living things could be patented; in my opinion, there was no adequate consideration of the question whether living things (i.e. micro-organisms) had been manufactured within the meaning of the term "manufacture".

Two matters were emphasised in the majority judgment which I do not consider that I am entitled to take into account in the present case. The first was that the processes whereby the micro-organisms were produced could be patented and that it would be inconsistent to refuse to patent the micro-organisms themselves. The second was that it was in the public interest to include micro-organisms within the meaning of the terms "manufacture" and "composition of matter". With regard to the former, it is to be noted that, in the Irish and American statutes, "processes" are not related to "manufacture" or "composition" of matter, from which it would appear to follow that a new and useful process for a purpose other than manufacture or composition of matter may be patented, and that there is a distinction in this respect between the grant of a patent for a process and the grant of a patent for the product of that process. With regard to the latter, I fully accept that it is, or may be, in the public interest to grant a patent for new micro-organisms but, as was pointed out in the dissenting judgment in that case, this is a matter for the legislature and not for the Courts. I have to decide what the legislature enacted and not what it intended to enact or ought to have enacted.

In *Chackabarty's Application* [1978] C.C.P.A. 77-535 which was decided in March, 1978, the United States Court of Customs and Patent Appeals, again by a majority, followed its decision in the *Bergy* case and adopted an argument, advanced on behalf of the applicant for the patent, that all things in the world are either the products of nature or things produced by man and that, as the micro-organisms did not occur in nature, they were produced by man and, therefore, were manufactured. Although current science fiction indicates that a time may come when living things will be manufactured by man and, therefore, will be patentable under the Act of 1964, the fact that a substance has been produced by man does not necessarily mean that it has been manufactured within the meaning of the statutes; this view was expressed in the dissenting judgments in *Chackabarty's* case.

CHAPTER 12

Remedies

Throughout the cases excerpted in the preceding chapters, there has been a consistent thread weaved of the breakdown of relations between parties requiring legal remedial action.   It is appropriate to outline now three of the most common legal remedies, the interlocutory injunction, the order of specific performance and the award of a sum of money in damages.

When something goes wrong in relations between business people, there are many ways in which the dispute can be resolved.   Some of these do not involve legal remedies, in the sense that a friendly chat or exchange of correspondence may clear up a misunderstanding. Nowadays also, many written contracts provide that, in the event of a dispute between the parties, a formalised arbitration procedure, outside the court system, should determine the matter. S.5 of the Arbitration Act, 1980 states that in such a situation court proceedings may, in general, be stayed by a party who seeks arbitration.   Thus, these different types of remedies may leave the courts without an input into a particular dispute, unless these alternative modes of conflict resolution fail to find a definite solution.

Assuming the courts are involved in the particular problem, it may be that one party feels that immediate action is required to preserve the position of both sides until the full court hearing takes place.   Bringing a case to full hearing can be a long process, involving the preparation of court documents which set out, and defend, a claim, consultation between lawyers and clients and obtaining a date for hearing a case from a (usually) overworked court system.   This is where one side may seek an interlocutory injunction, which can be heard by the courts on the basis of written, rather than oral, evidence, and on short notice.   It amounts to an attempt to achieve a rough holding operation.   One such instance was *European Chemical Industries Ltd.* v. *Bell* (1981) (Extract 5.4), where the employer successfully obtained an interlocutory injunction preventing its former employee from breaking the restraint of trade clause pending the full hearing of the case.   As that case shows, two issues are considered by the courts: whether the person seeking the injunction has established there is a serious issue to be tried if the case goes to full hearing, and where the balance of convenience lies between the parties in terms of granting or refusing the injunction. The fact that these are the only issues was confirmed by the Supreme Court in *Campus Oil Ltd. and Ors.* v. *Minister for Industry and Energy and Ors.* (1983) (Extract 12.1). The Court made clear that it was not its function to make any kind of final determination on the legal issues arising between the parties at the interlocutory stage. One point that marks out the *Campus Oil* case as different was the attempt to resist the injunction on the ground that it was mandatory rather than prohibitive in nature. O'Higgins C.J. points out that while that is normally the case in interlocutory proceedings, the mandatory injunction ought to be granted since if it was not the piece of legislation concerned would break down.

In contract cases, parties may enter into a definite arrangement from which one party may then attempt to remove himself. In that type of situation, an award of a sum of money may not adequately compensate the aggrieved person who wished to carry through the contract. The courts of equity responded to this with the order for specific performance which is, simply, an order requiring one party to carry through an agreement on the terms agreed, as occurred in *Nestor* v. *Murphy* (1979) (Extract 2.1). In many instances, such an order is given in relation to a contract for the sale of land. Indeed, there are certain types of contract in respect of which the courts are reluctant to order specific performance, such as contracts of personal service - the employment contract: see the interlocutory proceedings in *Fennelly* v. *Assicurazioni Generali S.p.a.* (1985) 3 I.L.T. 73 (H.C.); (1985) 3 I.L.T. 125 (S.C.). In *Roberts* v. *O'Neill* (1982) (Extract 12.2), the Supreme Court considered the question as to whether the equitable, and therefore undeniably discretionary, order ought not be granted where hardship arises after the contract has been entered into. McCarthy J. gave a definite "no" in response, while accepting the possibility of some exceptional instances.

The most common form of award, particularly in commercial cases, is one of damages to compensate for loss suffered. The general purpose here was discussed in the context of insurance in *St. Albans Investment Co.* v. *Sun Alliance & London Insurance Ltd.* (1983) (Extract 9.2). That part of a court's decision centres on what amount ought to be awarded in a given case. The other important question, in the context of breach of contract, is what type of loss can a person seek damages for. The courts have answered this by attempting to make an objective determination of what reasonable people would have foreseen as likely to happen if a contract was broken. This is what the foundation case *Hadley* v. *Baxendale* (1854) 9 Exch. 341 sets out as the basic test, and subsequent cases have refined this in particular contexts. In *Hickey & Co. Ltd.* v. *Roches Stores (Dublin) Ltd.* (1980) (Extract 12.3), Finlay P. applied this test in the modern context of a situation where the award of damages was given a considerable time after the breach of contract had occurred, with the intervening problem of inflation. Was the delay and the inflationary decrease in the purchasing power of money to be considered in deciding the amount of damages to be awarded? In concluding it was not, Finlay P. points up the common sense matters which must be considered in this context.

12.1   Campus Oil Ltd. and Ors. v. Minister for Industry and Energy and Ors. (No.2) [1983] I.R. 88 Supreme Court

[Under powers conferred by the Fuels (Control of Supplies) Acts, 1971-1982, the Minister for Industry and Energy made the Fuels (Control of Supplies) Order, 1983 by which he imposed an obligation on oil importers to purchase 35% of their requirements from the Whitegate oil refinery which was controlled by the State. The plaintiffs were Irish oil importers who challenged the validity of the order imposing the mandatory regime; the matter was referred by the High Court to the European Court of Justice. At this stage it became clear that the plaintiffs were not going to comply with the terms of the order and the Minister applied for an interlocutory mandatory injunction compelling them to comply.

The extracts from the Supreme Court judgments affirming the grant of the injunction discuss the principles on which such orders are granted. In particular, Griffin J. points out the complementary nature of the tests set out in the *Educational Co.* case (which is discussed in the extract from the judgment of O'Higgins C.J.) and *Esso* case and the English *American Cyanamid* decision.]

O'Higgins C.J.:

Interlocutory relief is granted to an applicant where what he complains of is continuing and is causing him harm or injury which may be irreparable in the sense that it may not be possible to compensate him fairly or properly by an award of damages. Such relief is given because a period must necessarily elapse before the action can come for trial and for the purpose of keeping matters *in statu quo* until the hearing. The application is made on motion supported by affidavit. It frequently happens that neither the applicant's right nor the fact of its violation is disputed by the person whose acts are sought to be restrained. In such case an injunction may be given almost as of course. The application for an interlocutory injunction is often treated by the parties as the trial of the action. When that happens, the rights of the parties are finally determined on the interlocutory motion. In cases where rights are disputed and challenged and where a significant period must elapse before the trial, the court must exercise its discretion (to grant interlocutory relief) with due regard to certain well-established principles. Not only will the court have regard to what is complained of and whether damages would be an appropriate remedy but it will consider what inconvenience, loss and damage might be caused to the other party, and will enquire whether the applicant has shown that the balance of convenience is in his favour.

None of these matters, however, are directly in issue on this appeal. Here interlocutory relief was granted to the defendants in pursuance of their counter-claim seeking a permanent injunction at the trial. The plaintiffs against whom it was granted contend that the learned trial judge should have required the defendants to establish a probability that their counter-claim would succeed at the trial and that the plaintiffs' claim would be dismissed.

Mr. Fitzsimons, on behalf of those plaintiffs, argued that the existence of such a probability test as a guide to the granting of interlocutory relief was recognised by the former Supreme Court in *Educational Company of Ireland Ltd.* v. *Fitzpatrick* [1961] I.R. 323. In particular, he relied on the judgment of Lavery J. in that case. I must say at once that I do not agree. In my opinion, the judgments in that case do not support this argument. It is true that there is one reference to "probability" contained in an extract from *Kerr on Injunctions* (6th ed.) which was quoted by Lavery J. at p. 336 of the report. That reference, in its context, is of doubtful significance. However, at p. 337 of the report, Lavery J. clearly laid down what he regarded as the proper test when he said:

> "The plaintiffs have to establish that there is a fair question raised to be decided at the trial. The arguments, lasting three days in this Court, show I think that there is such a question to be determined."

In any event, I would regard the application of the suggested test as contrary to principle. As I have already mentioned, interlocutory relief is intended to keep matters *in statu quo* until the trial and to do no more. No rights are determined nor are issues decided. I think that the principle is stated correctly in the following passage from *Kerr on Injunctions* (6th ed. p. 2), which was noted by Lavery J. in the *Educational Company* case:

> "In interfering by interlocutory injunction, the Court does not in general profess to anticipate the determination of the right, but merely gives it as its opinion that there is a substantial question to be tried, and that till the question is ripe for trial, a case has been made out for the preservation of the property in the meantime *in statu quo*."

The application of the plaintiffs' criterion on a motion for interlocutory relief would involve the Court in a determination of an issue which properly arises for determination at the trial of the action. In my view, the test to be applied is whether a fair *bona fide* question has been raised by the person seeking the relief. If such a question has been raised, it is not for the Court to determine that question on an interlocutory application; that remains to be decided at the trial. Once a fair question has been raised, in the manner in which I have indicated, then the Court should consider the other matters which are appropriate to the exercise of its discretion to grant interlocutory relief. In this regard, I note the views expressed by Lord Diplock, with the concurrence of the other members of the House of Lords at p. 407 of the report of *American*

Cyanamid Co. v. *Ethicon Ltd.* [1975] A.C. 396. I merely say that I entirely agree with what he said.

In my view, therefore, the learned trial judge, in considering whether the defendants had raised a fair question as to whether their rights had been violated, applied the correct test. I must add that, in my view, such a question had been raised and that the trial judge was correct in approaching the exercise of discretion on that basis.

The plaintiffs also argue that, in so far as the relief which was granted was mandatory in nature, such should not have been given by way of interlocutory relief. It is correct to say that a mandatory injunction does not usually issue prior to the trial of an action. However, there are exceptions and, in my view, this case is one of them. The order which is challenged was made under the provisions of an Act of the Oireachtas. It is, therefore, on its face, valid and is to be regarded as a part of the law of the land, unless and until its invalidity is established. It is, and has been, implemented amongst traders in fuel, but the appellant plaintiffs have stood aside and have openly defied its implementation. On the evidence, their action clearly threatens the continued operation of the regime established by the Order. This is so because the other oil companies, particularly the Majors, have threatened to pull out of the regime unless it is observed by all traders.It seems to me that in such circumstances it was proper to direct, by way of mandatory injunction, compliance with the order of 1983. If this were not done the existing position, in so far as the operation of the order is concerned, could not be preserved and, on the evidence before the learned trial judge, there was a grave danger of very great and extensive damage being caused to the Whitegate refinery.

Therefore, although one of the injunctions granted was mandatory in its nature, I think it was proper in the circumstances of this case that it should have been granted by way of interlocutory relief.

Griffin J.:

In *Esso Petroleum Co. (Ireland) Ltd.* v. *Fogarty* [1965] I.R. 531 Ó Dálaigh C.J., with whom Lavery J. agreed, accepted that the principles to be applied were well summarised in the passages from *Kerr on Injunctions* which were cited in the judgment of Lavery J. in the *Educational Company* case. Having stated that the plaintiffs were required to show that, in the language of *Kerr*, there were substantial grounds for doubting the existence of the alleged legal right, the exercise of which they seek to prevent, he said at p. 539 of the report: "The Court before stripping him of this right must be satisfied that the probability is in favour of the defendants' case ultimately failing in the final issue of this suit". On the other hand, Mr. Justice Walsh stated the principle applicable as follows at p. 541 of the report: "The principles upon which interlocutory injunctions are granted are well established and a Court will grant one when a case has been made out for the preservation of the property in statu quo pending the trial of the action if it is of opinion that there is a substantial question to be tried." That is a clear and concise statement of the principles to be applied in such cases.

The question was also considered by the House of Lords some ten years later in *American Cyanamid Co.* v. *Ethicon Ltd.* [1975] A.C. 396. It was there laid down that a court, in exercising its discretion to grant or to refuse an interlocutory injunction, ought not to weigh up the relative strengths of the parties' cases on the evidence available at the interlocutory stage - that evidence being then necessarily incomplete. Lord Diplock, with whose speech the other members of the House agreed, referred at p. 407 to what he called "the supposed rule that the court is not entitled to take any account of the balance of convenience unless it has first been satisfied that if the case went to trial upon no other evidence than is before the court at the hearing of the application the plaintiff would be entitled to judgment for a permanent injunction in the same terms as the interlocutory injunction sought." Lord Diplock then continued at pp. 407-8 of the report:

> "Your Lordships should in my view take this opportunity of declaring that there is no such rule. The use of such expressions as 'a probability', 'a *prima facie* case', or 'a strong *prima facie* case' in the context of the exercise of a discretionary power to grant an interlocutory injunction leads to confusion as to the object sought to be achieved by this form of temporary relief. The court no doubt must be satisfied that the claim is not frivolous or vexatious; in other words, that there is a serious question to be tried. It is not part of the court's function at this stage of the litigation to try to resolve conflicts of evidence on affidavit as to facts on which the claims of either party may ultimately depend nor to decide difficult questions of law which call for detailed argument and mature considerations. These are matters to be dealt with at the trial.
>
> One of the reasons for the introduction of the practice of requiring an undertaking as to damages upon the grant of an interlocutory injunction was that 'it aided the court in doing that which was its great object, viz. abstaining from expressing any opinion upon the merits of the case until the hearing': *Wakefield* v. *Duke of Buccleugh* (1865) 12 L.T. 628. So unless the material available to the court at the hearing of the application for an interlocutory injunction fails to disclose that the plaintiff has any real prospect of succeeding in his claim for a permanent injunction at the trial, the court should go on to consider whether the balance of convenience lies in favour of granting or refusing the interlocutory relief that is sought."

It was submitted on behalf of the plaintiffs that there are differences between the test applied in the *American Cyanamid* case and those applied in the *Educational Company* case and the *Esso Petroleum* case but any such differences are more apparant than real, as Mr. Justice Murphy noted in his judgmemt ruling the plaintiffs' application for an interlocutory injunction. The tests applied by Lavery J. ("that there is a fair question raised to be decided at the trial") by Kingsmill Moore J. ("that a serious question of law arose"), by Mr. Justice Walsh ("that there is a substantial question to be tried") and by Lord Diplock ("that there is a serious question to be tried") are essentially the same. ...It seems to me that the passage which I have cited from the speech of Lord Diplock has much to recommend it in logic, common sense and principle. I would respectfully adopt it as being a correct statement of the law to be applied in cases of this kind. In a number of cases in recent years this Court has applied as the true test, the test of determining whether a fair or serious question has been raised for decision at the trial and, if so, whether the balance of convenience was in favour of granting or refusing the interlocutory injunction sought.

12.2   Roberts v. O'Neill
[1983] I.R. 47 Supreme Court

[The defendants were the owners of the Silver Tassie, a public house. They entered into a contract of sale for the premises with the plaintiff. It then emerged that the defendants had been conducting negotiations for the sale of the premises with another party, a Mr. Carthy, who had issued proceedings for specific performance. When the plaintiff discovered this he also issued proceedings for specific performance. The action by Mr. Carthy was eventually dismissed by the Supreme Court: see *Carthy* v. *O'Neill* [1981] I.L.R.M. 443. The plaintiff then proceeded to claim specific performance, and the Supreme Court granted the order.

The extract from the judgment of McCarthy J. summarises the approach of the courts to a defence which relies on hardship as a ground for refusing specific performance. In this respect, the decision in *Lavan* v. *Walsh* [1964] I.R. 87 as to the date from which hardship is to be measured was crucial.]

McCarthy J.:

The argument
As I understand the argument advanced on behalf of the first defendant, and which I accept as being appropriate to be considered as if advanced on behalf of the second defendant, his case may be stated as follows:
1.   An order of specific performance is an equitable remedy and, accordingly, discretionary in all cases.
2.   There may be cases of real hardship caused by the grant of an order for specific performance.
3.   The time to test or measure the degree of hardship is not at the date of the contract which is sought to be specifically performed, but rather at the date of trial.
4.   In the instant case, there exists a circumstance over which neither plaintiff nor defendant had control and it prevented the closing of the sale until after the judgment of this Court in the *Carthy* case was delivered on the 30th January 1981, by which time the original purchase price was but half of the then current value of the property because of the huge nationwide increase in the value of licensed premises due to the high inflationary trends at the time.
5.   That is a circumstance over which none of the parties had any control; it effects a great hardship on the defendants because they cannot now afford to buy an alternative public-house such as would cater for their

plans to have their son continue in that business.   The only hardship on the plaintiff (and it, perhaps, a nominal one only, since he appears to have been buying in trust) is the very fact of not obtaining specific performance and having to settle for damages.

The plaintiff's answer is a short one.   He says that any hardship that exists has arisen after the date of the contract and after the date for its completion; and that he has not caused or added to that hardship.   In addition, it might be added that the defendants have been in receipt of the profits of the business since the original intended date for closing.   A further comment is made that the first defendant wanted initially, at least, to get out of the public-house business because of the unhappy burglary incident.   Neither the High Court nor this Court was given any information about the purchase price paid by the defendants in 1973 and, consequently, the degree of hardship neccessitated by them having to pay capital gains tax cannot be assessed.

The law
[Counsel] has argued that the correct approach is to measure the hardship existing at the date of the hearing.   That argument is unsupported by authority and is, indeed, contradicted by *Lavan* v. *Walsh* [1964] I.R. 87 in which Budd J. said at pp. 102-3 of the report:

> "The defendant in this case also relies on the plea that enforcement of the contract in this case would cause great hardship on her.   It is pointed out that the order is a discretionary one and it is strongly urged that the Court in the exercise of a proper judicial discretion should not grant the relief of specific performance because of the special facts of the case which I will deal with later.   Again, however, I must first refer to a matter of law.   The Court, it is well established, will not enforce the specific performance of a contract the result of which would be to impose great hardship on either of the parties to it.   It is conceded, however, that the question of the hardship of a contract is generally to be judged at the time it is entered into.   Change of circumstances taking place later, making the contract less beneficial to one party, are immaterial as a rule unless brought about by the action of the other party.   It is stated, however, in *Fry on Specific Performance* (6th ed., at p. 200):- 'It cannot, however, be denied that there are cases in which the Court has refused its interference by reason of events subsequent to the contract'.   From an examination of the cases of *The City of London* v. *Nash* (1747) 1 Ves. Sen. 12 and *Costigan* v. *Hastler* (1804) 2 Sch. & Lef. 160 it appears that this is so, but exceptions to the general rule appear very rare...   I must, however, approach the consideration of these matters dispassionately and exercise what I conceive to be the proper judicial discretion.   In the first place, as I have pointed out, it is undoubtedly the position in law that save in exceptional cases only a matter of hardship existing at the time of the contract can be taken into consideration.   Hardship existing at the time of the contract is out of the case.   It thus requires a strong case to be made before one should accede to a plea for the exercise

of judicial discretion in a quite unusual way, that is, by reason of hardship arising subsequently to the contract, and, the onus being on the defendant to satisfy me of the existence and genuineness of the alleged hardship on her, the proof of it should be strong and above suspicion."

Whilst, as Budd J. said, the relevant-time issue appears to have been conceded, I do not overlook the quite exceptional standing as a lawyer in which the late Mr. Roger O'Hanrahan S.C. (the counsel who made the concession) was held by Bench and Bar alike. Further, although Budd J. referred to the matter as being conceded, he expressed his own view in the most positive terms without reference to such concession. [Counsel] has suggested that there is an illogicality in taking the date of the contract as the relevant one, since it is unlikely that there would have been any contract if the hardship had been known then. This very argument perhaps answers the problem.

Hardship is permitted to defeat specific performance where an existing hardship was not known at the relevant time, being the date of the contract. While recognising that there may be cases in which hardship arising after the date of the contract is such that to decree specific performance would result in great injury, there must be few such cases and, in my view, they should not include ordinarily cases of hardship resulting from inflation alone. To permit, as an ordinary rule, a defence of subsequent hardship, would be to add a further hazard to the already trouble-strewn area of the law of contracts for the sale of land.

The application of the law

An examination of the evidence, including the summary at the commencement of this judgment, throws doubt upon the reality of the alleged claim of hardship. At all material times the defendants knew that they would have to complete a sale of the premises either to Mr. Carthy or to the plaintiff.

The plaintiff's advisers took meticulous care to make the plaintiff's position clear and, indeed, readily accepted that they could not press for completion until the *Carthy* case was resolved. The original motivation to leave the particular type of business was because of personal hazards; at no time from February 1978 to March 1981 was it ever suggested to the plaintiff or his advisers that there was any doubt about the eventual completion, assuming a satisfactory result to the first action. At no time did the defendants embark on any inquiry about a substitute public-house in order that their son might pursue what was alleged to be their wish for his career.

The second defendant, having dispensed with the services of her original solicitor, embarked upon a spurious defence based on an alleged absence of authority; she now seeks to join her husband in criticising the plaintiff (who is a vehicle builder aged 76 years, without any other connection with the licensed trade save that his daughter is married to one of the Madigans) because he assented in evidence to an extract from a letter dated 29 July 1979, written by his solicitors to Mr. Black specifying four items of alleged damages of which the fourth was "the difference in value between the premises as they are valued at the date of the hearing and their value at which we purchased them." It is to be noted that this letter, to which there appears to have been no reply, was written after the hearing of the *Carthy* case before Mr. Justice Gannon and before judgment was delivered in that case. I know little of what transpired at that hearing save for some extracts from the transcript of it which were used in evidence in the trial of this case, but it does appear that the second defendant did not give evidence at that hearing, apparently because she would have supported Mr. Carthy's claim.

The result

It may be that there are other circumstances surrounding the alleged hardship but I think that I have cited the salient ones. In my judgment they fall far short of establishing the type of case in which the Court should intervene to deny the ordinary remedy to one of the contracting parties in what was, at the time, a perfectly fair and proper transaction. There may be cases in which the Court should intervene or, to put it more crudely, interfere with the express wording of a contract, and in which the duty to do justice may override strictly legal principles and the well-recognised procedures of the courts of equity. Such is not the case here; indeed justice here demands that the contract be specifically performed.

12.3   Hickey & Co. Ltd. v. Roches Stores (Dublin) Ltd. [1980] I.L.R.M. 117 High Court

[The plaintiffs entered into a contract to retail fashion fabrics in the defendants shop on a profit sharing basis. The agreement between the parties broke down in 1972 and eventually the High Court was asked to adjudicate on the amount of damages payable to the plaintiffs for what the defendants in effect admitted was a breach of contract. In 1976, Finlay P. decided that damages were payable under various headings, but the parties were unable to agree on the amounts under these heads and the case was re-entered for decision by the President, who delivered judgment in May 1980.

The issue dealt with in the extract is whether the plaintiff should have the amount awarded increased by a percentage to allow for inflation between 1972 and 1976. Applying general principles as to the foreseeability of damage at the time of breach, Finlay P. declined to make such an allowance. His reliance on the propositions set out in the English *Victoria Laundry* case, which are regarded as a classic statement of the law, is of vital importance.]

Finlay P.:

Claim of plaintiffs for increase to loss
assessed to compensate for inflationary
decrease in the purchasing power of money

Mr. Liston, on behalf of the plaintiffs, stated this portion of the claim upon the simple proposition that the loss suffered by the plaintiffs, having been incurred by them in the years 1972 to 1976 and having been calculated in accordance with the figures actually lost during those years, bearing in mind the very significant decrease in the purchasing power of money since that period, if they are now paid by the defendants those figures only they are not fully and adequately compensated and in particular cannot be said to have been put in the same position as if the breach of contract had not occurred.

He relied in the first instance on the well known decision of the House of Lords in *Livingstone* v. *Rawyards Coal Co.* (1880) 5 App. Cas. 25 and in particular upon that portion of the opinion of Lord Blackburn in which he stated, at p.39:

> "The point may be reduced to a small compass when you come to look at it. I do not think there is any difference of opinion as to its being a general rule that, where any injury is to be compensated by damages, in settling the sum of money to be given for reparation of damages you should as nearly as possible get at that sum of money which will put the party who has been injured, or who has suffered, in the same position as he would have been in if he had not sustained the wrong for which he is now getting his compensation or reparation."

He relied in addition upon my own decision in *Quinn* v. *Quality Homes Ltd.* High Court 1975 No. 2242 P, 21 November 1977, in which, in a case concerning a warranty with regard to the structural condition of a house, I assessed damages on the basis of the cost of obtaining alternative accommodation at the time of trial rather than at the time when the faults were first discovered. He also submitted that the same principles appeared to have been accepted, if not expressly, impliedly, by the Supreme Court in *Munnelly* v. *Calcon Ltd.* [1978] I.R. 387 and pointed also to the decision of the Supreme Court under the Landlord and Tenant Act with regard to the calculation of rent upon renewal of leases in *Byrne* v. *Loftus* [1978] I.R. 326 which clearly involves an acceptance or an appreciation by the Court of the consequences of inflation.

Mr. Salafia, who on behalf of the defendants dealt with this portion of the argument, contended, firstly, that damages for breach of contract in a case such as the present are clearly confined on principle to damages within the contemplation of the parties and reasonably foreseeable by them having regard to their knowledge, and that the effects and extent of inflation could not come within that category. He further submitted, in the alternative, that the claim to apply an inflationary factor on the losses assessed was nothing more than a substituted form of claim for interest and that the decisions and principles applicable clearly inhibited the Court from granting interest in a case of this description. Neither counsel could refer me to any decision, nor am I aware of any, dealing directly with a claim for an increase in losses assessed consisting of a factor based on a decrease in the purchasing power of money between the date when the losses were incurred and the date when judgment came to be given.

I have considered the submission made to me on this issue and the cases to which I have been referred and I have come to the following conclusions. I am not satisfied that either the decision in *Munnelly* v. *Calcon Ltd.* or the decision in *Quinn* v. *Quality Homes Ltd.* is of any direct or real assistance to the resolution of this issue. Both of those cases appear to me to have proceeded directly upon the question as to the steps which the injured party might have taken to mitigate his loss rather than on any question of a simple or direct increase of the loss suffered as ascertained by an inflationary factor.

For the resolution of this issue, therefore, it is in my view necessary to return to the fundamental principles upon which damages in cases of breach of contract should be assessed. For the purpose of this case I would accept those principles as stated in *Hadley* v. *Baxendale* (1854) 9 Exch. 341 and re-stated in the judgment of Asquith L.J. in *Victoria Laundry (Windsor) Ltd.* v. *Newman Industries Ltd.* [1949] 2 K.B. 528 subject to the comments made on that decision by the House of Lords in *C. Czarnikow Ltd.* v. *Koufos; The Heron II* [1969] 1 A.C. 350.

In particular, as relevant to the issue now being considered, I would adopt the propositions set out at p.539 of the judgment of Asquith L.J. in the *Victoria Laundry* case, namely:

"(1) It is well settled that the governing purpose of damages is to put the party whose rights have been violated in the same position, so far as money can do so, as if his rights had been observed....

(2) In cases of breach of contract the aggrieved party is only entitled to recover such part of the loss actually resulting as was at the time of the contract reasonably foreseeable as liable to result from the breach.

(3) What was at that time reasonably so foreseeable depends on the knowledge then possessed by the parties or, at all events, by the party who later commits the breach."

The comments on these statements of principle arising from the decision of the House of Lords in *C. Czarnikow Ltd.* v. *Koufos; The Heron II* may be summarised as being restricted to the question as to what is reasonably foreseeable and as indicating that there should be considered as being reasonably foreseeable only such matters as were not unlikely to occur, excluding matters likely to occur only in a small minority of cases or being very unusual.

Adopting these principles, it is first necessary it seems to me for the resolution of this issue to consider whether the application to the figures assessed as loss incurred in years 1972 to 1976 of an inflationary factor is something which is necessary to put the plaintiffs in the same position so far as money can do as if their rights under the contract had been observed.

On the facts of this case I am not satisfied that the plaintiffs have established that this is so. What the plaintiffs lost in the periods concerned were trading profits. Had they been earned as the contract provided, they would have become part of the general income of the plaintiff and would presumably have either been applied in part or in whole as dividends to individual shareholders, towards defraying the company's debts, liabilities and running costs or towards the creation of some form of reserve. In the absence of proof, which did not occur in this case, of the manner in which the company's income was applied in the intervening period it would appear to me to be an unwarrantable assumption that such trading profits would now be held by this company in full, exempt from any intervening loss or depreciation, and so increased that their present value expressed in currency had the same purchasing power as would the profits have had when originally earned.

The second issue which arises, namely as to whether the defendants at least having regard to their knowledge at the time of the formation of this contract could reasonably have foreseen in the manner which I have outlined this particular consequence of its breach, depends upon the consideration of a number of different factors. The breach of this contract occurred in part at least upon the service of what was held to be the improper notice of termination in December 1971 and was concluded by the continued trading by the defendants in fashion fabrics after 2 February 1972. The plaintiffs cause of action for damages for breach of contract then clearly arose, and whilst it could only then be formulated upon the basis of estimates with regard to the amount of the loss as distinct from the way in which it has been formulated largely dependent upon actual experience, it was a cause of action which could immediately have been pursued. Under the terms of the agreement the first step in pursuance of the plaintiffs claim was to submit the question as to whether the defendants had been justified in their method and timing of termination to arbitration and the award of the arbitrator was not delivered until 12 July 1973. These proceedings were instituted in March 1975 by plenary summons and, an issue having been directed by the Court in March 1976 by way of preliminary issue on the principles applicable to the assessment of damages, judgment was delivered in that in July 1976. From July 1976 to July 1979 a delay in bringing forward the further assessment of the damages in pursuance of the principles decided in that judgment originated from the very practical and commonsense attempt of the parties by the exchange of figures and information to reach agreement on all or part of the damages. From August 1979 until the present the delay in determining this issue was due to an application in July 1979 by the defendants for an adjournment, which was granted by me on terms that they pay interest on the amount eventually recovered by the plaintiffs from that date until the final determination in the High Court, and therefore that period is not part of the claim in relation to inflation and the decrease in the purchasing power of money.

On this short recital of the facts, in which I do not suggest that there has been established to me culpable delay on the part of either the plaintiffs or the defendants, the question which seems to me to arise is as to whether not only what might be described as the ravages of inflation but also what is in fact claimed namely the effect of inflation over such a lengthy period could have been a heading of loss, within the principles which I have set out in this judgment, reasonably within the contemplation of the defendants. I have come to the decision that it could not. I think it reasonable to infer that any person engaged in trade as the defendants had been in the decade or so before 1969 would have been able to foresee as a not unlikely event that inflation and a consequential decrease in the purchasing power of money would probably continue. It is not, however, in my view on the evidence before me a reasonable inference to draw in this case that the defendants in 1969, at the time of the formation of this contract, could have reasonably foreseen even if they had directed their minds towards it that, in the event of a breach by them of the contract in 1971, the assessment of the damages recoverable by the plaintiffs as a consequence of that breach would not be determined until 1980.
On this basis I conclude that an increase on the loss assessed by me to compensate for the inflationary decrease in the purchasing power of money is not an allowable heading of loss in this case.